the legen—

wait for it

—dary story of

how i
met your
mother

an unofficial guide

Jesse McLean

ress

Copyright © Jesse McLean, 2014

Published by ECW Press
2120 Queen Street East, Suite 200
Toronto, Ontario, Canada M4E 1E2
416-694-3348 / info@ecwpress.com

Printing: Norecob   5   4   3   2   1

LIBRARY AND ARCHIVES CANADA
CATALOGUING IN PUBLICATION

McLean, Jesse, author
Wait for it: the legendary story of How I met
your mother / Jesse McLean.

Issued in print and electronic formats.
ISBN 978-1-77041-220-0 (PBK.)
978-1-77090-626-6 (PDF)
978-1-77090-627-3 (ePUB)

1. How I met your mother (Television program).
I. Title.

PN1992.77.H65M34 2014
791.45'72   C2014-902541-6
C2014-902542-4

Editor: Jennifer Hale
Cover images: Cobie Smulders © David
Gabber/PR Photos; Neil Patrick Harris, Josh
Radnor, Alyson Hannigan © Edward Le
Poulin/Corbis; Jason Segel © Byron Purvis/
AdMedia/Corbis; back cover © Monty
Brinton/CBS Photo Archive/Getty Images

The publication of *Wait for It: The Legendary Story of How I Met Your Mother* has been generously
supported by the Canada Book Fund for our publishing activities, and the contribution of the
Government of Ontario through the Ontario Book Publishing Tax Credit and the Ontario Media
Development Corporation.

PRINTED AND BOUND IN CANADA

table of contents

introduction

HAVE YOU MET *HOW I MET YOUR MOTHER?*

Fans of *How I Met Your Mother* shouldn't be surprised that the show's creators were drawn together by two loves: music and Wesleyan University.

Craig Thomas arrived at the campus of the notoriously selective school armed with drumsticks and a deep literary sensibility. By his own admission, the years he spent at Wesleyan produced a pile of "pretentious" short stories, but that's no surprise for a creative kid who came to the game (relatively) late. He didn't write much in high school, no doubt intimidated by his father's work writing ad copy (Mr. Thomas was responsible for the Foster's "Australian for Beer" campaign, so iconic to the brand that it is still being used some twenty-five years later). So, before the percolating desire to write was brought to a boil on the Wesleyan campus, Craig honed his drum skills.

This proved a social boon in the early '90s, as later related by his writing-partner-as-soul-mate Carter Bays. At a time when most kids showed up to university prepared to show off their fret-burning guitar chops, drummer positions were hard to fill in the bands that sprung up on campus like mushrooms. As such, Thomas found himself the attention of many would-be musicians and took up the drum kit in various post-grunge prog rock bands, like the divinely named "Grandma's Closet."

How could Carter Bays be anything but impressed?

Meanwhile, Craig was daunted by Carter when the latter finally arrived on campus. Bays had been writing throughout high school, where a number of his short plays were produced. He'd decided to submit a collection of these works to the Young Playwrights Festival, a competition started by Stephen Sondheim in 1981 to foster young writing talent. Carter's *Five Visits from Mr. Whitcomb* was selected for the festival and mounted off-Broadway, featuring Camryn Manheim (from TV's *The Practice* and *Ghost Whisperer*). This ate into his freshman year at Wesleyan, and he arrived two weeks into the first semester. While Bays has mused that he lost out on the important "making friends" introduction to university, Thomas has countered that his future partner stepped onto campus as a proven "bad-ass writer."

A multi-instrumentalist as well as a teenage Tennessee Williams, Carter caught a number of Craig's onstage attempts to end a nine-minute guitar solo with a drum fill. They met in class, both English majors with the vague notion they could somehow make a living in this quaint endeavor, writing "sweet, little stories in the *New Yorker* every couple of months," as Bays tells it.

Still, there must have been the lingering nag of future responsibilities as, unbeknownst to each other, they both landed internships in the development department at MTV. While the job consisted primarily of fetching coffee and making copies, they also enjoyed a sort of back-door TV boot camp at the network, which *used* to air these things called "music videos" — but that's a story for another time, kids.

Changing the world

Carter Bays

wesleyan alums you might know

The liberal arts college in Middletown, Connecticut, perhaps best known of the three "Little Ivies" (which also include Amherst and Williams), has proven a breeding ground for some of the most innovative and popular creative minds in film and television. Notable graduates include:

- Matthew Weiner, creator of *Mad Men*

- Dana Delany, from the television shows *China Beach*, *Desperate Housewives*, and *Body of Proof*

- Akiva Goldsman, the screenwriting giant behind such films as *The DaVinci Code*, *Cinderella Man*, and *A Beautiful Mind*, for which he won the Oscar for Best Adapted Screenplay

- Sebastien Junger, author of the nonfiction bestseller *The Perfect Storm* and co-director of the Academy Award–nominated war documentary *Restrepo*

- David Kohan, co-creator of *Will & Grace*

- Will Berman, Ben Goldwasser, and Andrew Vanwyngarden, collectively known as the band MGMT

- Amanda Palmer, singer-songwriter and one-time lead singer of The Dresden Dolls

- Zak Penn, screenwriter of *The Incredible Hulk* and *X-Men: The Last Stand*

- Paul Weitz, co-director of *American Pie* and *About a Boy*

- Mike White, the writer behind *School of Rock, Nacho Libre, Year of the Dog*, and creator and co-star of HBO's short-lived series *Enlightened*

- Actor Bradley Whitford, known for his work in *The West Wing, Trophy Wife, Saving Mr. Banks*, and *The Cabin in the Woods*, a film produced and co-written by . . .

- . . . perhaps the alum with the biggest impact on popular culture, Joss Whedon, who is also responsible for *Buffy the Vampire Slayer, Firefly, Dollhouse, The Avengers*, and providing many casting ideas to Carter Bays and Craig Thomas

    The school also turned out Michael Bay, the director of picture-and-noise art installations known as the live-action *Transformer* films. So, you know . . . otherwise, Wesleyan is *solid*.

In between the tasks of screening submission tapes from potential *Real World* cast members and signing the inevitable rejection form letters, they also learned about the development side of show business. It helped that they made friends with a vice president by the name of Jeremiah Bosgang who, in turn, knew a number of people in Los Angeles — including the agent who would represent Bays and Thomas from the start of their young careers, once again proving the adage that it's not what you know so much as *who* you know (provided that who you know is high-placed executives at major networks).

While still in their senior year at Wesleyan — and suddenly aware that their parents "weren't going to pay for us to play in a band and drink beers for another year" — the boys put their nights viewing *Late Night with Conan O'Brien* to good use. Not only did they study the fledgling show's development into a fully recognized cultural force, they spent a year working on their own material (known in the industry as a "packet") tailored to a show

Craig Thomas
JOSHUA TOUSEY / PR PHOTOS

that was blossoming with the appearances of Triumph, the Insult Comic Dog and the Masturbating Bear.

Sadly, after twelve months of crafting jokes for the irreverent environment where Craig and Carter *knew* they needed to work, agent Matt Rice dashed their dreams.

"You're never getting hired," he told them. "Everyone loves it there. No one's ever going to leave."

So, what are a couple of recent Wesleyan grads to do once their dreams have been shattered? Why, move into Mom's basement and play music, of course.

Craig's mother provided a soft landing place for both boys, not knowing whether they'd land on their feet and find jobs, or whether she'd have two shaggy English grads hitting her up for money to buy a sick twenty-four-track recorder to finally record their album.

Luckily for Mama Thomas, fate intervened when, in 1998, two writers left the staff of a highly regarded late night talk show.

Only this time, it was *Late Night with David Letterman*. And instead of a year, Carter and Craig had a mere forty-eight hours to put together their new packet.

As it turned out, this was perfect training for the fast-paced job. As Carter himself put it, "you read the paper in the morning and there's comedy on TV that night." After two sleepless days of writing and interviews with the head writer and the executive producer of the show, the boys were given their first big-time writing gig.

When fortune shines brightly on the young and naïve, it's easy to believe it will result in a lifetime of taking success for granted. But for these two kids from Connecticut, that seemed unlikely from the start. Once they left the executive producer's office and stopped to realize they'd secured a high-profile comedy writing job, they both became so excited that they got lost in the building. Unable to find their way back to the elevator, they had to ask the first person they saw in the hallway.

Who happened to be David Letterman.

An inauspicious show-business start, no doubt, but a start nonetheless.

Soon after, Carter and Craig drafted a plan for their future career trajectory. They considered working on a screenplay but decided that the security of writing for television appealed to them more (they were, as Thomas has pointed out, quick to sell their literary pretensions out to the first, if not even the highest, bidder). Talk of creating their own show came up early in the strategy sessions, but they both decided they needed to work as writers on other shows first, so they could truly come to understand how they worked. In particular, they would have to learn the differences between crafting the perfect Top Ten list and writing for a half-hour show with an established plot and characters.

Carter and Craig wrote for a show called *Quintuplets*, one of Conan O'Brien sidekick Andy Richter's many attempts at sitcom success, where he played half of a married couple who labor to raise their wildly different — you guessed it — quintuplet teenagers. The series lasted for twenty-two episodes.

They also wrote an episode of *Method & Red*, a series starring rappers Method Man and Redman (anyone remember their stoner comedy film *How High?*) as two streetwise hip hop artists who move into a tony white suburban neighborhood. It lasted for nine episodes.

Next the boys wrote five episodes for *Oliver Beene*, a comedy in same vein as *The Wonder Years*, with an adult narrator looking back at his quirky upbringing in 1962. It ran for a total of twenty-four episodes.

In hopes of avoiding the potential stigma of writing exclusively for short-lived television programs, they wrote an episode of *American Dad!* But even before they felt ready to start pitching their own shows to the networks, they were incubating their own ideas.

You know what comes next, right?

In 2002, Carter Bays and Craig Thomas pitched their big idea for a show: it would be about an Enron-type executive who gets sentenced by a judge to teach at an inner-city school to serve penance for his crimes but who, along the way, learns a little something about . . . *himself*.

Wait — that doesn't sound right.

Carter and Craig pitched this idea without any passion or verve. "From page one," Carter Bays once said, "neither of us wanted to do any research . . . and the whole thing just rang completely false." When asked if they had anything else, the boys trotted out another idea they'd been tooling around with for some time, one they thought would make for good sitcom fodder. It essentially boiled down to this: "Let's write about our friends and the stupid things we did in New York."

Before going in to pitch at CBS, Carter and Craig had been warned that the executives of that particular network only had two reactions: if they liked it, they would act very cool and remote and appear as if they didn't like it; if they didn't like it, they would be clear about how much they *really* didn't like it.

As it turned out, they liked it so much they greenlighted the show right there in the room.

Now is a point where we look at how much luck plays into fortune smiling brightly on the naïve. CBS had long been known as a network that catered to an older audience, the hard-of-hearing grump of the Big Three networks. What had once been the home of leading-edge quality network programming like *The Bob Newhart Show*, *M*A*S*H*, and *All in the Family* had became primarily known for reality programming like *Big Brother* and *The Amazing Race*, along with older-skewing shows like *60 Minutes* and *48 Hours*.

At a recent meeting, CBS executives had concluded that they were missing out on the lucrative 18-to-34 demographic and would benefit from having a show that appealed to a younger audience. Whether that meeting happened, as Craig Thomas suggests, the *morning* before their pitch meeting is hard to know. But the divine convergence of a network's need and a writing team's passionate pitch resulted in a pilot order for *How I Met Your Mother*.

Perhaps the most interesting connection between the pilot

episode and the time spent in New York that served as the boys' inspiration for the series revolves around the original pub, McGee's. Not only is it now a sightseeing stop on many NYC tours (it includes a full menu of *How I Met Your Mother* cocktails, including The Naked Man, Challenge Accepted, The Pineapple Incident, Robin Sparkles, and Daddy's Home), but it was the spot Craig and Carter went with the cast the night of the network upfronts, the annual announcement of a network's upcoming season.

What better way to celebrate the start of what would be a long-running series than back where it all began — with a bunch of friends doing crazy things in New York.

You could almost say they were destined to make beautiful music together.

Now all they needed to do was cast the project. I mean, what's the use of great songs if you don't have the perfect band to perform them?

have you met
. . . everyone?

josh radnor

On the surface, Josh Radnor's upbringing was not all that remark-able, and it certainly contained no indication that he'd go on to have a successful career in the arts.

Josh was born and grew up in Columbus, Ohio, which is about as Midwestern as a Midwestern state can get. His father, Alan, was a medical malpractice lawyer and his mother, Carol, was an elementary school teacher and homemaker who wound up as a high school guidance counselor. Josh went to Hebrew school in his younger years and eventually attended Bexley High School, spending his free time watching movies in the Drexel Theatre with friend Jesse Hara.

Throw in a dash of skipping stones down by the swimming hole, and you'd have the darn-near-idyllic childhood that properly

CHRIS HATCHER / PR PHOTOS

prepares a kid for a triumphant career as a mid-level corporate compliance officer.

Appearances, as we all know, can deceive.

Josh's father was a weekend sculptor during his law career and, upon retirement, took his accomplished handiwork seriously enough to take a class at the Cultural Arts Center in Columbus, where he crafted a bust of a desert Bedouin. His mother painted consistently throughout his childhood and into her later years, and she turned a fine hand at arts and crafts. His friend Jesse, who shared his interest in films like *Tootsie* and *Broadcast News*, would also have an impact on the future artistic endeavors Josh would undertake.

Before all that, however, Josh would have to attend a terrible open audition for *Oklahoma!*

During sophomore year at public school, Josh's friend Debbie asked him to accompany her to an audition for the chorus in the Rodgers and Hammerstein musical-theater classic. She needed moral support as she prepared for her time onstage and, while they waited, Josh watched the other young men strut and fret their hour upon the stage and came to a singular conclusion: "Maybe I should do this."

When the production's director pointed at Josh in the audience and asked if he was going to audition, he said it was like he was "pulled up by the lapels . . . next thing I knew I was onstage singing."

No word on whether Debbie made it into the chorus, but Josh landed the plum role of Will Parker.

Still, Josh was preoccupied with his love of competitive swimming. He juggled both pursuits until the following year when he played the Emcee in *Cabaret*, a more challenging and faceted role than anything found among the cowhands of the early twentieth-century Midwest.

Not only was he thrilled by the experience, but he found a fan in his high school guidance counselor. After one performance, she approached Radnor and insisted that he come see her first thing

Monday morning. While he may have been worried what fate awaited him, he was about to receive an early vote of confidence.

"I don't care if you become a lawyer," she said. "I don't care what you do, you are never to stop acting."

Even while attending Kenyon College as an English major, Radnor continued acting. He showed his range early on, from plumbing tragic emotional depths as Romeo to engaging in sparkling repartee as Jack Worthington in *The Importance of Being Earnest*. And despite his commitment to reading and discussing Updike and Carver with his classmates, he still made time to participate in the Kenyon Musical Theater program and the comedy improv group Fools on the Hill.

He switched to a Drama major and presented his senior thesis in a performance as Jonathan Waxman in *Sight Unseen*, the Pulitzer Prize–nominated play by Donald Margulies about a successful Jewish artist from Brooklyn who travels to London for a retrospective of his work and a reconsideration of his life.

For his work in the role, Radnor was granted the Paul Newman Award, an honor bestowed on the best male student actor of the year. Named after the Kenyon alum and former drama teacher, the award was instituted in 1958 to commemorate Newman's work on the campus and in Hollywood.

Emboldened by the acclaim, Josh enrolled in New York University's Graduate Acting Program at the Tisch School of the Arts, where he earned his MFA. Faced with the daunting prospect of actually making a go in the real world, and as an actor no less, Josh picked up small roles in film, including his first credit, as "Tour Guide" in *Not Another Teen Movie*, following uncredited spots in *Barney's Great Adventure* (where he appears with a purple dinosaur) and as Punk at Bar in *200 Cigarettes* (where he appears without any dialogue).

Midway through 2001, Josh had the good fortune to be cast as the lead in a new comedy series that promised to push his career to the next plateau. He waited to hear from the network when filming would commence, at which point all he would have to do is show up at work and watch the acclaim and praise pour in.

You can imagine his excitement when the show was picked up.

You can probably also imagine his despair when he was told that he had been dropped from the show and that his part had been recast.

Off Centre was billed as a comedy from "the guys who brought you *American Pie*," although the qualifying quotation marks might have been better reserved for the descriptor "comedy." The show was created by Danny Zuker (later a writer-producer on *Modern Family*), Chris Weitz, and Paul Weitz. Given that the brothers directed the wildly successful comedy film, it wasn't all that surprising that the lead role was recast with Eddie Kaye Thomas, otherwise known as Finch from the '80s throwback raunch-com.

The show aired on The WB and it was met with nearly universal derision and even vocal protest. A brand of comedy that was charmingly gross in the movies turned out to be crass and off-putting on the smaller screen. Stories involved the apparently inherent hilarity of circumcision, a sexual relationship with a "crazy" homeless woman, and endless synonyms for penis (both trimmed and untrimmed).

It's tough to know (or believe) when it happens, but sometimes being fired is the best thing that can happen.

One of the other supporting TV roles Josh landed was alongside Hollywood royalty Sally Field in the short-lived series *The Court*. He played law clerk Dylan Hirsch, and even though the show was pulled after only three of the seven filmed episodes aired, the experience served Radnor well in the long run.

When the producers of the Broadway adaptation of *The Graduate* were looking to replace Jason Biggs (also of the aforementioned *American Pie* films) for a six-week summer run in 2002, opposite Kathleen Turner and Alicia Silverstone, a recommendation from Field helped Josh through the audition process.

After submitting a tape and trying out for the casting team, Josh was brought in for a callback. If his nerves were frayed before getting into the room, they must have smoothed out when he realized he was the only actor reading for the part.

"I was starting to feel pretty good," Josh remembers.

Moving from recently unemployed television actor with a few off-Broadway credits under his belt to featured player in a major Broadway show was quite a transition.

"[Actually] playing the role didn't seem as weird as walking up to the theater and seeing my picture out front," Josh recalled. "And then, coming out afterwards and having all these people wanting your autograph, which was, I can assure you, totally new to me."

After his stint on Broadway, Josh landed television roles that helped pay the rent and plump up his résumé: on *ER*, *Law & Order*, *Six Feet Under*, and *Judging Amy*.

In 2004, Radnor took a role in Jon Robin Baitz's play *The Paris Letter* in a production at Center Theatre Group's Kirk Douglas Theatre in Los Angeles. He played a successful financier who has buried his true sexuality, only to have it confronted by an openly gay man in 1960s Paris. The suitor in this production was none other than Neil Patrick Harris. A month after the run of the play ended, Josh found that he was about to cross paths with the actor again when they were both cast in another project during TV's springtime pilot season.

"I heard he got the part," Radnor told starpulse.com, "and I called him, and I was like, 'Are you kidding me,' and he's like, 'I know, isn't this weird?'"

Weird or serendipitous?

More like "meant to be"; when Josh performed the big romantic monologue on Robin's stoop at his audition, he was so persuasive in the role that the casting director asked the actor, "Will you marry me?"

Starring on a successful sitcom didn't dampen Josh's writerly ambitions. He'd already worked on an unproduced screenplay titled *The Adulthood Project*, but when he finished an early draft of his next script, *Happythankyoumoreplease*, he knew that he wanted not only to act in it but to direct it as well.

Enter Radnor's old friend Jesse Hara who, fortunately enough, was running the management and production company Tom Sawyer Entertainment. And, in another splash of kismet, he had just moved into an apartment across the street from Radnor's. After reading and enjoying the screenplay (an ensemble piece about a group of tangentially related twentysomething New Yorkers teetering between adolescence and adulthood) and spending many hours discussing it with Radnor, Hara felt a need not only to help get the film made but to make sure Radnor was in the director's chair.

They met with much resistance. Many potential producers were eager to make a movie that featured that guy from *How I Met Your Mother* on the poster, but most were not anxious to take the risk of using an untested director. What Radnor and Hara envisioned as a small five-million-dollar film turned into a tiny one-million-dollar film.

Featuring Malin Akerman (*Watchmen*), Kate Mara (*House of Cards*), Richard Jenkins (*Burn After Reading, Step Brothers*, and an Academy Award–nominated performance in *The Visitor*), and Tony Hale (*Arrested Development, Veep*), the charming curbside chamber piece was nominated for the Grand Jury Prize at the 2010 Sundance Film Festival and won the Audience Award.

For his next script, Josh took inspiration from a trip he took back to Kenyon with his first film. He was amazed to find that even in his mid-thirties, he was one of the oldest people on campus. Caught up in the abundant optimism of the students around him, he wondered what it would be like if he met a female student and fell in love.

"That sounds like a great movie," Jesse told him.

Liberal Arts follows a disenchanted admissions officer in New York who travels back to his alma mater to attend the retirement dinner of his "second favorite" professor (Richard Jenkins). While there, he meets Zibby (Elizabeth Olsen from *Martha Marcy May*

Marlene and the remake of *Oldboy*), an old-soul nineteen-year-old who shakes him out of his existential funk and causes him to confront the forgotten dreams of his halcyon days. The film also features Zac Efron and fellow Kenyon alum Allison Janney.

While critics had been hard on Radnor's first film, what many assumed was a television star's shallow vanity project, acclaim was easier to come by for his sophomore effort. The late, great Roger Ebert went so far as to call *Liberal Arts* "an almost unreasonable pleasure."

Written during hiatuses from his day job, Radnor's script for *Liberal Arts* shares many themes with *How I Met Your Mother*. Both chronicle their characters' struggle to hold on to the shiny optimism of youth, but where the show makes a case for the happy co-existence of the past and the present, the film is more critical of the subterranean pull of nostalgia. The characters in Radnor's second film have difficult decisions to make, and nobody gets off easy, which leads to the sort of dramatic satisfaction that can be found in the longer form of a feature film, as opposed to a twenty-two minute sitcom.

As for his future film endeavors, Josh hopes to direct a film in which he does not feel compelled to appear. It is interesting to note that while *How I Met Your Mother*'s show creators and stars have battled *Friends* comparisons from the start (*much* more on that later), the similarities aren't limited to the show itself. Many have compared the development of Ted Mosby's career with that of Ross Geller from the '90s sitcom (both practitioners of highly specialized skills who go from working directly within their respective fields to holding professorships), but David Schwimmer, the actor who portrayed the hapless paleontologist, also pursued a directing career that has resulted in a few films in which he did not act (the comedy *Run Fatty, Run* and deadly serious *Trust*, about a teenage girl who falls victim to an online predator).

Whatever Radnor's next film is, we can assume that it will be filled with the type of hopeful if bittersweet longing we have come to expect from a filmmaker who once took a trip to Vienna and dragged his then-girlfriend around to all the locations used in the making of Richard Linklater's indelible *Before Sunrise*. It's no surprise that Radnor would make such a pilgrimage for a movie with a take on relationships that manages to be both sweepingly romantic and steadfastly clear-eyed.

Josh has also been working on a memoir, called *One Big Blissful Thing*, which details the author's search for enlightenment, which took him from his suburban childhood home to the Amazon, where he drank a hallucinatory tea called ayahuasca with a shaman.

The search for balance between the heart and the head continues to be the grand theme of Josh Radnor's life. Provided he gets to keep creating movies that can be shown at the old Drexel Theatre in Columbus, it's a battle well fought.

jason segel

While the title of Most Recognizable pre-*HIMYM* goes to Alyson Hannigan for starring in *American Pie* and geek culture watershed *Buffy the Vampire Slayer*, perhaps Jason Segel can comfortably take the honor of Most Successful during the series' run.

He will be saddened to learn that there is no award for this distinction — well, other than being in the position to reboot a beloved puppet empire and to go completely commando on the silver screen, to say nothing of his chance to follow where only Tiny Tim had gone before.

But we're jumping ahead a bit.

Jason Segel was born in Los Angeles to a Christian mother and a Jewish father. He experienced both sides in his upbringing, attending an Episcopalian school during the day followed by time at Hebrew school in the afternoon. The experience left Jason with a profound sense of spirituality. He certainly believed that there *was* a God, but the sense of exclusivity that exists in the different organized religion camps left him cold. He remembers, as a Christian student, hearing "if you're not one of us, then you don't

get it," while being told at Hebrew school that "if your mother's not Jewish you don't get it."

"I think I was very lucky that I got to have both experiences to see that it wasn't right," remarks Segel.

Perhaps it was this enlightened stance that allowed him to grow to such a towering height (the more progressive the mind, the closer to God?). And while his eventual height of six-foot-four, reached at the tender age of twelve, wound up working to his benefit, it resulted in terrible bullying during his time at Harvard-Westlake High School.

It is not just the small and weak who are terrorized in school; anybody who is seen as vulnerable or different is a target, and being adult-sized at such a young age certainly qualifies as being different. Being taunted for his height was bad enough, but it was the older kids circling him and jumping on his back while chanting, "Ride the oaf! Ride the oaf!" that really hurt.

Luckily, Jason made it through those difficult years and later demonstrated a talent for basketball. People tend to think anyone of a certain height is *naturally* good at the sport, but it was actually one of Jason's main interests throughout high school. He was a star high-school player at Harvard-Westlake School, though he was pulled into creative exploits as well. This might seem like an unusual way to go through those formative years — to have a foot in two wildly divergent streams — but it may have been the key to his success.

While he continued playing basketball, two friends showed him how the piano worked. Armed with a little information, he set about teaching himself to play. Even at a young age, Jason's work ethic was such that he could handle spending "two years being terrible at it until I was good at it."

He continued to play basketball for the Harvard-Westlake Wolverines, where he backed up future NBA star Jason Collins (who made headlines in 2013 by becoming one of the first major athletic stars to publicly announce his homosexuality), eventually winning a Division III state championship.

During his time on the hardwood, Segel was given the exquisite nickname "Doctor Dunk" (shades of "Big Fudge"?). He earned this stellar appellation when, during a two-week East Coast trip, he dominated a slam dunk contest. First, he called for silence from the crowd, and then he wowed them by completing a two-handed dunk with the front of his jersey pulled over his head. But he wasn't done after merely impressing with his skills. His showmanship pushed him even further, and he celebrated his dunk by diving headfirst into the crowd.

"I'm not nearly as skilled a basketball player as some of the other guys," Segel said at the time, displaying his trademark humility at a young age. "But I have a lot of bravado."

Segel's canny sideline impersonations of Arnold Schwarzenegger and Kermit the Frog not only kept the team loose, they also displayed his sharp ear and natural theatricality.

"I love getting up in front of people," the teenaged Segel admitted.

He kept up his artistic output by mounting plays on his own, perhaps spurred on by fellow student and friend Jake Gyllenhaal or by his worship of comedic chameleon Peter Sellers. It was one such performance at sixteen years old, in Edward Albee's *The Zoo Story*, that eventually set his acting career in motion.

The head of the drama department at Harvard-Westlake saw him perform Albee's first play and suggested that Segel give up sports for acting. Despite early misgivings, Jason decided to audition for that teacher, who happened to bring another woman along to the reading. Unbeknownst to Jason, this stranger was actually the casting president at Paramount. That audition led directly to Segel's being cast in the dark college comedy *Dead Man on Campus*.

At that point, Jason decided to forgo college entirely and focus on acting. He worked in local theater productions at the Palisades Playhouse and won roles in films like *New Jersey Turnpikes* and *SLC Punk!* But it was winning a role in a TV comedy, at the age of nineteen, that changed the course of his career forever.

No, not *that* TV comedy.

Freaks and Geeks was a whip-smart series about friends in the titular outsider groups going to high school in the 1980s. Critics fell for the show, but it was never given the time to find a large enough audience to allow it to survive past eighteen episodes (only fifteen were aired, with the remaining three not seen until shown in syndication on Fox Family in 2000). The critical acclaim for the series certainly helped — *Time* magazine included it in a "100 Greatest Shows of All Time" list, and *Entertainment Weekly* pegged it at number thirteen in its list of the best TV series of the past twenty-five years — but Segel's true success was the creative alliance he made on set with fellow cast members Seth Rogen and James Franco and with one of the show's executive producers, Judd Apatow.

There were other plusses from his time on this criminally short-lived series — he entered into a long-term relationship with co-star Linda Cardellini and was allowed to write a song that his character sang to hers, displaying another of his nascent talents.

When the series was canceled, it wasn't just the fans of the show who were crushed. The young stars were also devastated. Producer Judd Apatow felt a particular sense of responsibility to members of his young cast like Segel and Rogen, who were in the latter part of their teenage years and had abandoned plans for college (and, in Rogen's case, his home country of Canada) for a shot at show-business glory. Apatow encouraged both young men to focus on writing during their down time, believing that the improvisation skills they had employed on the *Freaks and Geeks* set were a clear indication that they could write.

Apatow marshaled them through comedy writing boot camp — everything from how to write an outline or a script to how to use the scriptwriting software properly — and urged them to keep working on projects until something clicked.

Jason secured a few acting roles in movies like *Slackers*, *LolliLove*, and *The Good Humor Man* along with an appearance on *Alias* and a three-episode run on *CSI: Crime Scene Investigation*, but by his own admission he was in a strange place. While most of his other young colleagues were able to be cast above and below their actual ages,

project. The Jim Henson Company had been contracted to make the puppets for the Dracula musical, and Jason took the opportunity to pitch himself as the writer and star of a Muppet movie reset. Unfortunately, all the characters had been sold to Disney, so the Henson Company had no rights to them at all. So he took his pitch to the studio, who overcame their apprehensions about giving the "penis guy" from *Forgetting Sarah Marshall* the keys to the Muppet legacy and bought his pitch right there in the room (for the record, Segel's favorite Muppet is Fozzie Bear, "the classic borderline hacky entertainer").

Roles in films like *I Love You, Man* (co-starring Paul Rudd) and *Bad Teacher* followed, along with voicing the villain in Steve Carell's *Despicable Me*. He also co-wrote another romantic comedy with his *Sarah Marshall* director, Nicholas Stoller. *The Five-Year Engagement* had all the makings of another hit for Segel but stumbled, struggling to find an audience in the face of the Nicholas Sparks romantic drama *The Lucky One*, starring Zac Efron, and an even bigger ensemble romantic comedy called *Think Like a Man*, based on the relationship advice book by comedian Steve Harvey, featuring comedian Kevin Hart.

Meanwhile, Segel continued his work on *How I Met Your Mother* but started to chafe a bit at the creative constraints and demanding schedule of such a show.

"When your idol is Peter Sellers, playing one character for eight years isn't what you're trying to do," he told *GQ* interviewer Alex Pappademas in July 2010. "I don't really feel like I have that much more to offer with this character. Maybe if we got divorced or something — but that's not gonna happen. It's gonna be some iteration of, like, my TV wife opens the fridge and she's like, 'What happened to the birthday cake?' And I walk in with a little frosting [points to corner of mouth] like, 'What birthday cake?'"

Segel repeated the line almost verbatim when he filmed his cameo in Seth Rogen and Evan Goldberg's *This Is the End*, in a conversation with Kevin Hart, coincidentally enough (although it's

Hart who walks away with the scene, missing out on Segel's disdain for his work and replying with an enthusiastic "That's why you guys are number one!").

Segel's candid words left many wondering if he would get fired for his apparent disregard of the show that made him a star. At the time, he was under contract up to the eighth season of the show and when talk of a ninth season started, all signs pointed to him not renewing. Whether due to pressure from other cast members or a change of heart, Segel did sign on for the final season. Yet despite talk of the planned *HIMYM* spin-off from show creators Carter Bays and Craig Thomas (*How I Met Your Dad*, natch), the likelihood of Segel appearing on weekly television again is remote — Alyson Hannigan made a joke about wanting to appear in the new series with her TV husband, saying that Segel agreed only if they called the show *Out by Noon*, so he could be finished work before lunch and free to focus on his other projects.

As for those future projects, it seems anything is possible. While he won't be a part of the Muppet franchise going forward, due to that old Hollywood saw known as "creative differences," he will likely focus on films. One possible role — and perhaps most surprising of all from this talented multi-hyphenate — is as an officiator of weddings.

While Tiny Tim appeared on *The Tonight Show* in 1969 to get married, Segel kicked it up a notch when he actually performed a wedding ceremony, marrying a couple on the same show in 2010.

For some reason, an about-to-be-married couple papered every lamppost leading from Jason Segel's home near the Chateau Marmont to his local pub with signs reading "Jason Segel: Will You Marry Us?" Segel took the request to heart and called Jay Leno's staff at *The Tonight Show* to ask if he could marry the couple on their show. By the very next night, Jason had become an ordained minister with the Universal Life Church, and he united the couple in holy matrimony on a national broadcast (the way God intended).

Make that *Father* Dunk, if you please.

cobie smulders

What do zooplankton, a British general known as "Bungo," international travel, indestructible bracelets, and same-sex attraction have in common?

Why Cobie Smulders, of course. In her formative years, that is to say.

Let me explain.

Born Jacobs Francisca Maria Smulders, "Cobie" received both her given name and her nickname from a great aunt. Of British stock on her mother's side, she likely inherited not only her elegant looks but also her interest in travel from this branch of her family tree.

Cobie's mother went traveling sometime in her early twenties and landed herself a job on a seafaring vessel. The dream of working her way across the Pacific Ocean failed to pan out, when a rusted cable speared a hole in the boat and it sank, leaving Cobie's mother adrift in a lifeboat with the rest of the crew. An American rescue vessel came to their aid and took the lot of them to Vancouver, which is where Cobie's mom fell in love with the "clean, green beauty of the Canadian coast."

Itchy feet didn't get to Cobie right away. She lived a fairly normal life in Vancouver, where she attended Lord Byng Secondary School (named after WWI British army officer Field Marshal Julian Hedworth George Byng, who served as the twelfth Governor General of Canada and, yes, received the affectionate sobriquet of "Bungo"). There she was an athletic sort who played tennis and soccer, but she also showed an interest in acting, which led to her appearance in a number of school productions.

By the time Cobie was twelve, she stood on the precipice of a life-changing decision. And, as these things often happen, it revolved around an unrequited crush.

While at summer camp, Cobie was smitten with a "tall, beautiful, funny" girl who used these attributes to further a career as a model. This girl approached Cobie and told her that she looked the part

JANET MAYER / PR PHOTOS

of a model, volunteering to facilitate a meeting between Cobie and her modeling agency.

"I would have done anything to hang out with her more," Cobie later said.

Modeling jobs followed over the next two years, and by the time she turned fourteen, Cobie spent her summers traveling with her stepmother or older sister to places like Greece, Italy, Africa, and Germany for modeling work.

Imagine living the life of a young, beautiful woman being whisked away to exotic locales just so a flock of make-up artists can flutter about to make you look as gorgeous and effortlessly stylish as possible, before turning to a photographer's camera that loves you so much the lens asks you out to dinner.

It doesn't get much better than that, does it?

Cobie's response was a pragmatic "meh."

"I'm in Japan, I don't know the language, and I'm standing in front of these businessmen who I'm hoping will hire me," she recalls of her tenure as a clotheshorse. After many years of experience entering rooms to have strangers judge her appearance quickly and coldly, Cobie grew tired of the callous and empty work environment that characterized the modeling world. She says, simply, "It just wasn't my bag."

Other than the hard work, long hours, and interminable travel, why did Cobie *really* dislike the life of a model?

"I hate having my picture taken," she told *Maclean's* magazine.

This is a jarring thought for those of us who understandably view the dazzling lifestyle of a globe-trotting international model as second only to flat-out membership in the monarchy — and it makes for a fine cover story for a super spy, by the way, not that I'm suggesting Cobie does black-bag work for The Agency . . . *or am I?* (I'm not.)

Cobie kept at her modeling work despite her misgivings because it provided opportunities to see places and meet people that would have otherwise been out of her reach. Despite all the international travel and "glamorous" work, Cobie managed to continue her high school studies and graduated not only on time but with honors in 2000, at which point she considered a career in marine biology. But when you're earning money to jet-set around the world, it's tough to convince yourself that you're better off elbow-deep in zooplankton.

Nineteen years old and a high school graduate, Cobie moved to New York to pursue her modeling career full time. It wasn't long before her debut trip down the catwalk at a runway show caused her to make another course-changing decision.

"It was a shoe issue," Cobie told the *New York Post*. "Also I think the runway was just tables stuck together length-wise. It was all very wobbly."

A few strides down the jerry-rigged catwalk and Cobie took a spill and landed face first into a decision that it was time to change careers.

"I didn't enjoy making a living off of how I look, so I bowed out," she says of that time in her life. "I was definitely using it to live in the West Village for free, to go to Paris or Germany for six months. But it had an expiration date."

Cobie returned to Vancouver with a few interests bidding for her attention. She registered at the University of Victoria with the intention of going into the marine biology field, but she couldn't shake the acting bug that had bitten her back at Lord Byng Secondary School. Cobie enrolled in acting classes and decided to give it a try for a year or two instead of diving right back into academics.

"I was looking into taking classes part-time," she told *Maclean's*. "But marine biology involves a lot of lab time."

Cobie grappled with the difference between acting auditions and modeling ones very early on. After years of being judged solely on her looks, Cobie suddenly realized, "Oh no, I have to actually perform. I have to do well, and I have to have a voice."

By the time she was twenty, Cobie started to land parts on TV shows. Her first role was in a show called *Special Unit 2*, a Syfy original series about Chicago cops hunting monsters. In the same year, Cobie landed a spot on the Luke Perry and Malcolm-Jamal Warner series *Jeremiah*, about a post-apocalyptic landscape in which the majority of the world's population has been wiped out by a virus. Add to that a day-player role on Eliza Dushku's *Tru Calling*, a show about a city morgue employee who can repeat the previous day and prevent people from meeting their grisly ends, and one could be forgiven for thinking that Cobie was destined to be a genre actress.

This typecasting continued when, in 2003, Cobie won her first recurring role in a television series: the part of Juliet Droil on ABC's short-lived *Veritas: The Quest*. The *Indiana Jones*–like adventure series lasted only thirteen episodes before cancellation. (Interesting note: the series pilot, about a teenager and his adventurer/archeologist father, contained a *crystal skull* as a plot point. I haven't seen the show, so I can't confirm whether anyone climbed inside a fridge to stay safe from a nuclear blast.)

After what felt like a good career roll, Cobie found her momentum stalled once *Veritas* was canceled. Minor setbacks are expected in the unreliable business of show, but after two years without acting work, it would have been understandable if she ditched it all and went back to marine biology.

Instead, she persisted. She waitressed around Vancouver and worked for her software engineer mother, a job that required her to drive around picking up damaged hard drives from various businesses.

"It was like a very small version of the Geek Squad," she told *Women's Health*.

This might have been a humbling experience — to go from playing a lead role in a major network television series to becoming an injured hard drive's medic — but she was compelled to keep moving.

Living in Vancouver allowed for quick trips south to Los Angeles for auditions, and the steady work at home allowed her to continue honing her instrument by appearing in local theatrical productions.

Looking back, most of us can point to a year that signified a profound shift in our lives. For Cobie, that year would have to be 2005.

She started to nab acting work again, first in a two-part arc on the sci-fi show *Andromeda* (based on an old treatment by *Star Trek* creator Gene Roddenberry), and also a multiple episode appearance in *The L Word*, where she played a young artist who catches the eye of Jennifer Beals' Bette Porter.

In real life, she caught the eye of a fella, and sparks immediately flew. Taran Killam, best known for his work on *Saturday Night Live*, where he was only the second cast member to have previously appeared on Fox's ersatz *SNL* sketch show, *MADtv*, met Cobie through a mutual friend at a birthday party. Cobie later said of the meeting, "It was one of those kismet things where you meet someone and you're immediately like, *Oh! Now we're dating exclusively.*"

They have been together ever since and have a daughter together, Shaelyn Cado Killam, born in 2009.

That's enough for one year, isn't it? Except for Cobie, it wasn't.

One week after meeting the man she would marry and go on to have a child with, she filmed the pilot for *How I Met Your Mother*.

Carter Bays and Craig Thomas must have been impressed by her audition because if they'd looked solely at her résumé, they would have noticed one thing missing from her repertoire: namely, comedy.

Despite having been raised in a family where a premium was placed on making people laugh, Cobie's screen credits were primarily in genre pieces and her stage work comprised mostly heavy dramas. Lucky for her, they not only noticed her inherent comic abilities, they felt that she was *perfect* for the role of Robin Scherbatsky.

"You *are* Robin," they reportedly told her. "You are Robin incarnate."

That type of unwavering support from the show's creators must have filled her with confidence, even when the role was offered to a "pretty famous actress" who, fortunately for Smulders, turned it down.

"Pretty famous" or not, it is hard to imagine anyone else inhabiting Robin's complex alloy of tomboy bluster and emotional vulnerability with such skill and charm.

Audiences agreed. The success of *How I Met Your Mother* has led to supporting roles for Smulders in many film projects, including the independent comedy-drama *Grassroots* (directed by Stephen Gyllenhaal, a film and TV veteran who once helmed a failed police procedural pilot that featured Cobie as the weekly criminal, in this case a set of twin sisters, one of whom might actually have been a *cold-blooded murderer!*), an adaptation of the Nicholas Sparks novel *Safe Haven*, and *Delivery Man* (an adaptation of the French-Canadian film *Starbuck*), in which she played Vince Vaughan's pregnant wife.

In 2011, Cobie got the role of Maria Hill in Joss Whedon's Marvel Cinematic Universe conduit *The Avengers*. She likely would have done anything to work with Whedon, though she may not have known that signing on as the right hand to Nick Fury (and future director of the planetary defense service *S.H.I.E.L.D.*) would require a nine-film commitment that covered not only sequels to *The Avengers*, but also appearances in the *Captain America* sequel and on the TV show *Agents of S.H.I.E.L.D.*

Even more tantalizing was the idea of a Joss Whedon–helmed *Wonder Woman* movie. When asked who he thought was best equipped to fill the red boots of the Amazonian warrior princess, Whedon suggested none other than Cobie Smulders.

"Yeah, well, he made mention of it," Smulders told *Maclean's*, downplaying the suggestion. "I don't know if I was his first choice, but it was a very kind joke."

Whedon walked away from the Wonder Woman project over creative differences with the studio and turned his attention to *The Avengers*, but was sufficiently impressed by Cobie's abilities to bring her along for the Marvel Cinematic Universe ride.

Don't worry that Cobie might still be smarting from losing the opportunity to play the statuesque heroine: in 2014, she voiced Wonder Woman in *The Lego Movie*.

Even in Lego form, the indestructible bracelets are still very impressive.

across the whedonverse with the HIMYM cast

One of the most interesting aspects of the world of *HIMYM* is the ongoing connection between *HIMYM* cast members and the Grand Geek Master, Joss Whedon.

- Alyson Hannigan starred in *Buffy the Vampire Slayer* and is a godparent to Whedon's son Arden

- Neil Patrick Harris starred in Whedon's *Dr. Horrible's Sing-Along Blog*

- The following *HIMYM* guest stars have appeared in the Whedonverse: Alexis Denisof, Amy Acker, Tom Lenk, Morena Baccarin, Harry Groener

- Cobie Smulders appeared in Whedon's *The Avengers* and *Marvel's Agents of S.H.I.E.L.D.* as Agent Maria Hill

- Jason Segel . . . well, he appeared alongside Joss when Neil Patrick Harris received his star on the Hollywood Walk of Fame

- Josh Radnor is still out of the Whedonloop, although I'm sure he would have made an excellent Avenger (considering his work in the controversial season nine Slapsgiving episode, maybe Shang-Chi: Master of Kung Fu?)

alyson hannigan

If, as a young girl in Atlanta, Alyson Hannigan ever thought about her career and worried about the possible geek credentials she might acquire, she would have been happy to learn that she would one day dive into something known as the Whedonverse and emerge with her place in the nerd pantheon firmly established.

Hannigan was born in Washington, D.C., and lived there with her mother, Emilie (a real estate agent), and her father, Albert (an overnight truck driver), until she was two years old. It was at this tender age that her parents got divorced and her mother moved to Atlanta, Georgia, to continue raising her daughter.

Alyson's charismatic presence was noticeable from a very young age, and she appeared in her first film before her first birthday. It was an instructional video for new parents called *Active Parenting*, and while it doesn't have the same mythic appeal as Jodie Foster's first onscreen appearance in a Coppertone ad, it's still an impressive start.

Early on, Alyson displayed a love for posing in front of a camera. As a print model (for "whenever they needed a baby," Hannigan has said) in Atlanta, she became highly sought-after, eventually receiving up to $130 an hour.

By the age of four, Alyson had moved on to television commercials. Her first national appearance was in a Duncan Hines spot, which was followed by work in ads for Oreos, McDonalds, and (fittingly) Mylanta. Her success on TV motivated her mother to move to California so they could better focus on young Alyson's career. The two moved to Hollywood when Alyson was eleven, and, as she settled into life at North Hollywood High School, she grappled with the challenges that may have prompted her to seek attention in the first place.

"I hated being an only child," she told *Parent & Child* magazine. "It was lonely and boring. But it also helped my imagination, because I had to entertain myself."

She also learned the value of being funny early on.

"Whenever I got in trouble, I always knew that if I could make my mom laugh, it would be better for me — it was a way to ease problems."

To make ends meet in between acting jobs, Alyson worked at a video store and as a babysitter. One of her clients was a famous TV dad who would figure largely — if absently — in Alyson's life later on. Proving that Hollywood is just as small as any other town, the young Alyson Hannigan was babysitter to none other than Bob Saget, the Future Ted who is heard but never seen on *How I Met Your Mother*. At one point, she even went to Hawaii on vacation with Saget's family.

At the age of fourteen, Alyson landed a role in the sci-fi comedy film *My Stepmother Is an Alien*, opposite Dan Aykroyd and Kim Basinger. Another co-star was Seth Green (*Family Guy*, *Robot Chicken*), who would later play her character's boyfriend on a certain little show about vampire slayers. And, in keeping with the supernatural vein, she also had a recurring role on *Free Spirit*, a sitcom for ABC about a good-hearted witch who moves in with a recently divorced dad to help raise his three kids. Once again she crossed paths with Seth Green, who guest-starred on one episode.

After appearing in a show that critics at the time voted "the worst show on television," Alyson knuckled down on her studies, graduated from North Hollywood High School, and attended California State University, Northridge. She continued acting in TV shows like *Touched by an Angel* but finished her studies in 1997 with a degree in psychology.

No doubt this experience would come in handy in the coming years, which found her playing a bookish nerd who blossoms over seven seasons, to say nothing of enduring the seven auditions required for her to secure the role. And even then, she was only given the chance after the actress (Riff Regan) who was cast in the role for an unaired half-hour pilot didn't work out. When the pilot was a hit but studio executives asked for a replacement for the role of computer nerd Willow, show creator Joss Whedon knew that finding the right actress to portray the character's complicated dramatic arc, one that sees her metamorphose from a shy girl to a woman of incredible power, would be key to the success of the series.

"Every line that somebody else would play like they were sad, Alyson was joyful about," said casting director Marcia Shulman. "That made her the only one for the role."

As for the much-talked-about same-sex relationship Willow started in the fourth season, Alyson was sanguine in the face of the heated debate that surrounded that very taboo prime-time kiss. "It's no different than when Willow fell for Oz really," Alyson said at the time. "It's just a relationship, a very sweet friendship."

Not only did *Buffy* change the direction of her career, it also changed her life. On set she met her future husband Alexis Denisof, who played Wesley Wyndam-Pryce on *Buffy* and its spin-off, *Angel*, and the two eventually became godparents to Whedon's son Arden. She and Denisof have two daughters, Satyana and Keeva.

During the run of this pop culture phenomenon, Alyson secured a role in the biggest cinematic throwback to '80s teen sex comedies since, well, the '80s, in *American Pie*, where her sweet and goofy recollections of summertime experimentations *still* have people yelling "Band camp!" at her in the street.

Once *Buffy* ended in 2003, Hannigan had to wrestle with that demon all actors dread: unemployment. Her ego and sense of self-worth were given a boost when she received an out-of-the-blue phone call while in the middle of making wedding plans with Denisof. Ubiquitous TV producer J.J. Abrams (*Felicity, Alias, Lost, Fringe, Revolution, Almost Human*) was a big fan of her work as Willow. When he heard that Hannigan was free, he courted her for a new show he was developing.

Unfortunately, it was another hour-long drama, the kind with fourteen-hour shooting days that made the likelihood of seeing her new husband remote, to say nothing of trying to start a family.

"I had to make the hardest decision of my life — telling J.J. Abrams I didn't want to do a one-hour show," she recalls.

At least the attention helped her survive the devastating end of *Buffy*, convincing her that people would want to work with her again. Fortunately, the show Abrams was pitching never made it to air, so Alyson didn't have to face the regret of turning down a show that turned into a massive hit.

"Could you imagine if I turned down *Lost*?" she later joked.

Instead, in 2004 she made her debut on London's West End in a stage adaptation of *When Harry Met Sally . . .* opposite another television icon, Luke Perry. But by 2005 she was anxious to get back to regular work on television and was attracted to the pilot script she read for *How I Met Your Mother*. She was also likely drawn to the multi-camera pitch of the show, although how she feels about its unorthodox shooting schedule (which more closely resembles that of a single camera show) is anyone's guess. After nine successful seasons, we can all agree that the long days on set were definitely worth it.

neil patrick harris

The biographies of many child stars have the type of arc that ends with a sensational hour-long *E! True Hollywood Story* episode, or at least a sunburst obituary on the bottom right-hand cover of *Us Weekly*. The Hollywood machine isn't known for being gentle, and countless child stars have been chewed up and spit out by it. The fact that Neil Patrick Harris managed to avoid the traps that snag many young actors has everything to do with his inherent talent, a solid grounding provided by his parents — and the pansexual master of ceremonies at a decadent, fall-of-man-style Berlin nightclub.

So, you know, pretty standard Horatio Alger fare.

Attorneys Ron and Sheila Harris from Ruidoso, New Mexico, were the parents of an energetic boy named Neil who, after a fourth-grade appearance as Toto in *The Wizard of Oz*, decided that he wanted to try his hand at the mysterious art of acting. He'd had a taste of performing for a crowd when he'd sung in front of the congregation of his Episcopal church. Around this time he also

found that he possessed a natural ability to pull a tune out of multiple instruments, including the oboe, the tuba, the xylophone, and the French horn (no word on whether it was blue).

Performing wasn't just a momentary fixation for the young Neil; he remained focused. He seemed ready to commit himself to a lifetime of pursuing his craft if it meant eventually finding success, but it didn't take nearly that long. His parents enrolled him at a week-long drama camp at New Mexico State University, where he caught the eye of a well-known playwright, sending the NPH rocket soaring.

Mark Medoff (*When You Comin' Back, Red Ryder?*, *Children of a Lesser God*) was working on the screenplay adaptation of a novel called *Clara's Heart*. The story of a loving but pragmatic housekeeper and her relationship with the child of a family broken by tragedy called for a precocious young boy who could hold his own in scenes opposite the formidable talent of actress Whoopi Goldberg. In a story reminiscent of the mythical discovery of Lana Turner at the soda counter of Schwab's Pharmacy (in truth, the sixteen-year-old actress was discovered at The Top Hat Café, just so you know), Medoff saw Neil performing at the drama camp and wielded his power as writer of the movie to secure the pivotal part for the young actor. Despite the limited influence usually afforded screenwriters, Hollywood allowed Neil to get the role.

Once released, the film garnered positive reviews for both leads (including a Golden Globe nomination for Harris), but otherwise failed to inspire much praise from critics. A lesser-known family film that he appeared in the same year, called *Purple People Eater*, is notable in that it co-starred two other child actors who went on to varying degrees of post-childhood success: Thora Birch (*American Beauty*, *Ghost World*) and Dustin Diamond (better known as "Screech" from *Saved by the Bell* and the featured player in a rather ill-fated celebrity sex tape).

With a steady stream of acting work starting to look more likely for young Neil, he and his parents decided that films were the best path for him and the family (which included older brother Brian).

The relatively short shooting schedule of a movie seemed like the kind of thing that could be easily fit into a summer break. This type of work wouldn't require the uprooting of the entire clan, the way a part in a television show might, and would save Neil the anxiety of the uncertain nature of TV work — Will we get picked up? Will we get renewed? Will my trailer get bigger?

Neil's parents had one exception to the no-television rule: if the part was *really* good, then they would consider it. The lawyer parents, having been big fans of *L.A. Law* and *Hill Street Blues*, agreed that on the remote chance that a Steven Bochco series came up, they would rethink their stance.

Well, wouldn't you know it . . .

Created by Bochco and David E. Kelley (*Ally McBeal, Chicago Hope, The Practice, Picket Fences*), *Doogie Howser, M.D.* seemed like a show tailor-made for the wise-beyond-his-years young actor. A connection between Neil's agent and the casting director provided the chance for the actor to meet with Bochco before the auditioning process began but that didn't secure him the part. The producers had him read for the role and, after not making a decision on the lead after a few months (and auditioning "hundreds of kids from everywhere," the casting director told *People* magazine), Bochco had him come in to audition again and eventually awarded him the title role two days before shooting began.

Before getting into the daily grind of shooting the half-hour dramedy, Bochco sat the family down and tried to prepare them for the tumult that being on a hit show can cause.

"This business is not unlike sets of waves," he told them. "You can ride one, and it's a great ride, but suddenly it crashes on the sand and you have to stand up and shake yourself off and swim back out."

He also warned that following the initial big wave of being on a popular TV show, it could be a long time before the next set of waves would start to crest.

"Trust that the business has lots and lots of waves. If you can wait it out, and hopefully hop on another wave later on," Bochco assured Neil, then a long-term career in show business was a definite possibility. Neil and his parents were thankful for the advice.

"It put things in proper perspective," he said later. And while the guidance was useful at the time, no doubt it especially helped Harris batten down the hatches once the show ended and he prepared for life after *Doogie*.

Following the abrupt cancelation of the show in 1993 after four seasons, Neil worked in assorted true-life TV movies like *Snowbound: The Jim and Jennifer Stolpa Story* and *Legacy of Sin: The William Coit Story* and the occasional theatrical release like *Starship Troopers* and *The Next Best Thing* (alongside Madonna and Rupert Everett). He also took guest spots on episodic television series including *Murder, She Wrote*, *Quantum Leap*, *Homicide: Life on the Street*, and *Will & Grace*.

From a distance, it is easy to suggest that these might represent Neil's "wilderness years." But he was a working actor who continually found roles. There is nothing too Grizzly Adams about that.

Still, the diminutive doctor cast something of a long shadow. Neil could easily have found himself consigned to playing figures that poked fun at his first big role (having played a version — or a lampoon — of Doogie in everything from an episode of *Roseanne* to an Old Spice commercial, wherein he claimed that he "used to be a doctor for pretend," which uniquely qualified him to "prescribe" an anti-perspirant).

Luckily, he always knew there was a place for him in the theater.

He once said that his stint as the adolescent doctor allowed him to bankroll trips to New York, where he would binge on a dozen shows over the course of a few days. In his twenties, Neil forged what he referred to as a "good workshopping relationship" with the Roundabout Theatre Company in New York, which included two go-rounds in Stephen Sondheim's *Assassins* in the dual role of the Balladeer and Lee Harvey Oswald.

Theater not only afforded Neil the chance to hone his dramatic abilities beyond the confines of a ripped-from-the-headlines TV movie, but also provided him the chance to be cast against type.

It was a slow process, but in Broadway dramas like *Proof* (opposite Anne Heche) and the Los Angeles company version of *Rent*, where he played Mark, the former television prodigy took on roles without the impediment of expectation that can occur when you appear in millions of people's living rooms over a number of years.

Then he was given a chance to play a role that would change everything for him.

"If the movie version . . . came up again," he once said of the role, "I'd never get the opportunity. That's why I'm so grateful to the Roundabout for giving me the chance to do something more extreme."

John Kander and Fred Ebb's musical *Cabaret* first debuted on Broadway in 1966, with Joel Grey originating the role of the Emcee, the omnisexual master of ceremonies at The Kit Kat Klub who beckons patrons to "leave your troubles outside," a wise bit of advice considering that the musical is set against the backdrop of the marching rise of the Nazi party that precipitated the fall of the Weimar Republic.

He had been considered for the role in the long-running revival for a couple of years before landing the part, but the timing hadn't been right, either from a scheduling perspective or from the view of preparedness.

"I'm more calm in my own skin, which I think is necessary for that role," he mentioned at the time in an interview with *Playbill*. "It's so physically specific, such a full-bodied ride for the actor playing the Emcee."

While Broadway audiences may have first been drawn to the idea of wholesome Doogie Howser slithering around the stage in ruby red lipstick and blue-and-black-dyed hair, they stayed for his towering achievement in a difficult role, one that had been played by a number of different actors during the show's long run. Harris became the top-drawing headliner for the revival, besting John Stamos as well as Alan Cumming, the actor whose incarnation of the Emcee had shone so brightly when the Sam Mendes–directed show debuted in London in 1993.

Not only did the darker role explode any preconceived notions the audience might have had regarding Harris' range, it gave him full license to use all of his considerable talents. While he is quick to note that he is not a classically trained singer, his self-identification as an "actor who sings" does a disservice to his talent.

Another fortuitous meeting of talents occurred when Neil took a role in the studio recording of Broadway legend Steven Sondheim's *Evening Primrose*, released by Nonesuch Records in 2001. But it was his portrayal of the simple-minded but sweet Toby in a Los Angeles production of *Sweeney Todd* that sufficiently impressed Sondheim and resulted in Neil reprising the role of Toby at the Lincoln Center.

Further collaborations with Sondheim followed, in the afore-mentioned *Assassins* as well as in a concert production of *Company* co-starring Stephen Colbert, Christina Hendricks, Jon Cryer, and Patti LuPone.

Harris also forged a personal relationship with Sondheim, one based upon a common love . . . of games and puzzles.

"He's a gamesman and I love me some puzzles and murder-mysteries," Neil has said. "So we started talking about computer games and crosswords . . . I think it's better to talk to someone as incredible as Stephen Sondheim about things other than his work."

Neil would have been forgiven for thinking that this type of *milieu* would constitute the rest of his life's work, and likely he would have enjoyed that immensely. But an unusual offer was to change the course of his career yet again when he was offered a role that challenged him like no other.

Harold and Kumar Go to White Castle tells the epic, heroic tale of two friends who get stoned and set out on a quest to find a particular kind of greasy hamburger. In the script for the film there was a part intended for Harris: he would play a character named Neil Patrick Harris, the one-time child star of a television show called *Doogie Howser, M.D.*

Of course, he was playing a cartoonish version of himself

(continuing a grand tradition of stars playing the "celebrity ass-hole" versions of themselves, something that Steve Martin has done to hilarious effect during interviews and cameos and a bit that Jack Benny built a whole career on). Harold and Kumar are excited to have picked up this treasured child star, and are understandably surprised to discover that he is "tripping balls" on ecstasy and in search of a strip club to escape the "sausage fest" inside the car.

The real question of assaying such a role was to determine if the joke was meant to be *with* Neil or at his expense. And as much as he wanted to distance himself from the image of a squeaky-clean child actor, Neil wasn't willing to do it at the expense of those who'd worked hard at creating and maintaining a show like the one that gave him his start.

"You want to have this extreme, messed up version of 'Neil Patrick Harris'? I'm down with that," Neil told Terry Gross on *Fresh Air*. "But is it going to be at the expense of a bunch of bad Doogie Howser jokes?"

The end result not only changed the way people looked at Harris but also helped pave the way for his longest acting role yet. He is quite certain that his appearance in *Harold and Kumar* helped him land the role of Barney Stinson, an equally horned-up character who swaps out ecstasy for Scotch.

It's interesting to note how the hypersexualized, womanizing version of NPH veered even further from the real thing after Neil came out to *People* magazine in 2006, a topic that was hilariously — if crudely — broached in *A Very Harold & Kumar 3D Christmas*.

The steady paycheck that *How I Met Your Mother* provided allowed the security for Neil and his long-time partner, David Burtka (Lily's long-suffering ex-boyfriend Scooter on *HIMYM*, and a successful chef in his own right), to start a family, having fraternal twins Gideon Scott and Harper Grace through a surrogate.

Neil also continued the collaborative link to Joss Whedon shared by most of his TV castmates when he starred in *Dr. Horrible's Sing-Along Blog*, a web-only musical miniseries in which he played a supervillain who battles a superhero (played by Nathan Fillion) to try to win the girl of his dreams, all through the magic of his freeze ray.

Harris took his talents behind the scenes when he directed a Hollywood Bowl production of *Rent* that raised eyebrows with the perceived stunt casting of non-theater stars such as Vanessa Hudgens (*High School Musical*) and Nicole Scherzinger (one-time frontwoman for the burlesque troop The Pussycat Dolls). He also helmed the show *Nothing to Hide*, a showcase for two of the world's most highly regarded sleight-of-hand artists, Derek DelGaudio and Helder Guimarães. Neil had seen the duo perform at Hollywood's Magic Castle and knew they deserved to be seen by a much wider audience.

Neil's love of magic has not only informed the character of Barney Stinson (whose magic skills were Harris' idea) but also put him in the position to serve as the President of the Board of Directors of the Magic Castle, the pre-eminent stage, restaurant, and private club for magicians and fans of illusions. Anyone who has seen his appearances on *Ellen* and *Late Night with Jimmy Fallon* can attest that Harris is a gifted magician in his own right, having won the coveted Tannen's Magic Louie Award in 2006, an honor that he perhaps treasures even more than the Emmy he won in 2010 for his guest spot on *Glee*. Although perhaps not *quite* as much as being named one of *Time* magazine's 100 Most Influential People in the same year. He was cited for his unflappable hosting stints on both the Tony and Emmy Awards but also for his pronounced effect on the way people viewed homosexuality, quietly changing minds without ever desexualizing himself so that he might appeal to a broader audience. He managed his most impressive trick when he came out — making it seem like no big deal at all.

Or, as he said with a shrug on a *HuffPost Live* appearance, "I fell in love with a dude."

season one (2005–2006)
LIFE IS JUST A LIVING ROOM SWORD DUEL

The gang's hold on youth is threatened

suit up! LEGEN . . . DARY THOUGHTS ON THE SEASON

Romantic comedy feels like a primarily cinematic term, but some of the greatest romances in popular culture have played out on television screens. The tension of a couple overcoming a seemingly impossible barrier plays quite well across several weeks, months, or even years of programming. Whether the quintessential will-they-or-won't-they of Sam Malone and Diane Chambers on *Cheers*, the on-again, off-again trials of Ross and Rachel on *Friends*, or even the actual impossibility of a union between Will and Grace on, well, *Will & Grace*, all these shows benefited from the comedic (and occasionally dramatic) fuel of the type of conflict once thought to be the exclusive domain of filmmakers from Preston Sturges to Woody Allen.

How I Met Your Mother is, in essence, a long-form romantic comedy. Like many of the best films of this kind, it is set in New York, which has the breakneck pace that best suits the quick wit of the best rom-coms. And while there is more than one couple at the center of the proceedings, we find our hero in Josh Radnor's Ted Mosby, who has great chemistry with a number of potential mothers of his children. But the best chemistry is reserved for what plays out over the length of this first season: his romance with Cobie Smulders' Robin Scherbatsky.

While the show ticks off a number of boxes on the rom-com genre's list, the most interesting part is a very simple inversion. The fact that the romantic fool at the heart of the story is a guy and not a girl is a great indication of Carter Bays and Craig Thomas' unconventional worldview, one that would bring so much freshness and invention to the romantic comedy in general and the network sitcom in particular.

One of those innovations has to do with how the show is made. The multi-camera setup of *How I Met Your Mother* will look familiar to fans of shows that shoot in front of a live studio audience (*The Big Bang Theory*, *Two and a Half Men*). Actors generally prefer working on these type of shows as opposed to the more cinematic single-camera ones (*30 Rock*, *The Office*) because the hours are more sensible. Instead of shooting twelve- to fourteen-hour days like the single-camera shows, multi-cam shows shoot for one day and, with only a few days for read-throughs and rehearsals, make for a more human- and family-friendly schedule.

What Bays and Thomas did, however, was promise a multi-camera show but deliver what was in essence a single-camera script. With as many as sixty scenes, many of them flashbacks and flash-forwards, in each episode, *How I Met Your Mother* more closely resembles *Parks and Recreation* than *2 Broke Girls*.

While this means that one episode takes three days to shoot, it also means that the producers couldn't imagine how to film an entire script in front of the same crowd from start to finish (prompting Thomas to suggest that such a situation "would blur the line between 'audience' and 'hostage situation'"). The innovation becomes clear when you consider that Bays and Thomas have made a show that looks as familiar and welcoming as a multi-camera show (with the standard laugh track obtained by airing the cut episode to a full audience) but with the smash cuts and quick cutaways of a single-camera program.

The creators also breathed life into the sitcom setting and the rom-com genre by putting a man at the center of the matrimonial time clock countdown. How many times have we seen women saddled with this type of premise, from the disconcerting man-trap angle of *How to Marry a Millionaire* all the way to the modern-day exploits of Bridget Jones or Carrie Bradshaw on *Sex and the City*? While the motivations may differ (to be set up for a comfortable life in the 1950s, versus finding true love while managing a satisfying career in an effort to "have it all" in a post 9/11 world), it has generally been considered the domain of female characters to fret over the romantic future and to pine over an as-yet-unmet spouse, that elusive person known as The One.

Another benefit of investing all these attributes in a male character is that it allows for all manner of neurotic complications and grand gestures that, if foisted on a woman, might feel unseemly at best and pathetic at worst, especially after we've all endured a lifetime of scatterbrained rom-com heroines. While much of the credit for the show's freshness is rightly assigned to the creators, Josh Radnor had the unenviable task of acting like a foolish romantic whose actions could easily be mistaken for those of a stalker. His considerable nebbish charisma certainly owes much to the modern romantic-comedy hero mold cast by Woody Allen, but archetypes don't help an actor who has to tell a character he barely knows "I love you" and make it seem adorable rather than creepy. That he can pull this off, along with an earnest confession at Robin's brownstone stoop that he's not really sorry for being such a romantic goon (a speech that would likely stand as Exhibit A in a restraining order case), is a testament to Radnor's skill and Ted's inherent charm — and a good reason to stick around to watch these twentysomethings start to grow up.

For a season about the bumpy road from youth to adulthood, complete with all the skyrocket highs and shoe-leather lows that come from the dreams of youth being exceeded or dashed, it is no surprise that the pilot episode opens with a marriage proposal. Sure, it's a practice run with Marshall trying out his approach on his best friend, but it solidifies Ted's desire to be a married guy like his college buddy and roommate is about to become. It also signals that the next phase of adulthood is upon them — whether they struggle to succeed at it (Marshall and Lily) or maintain a seemingly primal urge to fight against it (Barney), they all must accept that life is moving forward.

Although Marshall and Ted *claim* to want things that would indicate adulthood, they have in effect extended their college dorm days by remaining roommates now that they're finished with school and focusing on their careers. Funny how a previous generation (denoted by the letter *X*) was once taken to task for boomeranging back to their parent's basements in their twenties, especially when compared to previous generations who tamed the West or fought in wars. Funnier still that the idea of the extended adolescence has become a much more acceptable phase of growing up, to the point where people these days routinely refer to people in their twenties as "kids."

Millennials don't have it any better, but this begrudging shift in the way that time in our lives is viewed helps to explain the enduring appeal of a show like *How I Met Your Mother*. Even if we didn't all spend our twenties in the Greatest City on Earth (I believe there's a ™ pending on that), most of us can recall a time when there was a large gulch between who we were and who we thought we would become, and the primary task was to figure out how to get there.

Kids, back in my day (he said, in his best Future Ted Mosby voice) I remember seeing a movie called *St. Elmo's Fire*. It presented such a dreamy, improbable picture of that very time in your life that I, a teenager at the time, couldn't wait to get there. Struggling law students and would-be writers lived in charming exposed-brick apartments, and couples worked for politicians and lived in apparently undervalued loft spaces (how else could they

afford them?). Imagine my surprise when I arrived at my twenties only to find that the only loft apartments I would ever spend any time in were in the movies.

While *St. Elmo's Fire* and *How I Met Your Mother* share surface similarities — the age of their protagonists, the ensemble dynamic, and even the bar that serves as a nucleus for their respective groups — the television show doesn't make things easy for the characters. Ted's struggle to find the future Mrs. Mosby while simultaneously succeeding at his architecture career feels very relatable (although I'm still not sure how he and law student Marshall can afford their apartment — maybe we'll go with a rent-control explanation). Similarly, Lily's initial reluctance to marry Marshall stems from worries that she's sacrificed her childhood dream of becoming an artist instead of the kindergarten teacher that she's ended up. Fans of the show are quick to point out that these are dilemmas that resonate with anyone who had grand dreams for their future self. And, in the end, isn't that most of us?

remember the time . . .
HIGHLIGHTS, RUNNING GAGS, AND CATCHPHRASES

Any good comedy series will have recurring gags, but it's amazing to think of how many elements that appeared in the pilot episode have featured throughout the series. It's a testament to the vision of Carter Bays and Craig Thomas that the premiere episode featured the blue French horn, the appearance of driver/guardian angel Ranjit, laser tag, "Suit up!," "What up?" and Barney's Blog.

Other memorable happenings from the first season:

- The live-action version of Linus and The Great Pumpkin in "The Slutty Pumpkin"
- Learning exactly what liberty tastes like in "Sweet Taste of Liberty," only to be disappointed that the answer is "pennies"
- One of Barney's best *legendary* lines in the show's entire run: "It's going to be legen— wait for it . . . I hope you're not lactose intolerant 'cause the second half of that word is —dary!" ("Sweet Taste of Liberty")
- The mysterious pineapple from "The Pineapple Incident": this episode is the most-watched episode of season one and the second highest of the series, after the season finale "Last Forever"
- Robin's inability to turn down Barney's bets to say inappropriate things on the air ("Return of the Shirt")
- The first appearance of the dreaded Cockamouse in "Matchmaker"
- Poor Lily dwarfed by the giant Eriksen clan in "Belly Full of Turkey": this episode is also notable for the first appearances of jokes poking fun at Canada and Canadians, including the obvious pronunciation of *about* as *aboot*
- The story Marshall tells in "Life Among the Gorillas," which is reminiscent of the "naturalistic as hell" story Tim Roth tells lead thug Lawrence Tierney in *Reservoir Dogs*

- Ted's statement in "Milk" that his perfect woman would play bass like Kim Deal (Pixies and The Breeders) or Kim Gordon (Sonic Youth), which leaves us to wonder if this might offer a clue about the identity of the Mother
- The start of Lily's not-so-secret attraction to Robin in "Best Prom Ever" when Robin kisses Lily to give her the "lesbian experience" she never had in college
- The telepathic conversation Marshall and Lily have in "Mary the Paralegal," in the first in a long line of such conversations between the two soul mates
- The suggestion in "Okay Awesome" that Marshall looks like a third Affleck brother (". . . Brian Affleck?")

taking life and turning it
into a series of crazy stories
THE EPISODES

For each season, we will take a look at selected episodes from the year: the funniest, the ones that add the most to Ted's search for the ever-elusive girl of his dreams, or simply the most memorable — those that have won this series a warm place in the hearts of so many. Also, wherever there are slaps, this guide will be there.

1.05 okay awesome

The whole notion of losing one's youth is interesting, but never more so than in this episode, where there is a concerted interest in *trying* to shed those early years. Well, even if it's only Lily, who decides she wants to try being a grown-up after lying about her beer-guzzling weekend to a coworker. Marshall agrees, if only to make her happy (as always) and pledges to "rock it, maturity style!" at an upcoming wine tasting the couple will host.

Meanwhile, Robin represents the pull of younger days when she invites Ted and Barney to an exclusive club called Okay. The allure of these clubs (with their ear-splitting volume and wallet-splitting drinks) always seems to me to be for those who have just started going and those who used to go and now look back on those days nostalgically.

Either way, a lot of this episode is about not only how to grow up (and how not to) but also the difficulty of communication, whether at a thumping bar or a snoozy grown-ups party (the high five that fellow wine tasters share after the line "You gotta go for the thirty-year fixed mortgage" is heartbreaking). The subtitles over the deafening music work well (and are used to great comic effect, reminiscent of Woody Allen's *Annie Hall*) and provide what is likely network television's most accurate portrayal to date of a night in a club.

Even more realistic is what Marshall goes through when he arrives at the club after ditching his own wine tasting through the bathroom window. He gets a temporary crown knocked loose just as he is ready to bust a move and goes into the bathroom to search for aspirin. What he does in there is not shown, but the wide-eyed and invigorated Marshall who exits makes us wonder what exactly was going on in that bathroom. Cocaine? Ecstasy? Or, as Josh Radnor posits in the DVD audio commentary for this episode, a "cup of coffee"?

Ted realizes that he hates clubs and only goes out of a sense of obligation to the effort to meet the future Mrs. Ted Mosby. When he strikes up a conversation with the club's "coat wench" (Jayma Mays, who would later find stardom on *Glee* as well as with roles in *The Smurfs* and *Epic Movie*) she neatly sums up everything that's wrong with growing up: "Everything you're supposed to like actually sucks."

Naturally, the gang discovers that youth isn't so easily discarded — and that the quality of your life is determined not by where you spend it but by who you spend it with. At the very least, they discover that the club is no place to find true love or, in Barney's case, grind with a "fine cutlet" for a one-night tryst — especially when that cutlet turns out to be your cousin Leslie.

empire state building fun facts

- Barney's cousin is played by choreographer Kristin Denehey, who choreographed Marshall's late-episode dance number in this episode, as well as the rain dance Ted performs later this season in "Come On" (along with appearing in the film version of *Rent* and orchestrating

dance moves on *Entourage*, *The Sing-Off*, and the dance movie *Go For It!*).
- One of the three geeks outside of the club is played by Samm Levine, another ex–*Freaks and Geeks* cast member, a further sign of Bays and Thomas' devotion to that series.

1.08 the duel

Growing up is a concern in this episode, but even more so is the idea of independence. And as usual for *How I Met Your Mother*, the standard tropes are inverted and it is the women who are more concerned with life outside of their relationships than the men.

It turns out that Lily has maintained an apartment of her own in New York despite her de facto role as fellow roommate of Marshall and Ted. It's no surprise that this *is* a surprise to Robin, but when Lily returns after a three-month absence, she is shocked to learn that her apartment is no more. Even more surprising, it has turned into a Chinese restaurant that uses her furniture to complement the eatery's décor.

The idea of not letting go of the past is also prevalent in this episode. Ted doesn't want things to change, an outlook best epitomized by his love for a fifty-year-old coffeemaker he affectionately calls "Shocky," which, true to its nickname, zaps him every time he plugs it in and produces coffee that tastes a little "rusty." When Lily officially moves in with the boys and throws out Shocky in favor of a machine that makes coffee that tastes good *and* doesn't electrocute the intended drinker, Ted thinks he's being edged out of the apartment and, along the way, the life to which he's become accustomed.

The question of who will get the apartment when Marshall and Lily wed is one that the boys have deferred to Future Ted and Marshall for consideration, but when the likelihood of living arrangements having to change becomes too vivid for them to ignore, Present Ted and Marshall decide the fate of the pre-war apartment in the only sensible manner: a duel.

If the apartment is, as Lily says, a guy's place that "smells like dude," the presence of crossed swords over the piano shouldn't come as a surprise. What's even less of a surprise is Marshall and Ted's inability to communicate unless it's accompanied by a clash of sabres. Their *bro*lationship is due to change with Marshall's impending nuptials, and they will have to learn to talk things out without engaging in swordplay that will end up injuring innocent bystanders like Lily, who is accidentally stabbed by Marshall when the poorly constructed coffee table collapses under his weight (a pirate-style *contretemps* isn't really convincing unless you're up on a table jumping over a sword slash, is it?).

Things change, as Lily notes in a toast at the Chinese restaurant that used to be her apartment (and we've all been there before, haven't we?), but as long as the important things remain the same, the little things won't matter. That's what becoming an adult is all about — that, and getting used to that barnyard dude smell.

empire state building fun facts

- Another *Freaks and Geeks* alert: when Robin takes a date with a nerd at MacLaren's to prove Barney's Lemon Law (the judgment-free ability to step out of a date five minutes in, no hard feelings) wrong, he is played by Martin Starr, who was geek Bill Haverchuck for eighteen episodes on the much-loved show. Starr's relationship with producer Judd Apatow continued with appearances on *Undeclared*, *Superbad*, *Knocked Up*, and *Walk Hard: The Dewey Cox Story*.
- Plot hole: during their sword fight, Marshall tells Ted that Barney would be a poor roommate choice due to his proclivity for cooking naked, but it is established later on that Barney doesn't cook at his apartment.
- Possible plot hole: also, during the duel, Marshall suggests that Ted is "anhedonic," and Ted claims not to know what that means; but with his already-established pseudo-intellectualism further confirmed in later episodes,

wouldn't he already know that this ten-dollar word means "unable to experience joy"?

hey, kids!

For those wondering, the actors who appear as Ted's daughter (Lyndsy Fonseca from *Big Love*, *Desperate Housewives*, *Hot Tub Time Machine*, and the *Kick-Ass* movies) and son (David Henrie from *Wizards of Waverly Place* and *That's So Raven*) are not trapped on an age-defying TV set in Hollywood. They remain free from the ravages of time in their appearances on the couch because all of the reaction shots were filmed early in the show's run. As Carter Bays remarked, they are the "luckiest kids in show business. We've been sending them paychecks for eight years." Perhaps most impressive (from an overall view of the show) is that the last segment they filmed with these young actors was at the end of season two and features prominently in the end of the series.

1.11 the limo

Is there anything more fraught with high expectations and morning-after regret than New Year's Eve? Instead of being the kind of time that looks better upon reflection, it tends to be one hundred times better in anticipation. Or on TV. When you're home on the couch with another warm body.

Some people may look at the eventual nesting tendencies that set in when a person encroaches on middle age as a desperate development, but the minds behind this episode (and "Okay Awesome") illustrate instead that going out and spending time with large groups of people tends not to mitigate loneliness so much as magnify it. The ability to enjoy a "magical, perfect New Year's," as Barney suggests, is almost impossible because it doesn't exist. The night is usually overstuffed with disappointment, filled as it is with dates who stand you up, drunk Russians, and fake recording artists who totally steal your *Get Psyched* mix CD.

Ted realizes this, but what he doesn't realize is that an overly planned evening does not ensure a smooth night's entertainment. In fact, the tighter the schedule, the more likely it is to go off the rails.

Ted brings along a date from the office who he thinks is into him because she's always finding reasons to hug him. He doesn't seem all that fazed when it becomes clear that she is a friendly person who hugs people instead of offering a brisk handshake. She *is* fazed when Ted bends the night's otherwise rigid itinerary to include Robin, stood up by her work-focused boyfriend.

Things look good for Ted and Robin when his date leaves early, and Ted thinks he might have a reason to like New Year's after all — he should have known better. But when Robin's boyfriend shows up out of nowhere and Robin still gives Ted a kiss at midnight, it can't help but feel bittersweet: he's been looking for a magical night all over New York and found it with one of his best friends. But how can it happen with another guy in the picture?

Just like Barney's missing mix CD, you have to let things go sometimes. And like Barney's CD, those things might just come back to you — and give you a warm kiss just after midnight on New Year's Eve.

Likely they'll just play music, but it never hurts to dream.

empire state building fun facts

- "Not Moby" was played by J.P. Manoux, a TV regular known for appearances on *Community* (where he played a character named Faux-by), *ER*, and *Wilfred*, as well a role in Judd Apatow's *Knocked Up*.
- Carter Bays and Craig Thomas thought that setting an entire episode inside a limousine would make for a quick shoot (for once), but it turned into a logistical nightmare,

trying to fit actors into the space and choreograph their movements. It's no surprise that the gang stuck pretty much to the bar after this episode.

1.14 zip, zip, zip

Inevitably, the whole "let's keep things young" dynamic plays out not only on a personal level but in relationships as well. Not only do we hold onto youth as long as we can, we try to do the same with our partners — to keep the flame burning with a never-ending list of "firsts."

Usually those "firsts" include falling asleep in your loved one's arms and meeting their parents, not peeing in front of them. But youth takes funny forms sometimes.

With Ted having met the possible love of his life in Victoria (Ashley Williams) in "The Wedding," he is consumed with taking things to the next level. Funny how the introduction of a possible candidate for the role of The One can make you want to burn through days and experiences instead of holding onto them for dear life.

Ted and Victoria try to preserve some mystery by holding off on making love for the first time, only to jettison that plan when Victoria's schedule is packed on their one-month anniversary. It doesn't take long for anticipation to become a hurdle to clear instead of a roadblock to cherish.

Marshall and Lily are still trying to achieve a tier of grown-up sophistication with their weekend getaway plans. Instead of jetting off to Paris, they opt for a dusty-sounding bed-and-breakfast that was picked as one of New York's "Top Five Vacations on a Budget." No wonder they blow the whole thing off for a *Quantum Leap* marathon.

Trapped in the bathroom while Ted and Victoria take *forever* to get down to business (by way of no small amount of bad eighth-grade love sonnets), Marshall and Lily are forced to confront the fact that even before their wedding, they are already like an old married couple. Lily in particular is worried about the romance in their lives, and watching her fret makes us realize the interesting thing about their relationship in this show. While most long-running couples make for comic fodder through their antagonistic relationship, *How I Met Your Mother* wrings laughs out of how well these two get along. Another happy inversion in this deceptively approachable series.

As much as Lily tries not to pee in front of Marshall, there is no holding back primal urges (see Ted and Victoria and their slow-motion display in the living room). But Marshall saves the day by pointing out the one mystery left in their relationship: his explanation puts one in mind of Shakespeare when he wrote, "summer's lease hath all too short a date," a sonnet he originally closed off (true fact) with "keepeth thine love alive by ever-reserving the deuce."

empire state building fun facts

- Ted hastily reveals the location of the apartment when it looks like things are getting steamy with Victoria: the apartment (and bar) is at 75th and Amsterdam, which is a relatively laid-back intersection in New York with (as of this writing) a number of apartment buildings (brownstone and otherwise, but no stoops), a restaurant named Fusha, a little spot called Candle Bar, a Chinese restaurant called Grand Sichuan (and *not* the Szechuan Garden Marshall references in this episode), and the back of the legendary Beacon Theatre.
- While the physical existence of the Bro Code isn't confirmed until the third season ("The Goat"), I believe this episode contains the first official reference to it. ("First rule: leave no bro behind. Either we all score or no one scores.")

1.18 nothing good happens after 2 A.M.

In many ways, this is the episode where the show really hit its stride. Carter Bays and Craig Thomas wanted to have a show that was a comedy but "about something" as well, something they thought was sadly lacking in current sitcoms. This episode accomplishes their desire to anchor the wacky sitcom shenanigans with real emotion. This was one of seven episodes the duo wrote for the first season, and it serves as a prime example of their goals for the series.

In particular, this story explores the growing pains of relationships and how they mature the same way people do. Or, in Ted's case, the same way people *don't*.

Ted and Victoria are trying to negotiate the pitfalls of a long-distance relationship as she furthers her baking studies in Germany. She mentions that she wants to have a serious discussion, which leaves Ted twisting in the wind, certain that she's going to break up with him.

Robin has had one of those days completely free of monumental events that still somehow manages to shake you to your core and make you question every decision you have made in your life. She's pining over Ted (secretly, she thinks) and is in a very vulnerable state when she calls him after 2 a.m.

Ted goes against his mother's advice to "just go to bed" after that hour because all good judgment goes to sleep even if you don't. He makes a terrible decision that involves deceiving Victoria and outright lying to Robin.

It's another tough road for the audience's relationship with Ted. We like him a great deal, but a morally compromising call that involves sex with one woman while still attached to another is the kind of move that could make any audience/protagonist relationship go bust. Again, the fact that we don't immediately hate him owes much to Josh Radnor's charm but also to his vulnerability. Bays and Thomas' ability to write about such a situation without moralizing allows the audience to identify with the main character even more, compelling us to sift through the bad calls we've *all* made after everyone else has gone to bed at a respectable hour.

empire state building fun facts

- Robin's colleague and co-anchor, Sandy Rivers, is played by Alexis Denisof, Alyson Hannigan's real-life husband and former *Buffy the Vampire Slayer* castmate.
- George Kee Cheung guest-stars as Korean Elvis ("remember the time that Lily kicked Korean Elvis in the nards?"): he is a Chinese performer with a long list of credits to his name, from *Matt Houston* to *RoboCop 3*, and has worked as a stuntman in everything from *Knight Rider*, *Riptide*, *The Fall Guy*, *Big Trouble in Little China*, *MacGyver*, *Lethal Weapon 4*, *The West Wing*, to the intriguingly titled *Bring Me the Head of Lance Henriksen*.
- Ted barks out Robin's address in a late night taxi-cab (funny how he keeps doing that every time he might get laid): she lives in the Brooklyn neighborhood of Park Slope at Eighth and 8th, where there are a number of charming brownstones (complete with stoops!), the Park Slope pharmacy, and, conveniently enough for a lady who owns five dogs, a Pet Boutique & Supplies store at 724 Eighth Avenue.
- At career day in Lily's class (wait — career day in *kindergarten?*), not only do we not get any closer to finding out what Barney actually does for a living, we also see on the blackboard that among the list of presenters he is announced as "Barney — not the purple one."

Alyson Hannigan with Alexis Denisof
CHRIS HATCHER / PHOTORAZZI

1.22 come on

The first season winds up with Ted making another grand romantic gesture involving blue instruments — in this case, a blue string quartet smuggled into Robin's apartment. When it doesn't go the way Ted hoped for (that is, with a resounding "Yes I'd like to jump into a serious relationship, you big romantic knucklehead!"), an argument ensues that might not have been possible if not for the similar tone deftly displayed in "Nothing Good Happens After 2 A.M." It's not often in a sitcom that long scenes, let alone dramatic ones, are allowed room to breathe. Silence is deadly in television comedy, but Bays and Thomas display a confidence brushed up against in previous episodes that is given full strokes in this first season finale. They seem not only sure of themselves, but sure that their audience will follow along for a few minutes without any punchlines.

Also bucking the standard Hollywood convention, it is a woman who has difficulty letting go of her youthful dreams. Lily has applied for a painting fellowship in California without telling Marshall, who only finds out when her acceptance message is played on the answering machine.

The one glitch in the episode is that Ted isn't his usual charming-despite-his-questionable-tactics self. When Ted makes his decision to lie to Robin about breaking up with Victoria, we still like him because we've all been in situations where we haven't made the most upstanding judgment calls. However, when Ted uses a rain dance to try to get Robin (an act that is immature at best, cultural appropriation at worst) it doesn't feel all that relatable, and we're less than charmed. Grand romantic gestures are fine but it still strikes me as a point where that delicate balance of zany comedy and human drama is lost. It is only regained when the jubilant Ted meets up with Marshall, miserable and holding the engagement ring from an absent Lily, on the stoop of their apartment.

All in all, a lot happens in this episode — which leaves us with as Trudy in "The Pineapple Incident." McKellar became famous at an early age and then . . . graduated *summa cum laude* from UCLA with a degree in mathematics and co-authored a paper entitled "Percolation and Gibbs states multiplicity for ferromagnetic Ashkin-Teller Models on Z^2," resulting in the Chayes-McKellar-Winn Theorem . . . you know, like so many child stars before her

- Taran Killam (*SNL* and future husband of Cobie Smulders) as Gary Blauman in "Life Among the Gorillas"
- Bryan Callen (*MADtv*, *The Hangover*, *7th Heaven*, and the unfortunate parody film *The 41-Year-Old Virgin Who Knocked Up Sarah Marshall and Felt Superbad About It*) as Bilson in "Life Among the Gorillas"
- Show creators Carter Bays and Craig Thomas as fake paramedics in "Milk"

maybe it's the booze talking
REACTIONS TO THE SEASON

In this section, we will look at the overall reactions to each season, from both the critics and the fans, as well as any awards bestowed upon the show.

The first season met with generally good critical reviews, although comparisons to the recently concluded *Friends* started right from the pilot. Sentiments ranged from Hal Boedeker at the *Orlando Sentinel*, who wrote, "for anyone longing for the next *Friends*, CBS offers a worthy candidate," all the way to James Poniewozik, who wrote in *Time* magazine, "witty, good-looking people dating, hanging out and trading quips in Manhattan . . . it's a revolutionary idea for a sitcom — in 1994."

Many people cited Neil Patrick Harris' Barney Stinson as one of the show's main draws, prompting Jamie J. Weinman of *Maclean's* to suggest that "Barney is the new Fonzie." Robert Bianco, writing for *USA Today*, said the "inventive" show "boasts a fine cast that could, with time, jell into a great one." Bianco singled out Neil Patrick Harris' "change-of-pace" role as well as Alyson Hannigan, saying that she was "as delightful here as she was in *Buffy*, which is high praise indeed."

It's also true that the online presence of *How I Met Your Mother*, which helped to establish a very strong fan base, all started with the actual appearance of "Barney's Blog," an idea first mentioned in the pilot episode. What later became a full-fledged trend of registering domains and creating real-life versions of websites seen in the show started with these blog entries.

Harris' pole position of popularity led some to consider that the show — with ratings that were OK but not solid, ranking 51st out of 156 shows during the 2005–2006 season — might wind up being retooled to focus on Barney's sleazy antics, in much the same way things shifted on *Happy Days*. But Bays and Thomas stood fast with their dedication to the romantic-comedy leanings of the show.

As for awards, it was a slow start for the series. The show won two Emmys, for Outstanding Art Direction and Outstanding Cinematography, both in the Multi-Camera Series category. The show also won a People's Choice Award for Favorite New Television Comedy and, perhaps most telling, a nod from the Casting Society of America for Best Comedy Pilot Casting.

The other relationship that takes up much of the second season is the one between Marshall and Lily. Even though we watch as Lily tries to make a go of things, first in San Francisco and then on her own in New York, and even though Marshall casts his line out into the dating waters, we are quite sure that these two are going to wind up together because, dammit, they *belong* together. As a result, we don't invest a lot in the idea of these two apart, and even when Marshall looks to hook up with a beautiful barista in the seventh episode of the season ("Swarley"), we're not at all surprised when Marshall and Lily are back together by the end of the episode.

Less expected is the humanization of Barney Stinson. The idea of a manipulative shark who lives, as the creators suggest in the pilot script, "on steak and cigars" can last a few episodes, maybe even one season, but if we're going to spend longer with this guy than drinks up to last call, we'll have to know more about him. The developing backstory is a little dark (a promiscuous mother constantly on the hunt for Barney's new daddy) but still manages to be funny — if you don't mind laughing at a kid throwing a ball at the man on the television that his mom says is his father. *The Price Is Right* is usually good for a few laughs and tears, but even more so when considering how Bob Barker factors into *HIMYM* this season.

Continuing from its beginning in season one, the ongoing Canadian jokes at Robin's expense continue to be worth their weight in Tim Hortons double-doubles, especially when it is revealed that Robin is a gun nut. Sure, this fact provides some dramatic grist to the relationship ups and downs between her and avowed anti-gun Ted, but it also flies in the face of what we've come to expect from a peace-loving, universal-health-care-having Canadian character. It makes sense as we learn more about Robin's background and rough relationship with her father, and it is even more in keeping with the show's focus on flipping the norms of the standard male-female romantic comedy dynamic. Only on a show like this — and only in an American city like New York

— could a square-jawed beauty from above the 49th Parallel be the gun-nuttiest member of any particular group. This is clearly a storybook version of the Greatest City on Earth and not the real one, where you're likely to get shot by a certain ex-mayor if he finds you drinking a high-fructose corn syrup–based beverage. Or so Fox News would have me believe.

By the end of this season there are few surprises, none that would shock us if we've been paying attention. But that's the funny thing about this show: we know where we're going, but we're happy to be along for the ride. In this, *How I Met Your Mother* teaches us the difference between plain reminiscence and nostalgia — one is nothing but a colorless recitation of the facts while the other is bittersweet, like the pain from an old wound, as the Greeks said. And we will happily pick at that old wound, provided it yields as much fun as a round of laser tag with Barney.

So far, so good.

remember the time . . .
HIGHLIGHTS, RUNNING GAGS, AND CATCHPHRASES

- Barney's *Grapes of Wrath*–inspired speech in "Where Were We?" in which he vows not to take up the fight of the Dust Bowl Okies, but instead to assist women with their daddy issues through promiscuity and casual sex. While the sentiment isn't quite the same, it is still stirring to hear Barney swear that "we'll be there" . . . even if it is to exploit his conquests and not so much to set them up with jobs, land, and dignity

- The long cut in "Swarley," where the three guys sit stone-faced in a coffee shop for almost a full minute before deciding that hanging out in a bar is *much* more interesting. Many have seen this as a rejoinder to those who saw *How I Met Your Mother* as a *Friends* knock-off. The episode's writer, Greg Malins, swore that it was never his intention to summon comparisons to the Central Perk gang, a protest that feels a little suspect when you consider that Malins was a writer/producer on *Friends*

- The *Cheers* references in the same episode, from the entirety of MacLaren's hollering out "Swarley!" to the use of the *Cheers* theme song, and the end credits being set in the same font as those on the long-running bar-set comedy
- Barney's mistaken ideas about his true lineage in "Showdown" — am I the only one who thinks Bob Barker makes perfect sense as his father?
- Marshall's fear of ferrets, which he says are nothing more than "tube-shaped rats," a view that turned more than one viewer against these land-based otters ("Where Were We?")

taking life and turning it
into a series of crazy stories
THE EPISODES

2.01 where were we?

Sure, his kids show the first signs of getting restless ("It feels like you've been talking for a year."), but Future Ted still has a lot to say about his time in New York.

Ted and Robin are in the opening movements of their new relationship, where everything manages to be sweet and cuddly as well as hot and heavy. It's called the honeymoon phase for a reason, because not only will it not last, but who could possibly maintain that kind of energy over the long haul? (Seriously, every time you make love it can't end like Beethoven's "Ode to Joy.")

For now, though, they can't get enough of each other. Marshall is also unbearable to be around, but for the exact opposite reason. With Lily gone to San Francisco for an art fellowship, Marshall is forced to consider a life without her and what that future might look like. Well, not quite yet — he's still in the moping and drinking beer for breakfast stage. But how he envisioned his adulthood has shattered; doesn't that entitle a guy to some inappropriate drinking?

In fact, the changed face of his adulthood messes with Ted and Robin's relationship: despite an oath to take it slow, they have a de facto baby in Marshall. He can't feed himself, cries all the time, and keeps the new couple up all night — so we shouldn't judge if Robin's idea of new parenting includes feeding the baby beer until he passes out.

Barney, ever the histrionic child, is excited by the idea of

David Henrie

Marshall's single status. He sees it as the potential for a blank slate, to say nothing of a new wingman, if only they can erase from Marshall's mind all the images of Lily's naked breasts, or "BPEGs." Early into the breakup Marshall is still terribly depressed, which in turn is depressing to Barney, whose sensitive suggestion to fight this affliction — "stop being sad and be awesome instead" — is worth its weight in cognitive behavioral therapy. (This is also Freud's take on how to battle the post-breakup malaise, buried in the back of his *The Interpretation of Dreams*. Although now that I think of it that *might* have been a handwritten footnote. Is it possible that Barney Stinson took psych in university?)

The gang's tussle with encroaching full-on adulthood continues, as Ted and Robin find themselves at their first disagreement as a couple (minor though it is, regarding Lily's role in Marshall's morose downward spiral, although they do differ on the idea of gun ownership) and Barney learns that while combatting all the pain and inner turmoil by going to a strip club may work for him, it is not a fighting stance that works for everyone, especially Marshall.

empire state building fun facts

- While we know Robin is a gun nut, actress Cobie Smulders never fired an actual gun until training with a guy who puts Los Angeles SWAT teams through their paces for her role in *The Avengers* movie. Cobie thought she might walk away from the experience full of adrenaline and a desire to buy a gun, but instead left with a healthy respect for the damage a gun can wreak and a distinct "It's not for me" vibe.

2.08 atlantic city

The commitment to inverting romantic comedy tropes is in full effect so far this season, with Lily being the one who calls off the wedding and Marshall the one who is reluctant to take her back for fear of the hurt it might cause. Once he gets past that (and they have some let's-get-married kitchen sex that includes flour, tousled hair, and Mrs. Butterworth), Lily is very anxious to get the wedding over with. While that might not be the most romantic notion, Marshall seems on board, if only to hold onto his once-itchy fiancée (and keep the syrup flowing, if you know what I mean).

This episode isn't only about Marshall and Lily getting back together; we also see Barney reconnect with an old love. It's almost sweet to see Barney meet up with the flame he left behind, notwithstanding his lecherous comment that she is "always in decline, never hitting bottom." Did I mention that his ex is Atlantic City and, more specifically, gambling? It's no surprise that a high-powered executive like Barney (again, we're not sure what he does, but it requires a big office, so I guess "executive" should cover it) would be taken in by the thrill of winning it all. Of course, you might think his ardor would have been stunted somewhat when he lost his entire life's savings, but then you would have a poor understanding of the compulsion to gamble and the almost sexual pull of putting everything on the line (a pull that Barney, of all people, can't resist).

Even more puzzling are the rules of the Chinese game that Barney frequented during his days as an Atlantic City regular (clearly he was a high-roller in the old days, given his great treatment at the casino and his deep knowledge of conversational Cantonese). Apparently one can win enough money to fund a wedding in international waters in a game that appears to be a nail-chewing combination of poker, mahjong, musical chairs, roulette, and Yahtzee (the creators of this game apparently never saw *The Deer Hunter*).

It becomes clear that Lily wants a quickie wedding so she can avoid facing the Eriksen clan and their likely-to-be-disapproving glares. After all, she did jilt their sweet Midwestern son Marshall and leave him to cancel all the wedding arrangements. (Side note: shouldn't it be the job of the one who high-jumped the altar to make those calls?) But does that mean that Marshall should be deprived of the joy of seeing his family at his own wedding, even if their loving looks are punctuated by eye-daggers flung at Lily? The bride-to-be doesn't think so, and if she's willing to take that kind of hit for the guy she loves (which she is), then isn't she showing her own grown-up stripes and proving herself, once again, to be the right woman for Marshall to marry?

empire state building fun facts

- The baffling game that Barney plays is called *xíng háishì bùxíng*, which translates to "Deal or No Deal," so it must easily date back to the Tang Dynasty, which boasts a direct line to comedian and rubber-glove-as-hat-wearer Howie Mandel (... please don't ask for verification of this fact).

2.09 slap bet

The fears, irrational or otherwise, of being in a serious relationship litter this episode, despite the attention to the machinations of the Slap Bet, the role of Slap Bet Commissioner, and the adherence to moral absolutes that holding that office requires.

The opening of a new Sharper Image store is enough to garner Barney's interest, and the possibility of him buying them foot massagers sparks the interest of the gang. Everyone, that is, except Robin, who seems to have a preternatural aversion to malls (with her dread of Doc from the Seven Dwarfs placing a close, if bewildering, second in the irrational fear department).

Speaking of irrational fears, we learn in this episode that Marshall apparently not only believes in the existence of Sasquatch, but avoids the Pacific Northwest out of concern of running into the cryptozoological beast. Given Marshall's height, is it possible that what he truly fears is encountering a hairy beast who thinks Marshall is a long-lost brother?

More important is Robin's fear of giving too much of herself in a relationship. Marshall notes that she is a "really private person," but Ted can't let his curiosity go, and believes the lawyer-in-training's initial assertion that Robin must have a husband she abandoned in Canada.

The Canadian jokes don't stop there, with the eerie echoes of Alanis Morissette in Robin's Canadian pop star career playing an even bigger role. That reference may have a more direct resonance in later seasons (when Robin references her ill-fated serious and grunge-inflected follow-up album), but those unfamiliar with the Jagged Little Pill's early incarnation are missing out on the Robin Sparkles–type arc of the real singer's early career.

Not only did Morissette enjoy a modicum of success as a one-name dance-pop singer in Canada (just "Alanis" for those who are curious), she was known for hit songs such as "Too Hot" and "Walk Away," notable for a pre-*Friends* appearance by Matt LeBlanc in the accompanying video. While there are no direct references to "going to the mall" in the early Alanis repertoire, "Too Hot" was a perfect encapsulation of the mall-pop sound during her first reign atop the Canadian charts, before she attained worldwide acclaim for singing about going down on someone in a theater.

Ted puts up a good front trying to honor Robin's desire to keep her past secret, but she soon realizes that letting him in, letting him know her better, can only strengthen their relationship, not hinder it. Even if it means listening to Robin Sparkles rap.

If you watch the full video for "Let's Go to the Mall," you might even see a cameo from that famous cryptid himself, Sasquatch. Or that might just be Alan Thicke.

empire state building fun facts

- This episode features two occurrences of what I like to call the Expository Inquisition: that is, the introduction of a pre-existing theory held by one of the characters that can only be explained by one of the *other* characters asking a question that simply rephrases the title of said theory ("What's a 'Slap Bet'?" or ". . . the 'Oh' Moment?").

- It is also important to note that the Canadian jokes in this episode really hit their stride, from the general bemused ignorance of most of the gang to the jingoistic disdain Barney holds for what he believes is a backward country full of porn that features "flat-chested Nova Scotians grinding up against Mounties."

2.16 stuff

What it means to be a good friend — whether girl, boy, or platonic — is at the heart of "Stuff." On the one hand, it might mean throwing out a rare Bolivian cactus; on the other, it might mean sitting through an excruciatingly long one-man show about a robot that falls in love with a toaster.

Wait. I'm getting ahead of myself.

Everything is going great between Ted and Robin until all the items around the apartment come to life as his ex-girlfriends. It becomes clear that Ted holds onto a lamp or a throw pillow not because they hold sentimental value but because they mark biographical points that he'd like to remember, without attaching any feelings to the person who bought them. Also, as Robin remarks, he seems incapable of buying anything for himself. And if he's like most guys I know, she probably wants to steer clear of his underwear and sock drawer.

Robin knows that she can't pretend that Ted never had other girlfriends, but evidence of those relationships dangled in front of her is too much for her to stand. She goes to the gang for a ruling and comes out ahead. Clearly, Ted should have thrown out those items already or, at the very least, lied about where they came from (so says the married writer who believes that relationship trouble is best approached with the *honesty is the best policy — unless lying can get you out of a jam* rule). However, Robin's moral high ground becomes shaky when it is revealed that all her dogs are gifts from previous boyfriends. And, like Ted, what guy hasn't imagined his paramour's exes as impossibly hot guys acting like dumb, slobbering dogs at the end of a leash? (Yes, I'm seeing a therapist about this entire paragraph. I mean, I'm not, but that lie made you feel better for a minute there, didn't it? I win!)

There's a funny subplot about the group going to a dreadful "artsy" play that features Lily, but while there are some broad swipes at terrible art (possibly second to airplane food as the oldest standby for jokes), they are mostly distractions from the main plot, where Ted can't help but see all of Robin's dogs as her hunky ex-boyfriends. This leads to some strange, surrealist sights like Ted and Robin walking a quintet of guys in dog collars down the street, the kind of imagery one might see in a play where the main characters are Rage, Greed, and Envy.

In the end, the key to being a good friend, whether platonic or romantic, is to think of another person's feelings ahead of your own once in a while. Except if you're Barney. After enduring Lily's interminable play, Barney puts on his own one-man show (complete with recorder solo), in which a lovestruck robot discovers his circuitry is overloaded . . . with feelings. A little like the womanizer himself, as we'll learn in later seasons. And that, kids, is what they call "foreshadowing."

empire state building fun facts

- After a season and a half of housing five dogs in a cramped Brooklyn apartment, this is the first time we see Robin walking them.
- Robin sends her dogs to live with her aunt upstate, which was a concession by the show's creators to actor Josh Radnor — who only divulged his intense dog allergy after he got the part of a guy who, for a couple of seasons, is in love with a multi-dog owner: for Carter Bays and Craig Thomas to do that shows they've taken the moral of this episode to heart.
- Barney tells Lily that friendship is fine "if you're a Smurf":

it's an interesting quip given that five years later, Neil Patrick Harris would star in the big screen adaptation of *The Smurfs*, along with Katy Perry (who appears in season six's "Oh Honey") and Jayma Mays, who appeared as the cute coat check girl in season one's "Okay Awesome."

2.17 arrivederci, fiero

True to *HIMYM*'s fixation with the intoxicating (some might say stupefying) allure of nostalgia, everyone in the gang is forced to look back when Marshall's car — a rickety Fiero held together with epoxy and youthful idealism — gives up the ghost just shy of clicking over 200,000 miles. As Future Ted remarks early on, we all hold onto things that signify the person we thought we were going to be — instead of the compromised and likely unfulfilled adult we've become. And isn't that the crux of the pragmatism of adulthood?

Lily didn't become a world-renowned artist. Ted didn't become a philosopher. Barney never learned to *actually* drive. And Marshall is on his way to taking a "sell-out corporate" job at a huge law firm instead of following his dream of working in environmental law. One thing this episode doesn't touch on is the irony that Marshall's beloved link to the ideals of his youth is exactly the kind of gas-guzzling, exhaust-belching monstrosity that, as an environmental lawyer, he would have fought to get off the road.

Of course, he has nothing but fond memories of the car, especially when he and Ted look back and remember how a college-era road trip and subsequent stranding in a blizzard brought them closer together. Marshall looks past Ted's nascent show-offy intellectualism (one of the first times this is hinted at with regard to Ted's character, complete with a Robert Frost quote) when he offers up his flesh for Marshall's survival, should the bespectacled mop-head die first. Marshall doesn't return the favor, as the idea of someone eating or splitting open his body like a tauntaun "skeeves" him out, but the dramatic sacrifice (along with a long night in each other's arms — you know, to conserve heat) goes a long way to bringing them together as best friends.

When it comes time to let go of the near-mythic Fiero, still 0.7 miles short of the 200,000 milestone, Marshall has to accept that things change, and that includes who we become. As the gang accepts that they won't see the odometer flip over, and instead settle for a triumphant clarion call of "close enough!" it reeks of contented compromise, which is a cornerstone of adulthood. I mean, as far as roads taken goes, it's no "one less traveled," but it'll do.

empire state building fun facts

- The running gag of The Proclaimers' song "I'm Gonna Be (500 Miles)" playing over and over in the Fiero's stereo manages to encapsulate the entire lifespan of an earworm pop song and the many stages of one's relationship with it: love it, like it, hate it, it's not so bad, love it!
- Also, it is revealed in the closing flashback scene that Marshall purchased the song on "cassingle," which, in a world of digital music, is exactly the sort of blast from the past that makes certain writers of certain television series guides bend over at the waist, winded, wondering what the hell happened to the last twenty-five years.

2.18 moving day

Never mind that they arrive at the decision to move in together at the end of their longest fight ever (see "Stuff"), Ted and Robin are convinced that to do so is the appropriate next step in their relationship. Nobody else does, whether they appear supportive at first (see Marshall and Lily) or dead-set against it from the outset (see Barney and his "The 'Are You Ready to Move in Together?' Quiz"). Even we in the audience can see that these guys are treading water, fooling themselves into thinking they are even ready for a relationship, never mind cohabitation.

That is part of the enjoyment of the series though, isn't it? That level of dramatic irony, where *we* can see that the road they are taking leads nowhere, but they remain blind to it. It has a bittersweet sting, like the nostalgia that permeates the whole series.

Also part of the enjoyment of the show is the combination of narrative inventiveness with the comfort of characters we've come to know and love. While Marshall and Lily may convince themselves that they are excited at the prospect of having the apartment to themselves, we're not surprised to learn that with the empty room comes a Ted-sized hole in their lives. If Ted is the one who does all the grocery shopping and owns all the bath towels, how will these two succeed as a married couple? They can't even stock their bathroom with toilet paper.

Marshall comes to the conclusion that they need Ted in their lives and wonders if he and Lily can marry Ted, in effect morphing from a couple to a "triple," hopefully enjoying all the rights and privileges of other married couples and being recognized as such by the City and State of New York (given how successful the show is, I think they've got the votes).

The triple marriage idea floated by Marshall — who uses the story of the codependent Amazonian rainforest to convince Lily that without Ted they will wither and die — forces viewers to wonder if they are completely bonkers, if their marriage is already doomed . . . or if we need to rethink our take on "traditional" marriage.

Given the ultimate fate of Ted and Robin's plan to move in together, I'd go for the latter. As is often the case in these situations, the principals are the last to see the plain truth: they are not ready to move in together — something Ted realizes when Barney points out that he keeps calling his future home "Robin's place" and not "our place" or even "home."

The inventiveness of the episode is an elegant creation on Barney's behalf, when he not only steals the moving truck filled with Ted's belongings but turns it into what is, in effect, a mobile swinging bachelor pad. Despite the fact that Ted and Robin consummate their amicable decision to live apart by having sex in Barney's cube-van version of the Playboy Mansion's grotto, the couple still feels like they are on the road to nowhere. Barney sees it too, and even though his efforts to keep the two apart are dysfunctional and destructive, he's on the right track. Even if he isn't able to see his own emotional investment in these two breaking up.

But more on that later.

empire state building fun facts

- It makes perfect sense that Barney delivers a Top Ten list ("Top Ten Things I Would Have Called My Truck if Ted Hadn't Been a Jerk and Given it Back") in a note-perfect David Letterman impersonation (right down to the number-three slot utterance of "Hee hee hee"). Given Bays and Thomas' history on the writing staff of *The Late Show*, it feels as if they've been sitting on this kind of gag for a long time: it's too bad they didn't institute a rule ending each episode with a Top Ten list, if only so we could have looked forward to more "The Eighteen Squealer" jokes.

mother herrings
THOSE WHO WOULD BE MOM

As the bulk of season two is taken up by Ted's relationship with Robin, we are left to think that there aren't any mother herrings this season. Or are there? We do get to see a trio of ex-girlfriends morph out of household items in "Stuff," but viewers think enough of Ted that we assume he wouldn't choose the mother of his children based on the size of her rack.

house guests

- Funk legend George Clinton from the P-Funk All Stars as himself in "Where Were We?"
- Morena Baccarin (*Firefly*, *Homeland*) as the "crazy eyes" barista in "Swarley"
- Bryan Cranston (*Breaking Bad*, *Malcolm in the Middle*) as architect Hammond Druthers in "Aldrin Justice" and "Columns"
- Wayne Brady (*Whose Line Is It Anyway?*, *Let's Make a Deal*, and a memorable guest spot on *Chappelle's Show*) as Barney's brother, James, in "Single Stamina"
- Jane Seymour (*Live and Let Die*, *Dr. Quinn, Medicine Woman*, *Wedding Crashers*) as Professor Lewis in "Aldrin Justice"
- Bob Barker (*The Price Is Right*) as himself — and the father Barney *thinks* is his — in "Showdown"
- David Burtka (Neil Patrick Harris' real-life partner) as Lily's ex-boyfriend and hapless stalker, Scooter, in "Something Borrowed"
- Lucy Hale (*Pretty Little Liars*) as Robin's little sister, Katie, in "First Time in New York"
- Michael Gross (*Family Ties*, *Dan Vs.*, and *Tremors*, on the big screen, direct-to-video, and as a TV series) as Ted's father in "Brunch"

David Burtka and Neil Patrick Harris
CHRIS HATCHER / PR PHOTOS

maybe it's the booze talking
REACTIONS TO THE SEASON

The ratings for the second season were consistent overall with the first season, but by the end of the year it had managed to slip ten spots to 61st place out of 142 programs. While each episode fluctuated between nine and ten million viewers, it couldn't make much ground against the ratings leviathan that was *American Idol*. Funny, given that Neil Patrick Harris would later appear as a guest judge on season nine of the show in 2008, which goes to show that the television game makes strange bedfellows — and guest judges — out of almost any of its players.

Fans understandably worried about the dramatic thrust of the show in the second season. Ted's search for love was the primary force behind the series. But with Ted attached to Robin, the concern was that the series was sputtering out only two seasons in. Can Ted be interesting outside of being in a state of romantic yearning? We'd have to wait to find out.

The awards started to come a little more easily. The show won Emmys for Outstanding Art Direction and Cinematography for a Multi-Camera Series, and for the first time Neil Patrick Harris received a nomination, this time for Outstanding Supporting Actor in a Comedy Series. Harris also nabbed a nomination at the Teen Choice Awards for Choice TV Actor: Comedy and the episode featuring Barney's gay brother, "Single Stamina," was nominated for a GLAAD Media Award.

a quick refreshment
ENSEMBLE TV COMEDIES

Despite being founded in 1933, the Screen Actors Guild didn't enter the accolade-and-statuette business until 1994. Along with showing the wisdom to extend the award-dispensing to both TV and film, SAG (known since 2012 as SAG-AFTRA, having merged with the American Federation of Television and Radio Artists) also seeks to recognize achievements in both comedy and drama.

In a decision that out-distances the Emmys, Golden Globes, and even the Academy Awards, the Screen Actors Guild also rewards the highest achievements in ensemble acting, a boon to television endeavors that draw on the resources of a rich, well-rounded cast.

A true ensemble is more than a flank of supporting characters simply attending and commenting on the actions of the main characters. The dynamics of ensemble are far deeper, far subtler than that. For a cast to truly be considered an ensemble, the relationships between each of them must be fully considered and dramatized. A fan should not think of one character without immediately reflecting on their dynamic with another, whether played out in grand dramatic gestures or slight facial tics. Each character works as an interlocking piece of the puzzle, like gears in a machine that drives not only the forward momentum of the story but a deeper understanding of the people involved.

A review of the winners of this award since its inception strongly indicates that solid ensemble work has been central to the success of some of the most historically resonant TV comedies — and that the cast of *How I Met Your Mother* can neatly assume a place among these lauded enterprises.

Seinfeld 1994, 1996, 1997

While it is easy to think of *Seinfeld* as existing in a bubble of observational humor that distances it from the times in which it was created, a look at the fellow nominees that first year provides an interesting snapshot: *Frasier*, *Mad About You*, *Murphy Brown*, and *Northern Exposure* fix the show squarely in the '90s.

Watching any of the episodes from the series' golden years (like most shows, located somewhere in the middle of its run), the show feels timeless. It doesn't seem to have lost any of its humor or insight despite the marked lack of modern wrinkles like smartphones, Skype, and Facebook — for that, we thankfully have Modern Seinfeld on Twitter (@SeinfeldToday), which takes up that slack to hilarious effect. Instead, the show (essentially about the bristling selfishness that lurks beneath the veneer of politeness) continues to feel fresh and current.

More than that, despite ostensibly being created as a starring vehicle for veteran stand-up comedian Jerry Seinfeld, it is a quintessential ensemble piece. Not so much for the interplay between the characters (in fact, there is a complete lack of hierarchy or social stratification among the four) but borne out by the fact that it seems as if every episode contains a well-defined storyline for every character. Add to that the elegant convergence of plot threads (unseen since the finer episodes of *Fawlty Towers*), and a solid four-legged table of a show is the result. If you think otherwise, try to imagine just about any episode without one of the four characters getting involved. For a show legendarily about "nothing," the audience was invested in each character, and every chapter of the series felt like a make-or-break proposition.

Friends 1995

Fans of *How I Met Your Mother* (and those who bristle at the constant comparisons to that *other* show about twentysomethings wrestling with love and career in the Big Apple), will be happy to learn that *Friends* only won this award once, a year after it premiered and well into the cultural explosion that surrounded a show that, at the time, seemed revolutionary in its appeal to a younger demographic.

In addition to its *it's-like-they-put-a-camera-in-my-coffee-shop* appeal to Generation X–types (They don't have their lives figured out! They have McJobs!), *Friends* must be recognized for its ability to make an intrinsically ensemble concept work over the long haul of a ten-year run by constantly rewiring the relationships between the characters. Other than the ultimate union of Rachel and Ross, there were a number of shifts in the connections between them. Who knew from the first season that Monica and Chandler would make such a happy couple? Who could have guessed that Joey would fall in love with Rachel in the later years? And who among us would have guessed that Gunther would have made it all the way to the series finale?

Ally McBeal 1998

A workplace comedy known as much for the creepy CGI of a metaphorical dancing baby as for *Time* magazine wondering if it was the death knell of feminism, *Ally McBeal* is a time capsule of the '90s, and, as such, is almost the polar opposite of *Seinfeld*. Remember when Vonda Shepard was a big star? Remember when Robert Downey Jr. was still wrestling with his demons? Remember Jane Krakowski before *30 Rock*?

If you don't, then you were probably born in the '90s and likely wouldn't think much of the canned quirk David E. Kelley (*Chicago Hope*, *The Practice*, *Boston Legal*) doled out. Sure, the cast of regulars like Krakowski, Portia de Rossi, Lucy Liu, and Peter MacNicol broke a sweat to entertain us, but if timelessness is the target then *Ally McBeal* doesn't even hit the tree.

Frasier 1999

The term *ensemble* best applies to this show in the later seasons of its eleven-year run (for those counting, that means Kelsey Grammer played the titular character, between the spin-off, *Cheers*, and a one-time appearance on *Wings*, over a period of twenty years).

While this continuation of the Frasier Crane character might stand as the pre-eminent how-to for any future spin-offs of long-running sitcoms (new city, new start, old family dynamics to sort out), *Frasier* is better remembered for its champagne wit and sparkling repartee than for the graceful yet frenetic farce of *Cheers* or the truly close-knit, interdependent storylines of genuine ensemble comedy.

Can you imagine any episode of the series without Niles or Roz? I think so. Can you imagine an episode of *Frasier* without Frasier himself? You should be able to, because David Hyde Pierce took over for at least one episode while Kelsey Grammer took care of personal issues in rehab. It's a terrific show (having won the most Emmy awards — thirty-seven — of any comedy series), but it's not the finest example of true ensemble work.

Will & Grace 2000

A romantic comedy with the mother of all obstacles to a happy ending — incompatible sexual orientations — on the surface *Will & Grace* looks like another sturdy four-post ensemble cast. However, this show is more of a study in duets, with the most memorable storylines involving Will-and-Grace pairings as the main plots, with Jack-and-Karen hurly-burly providing farcical fuel for the secondary subplots.

Will & Grace certainly had enough work to do featuring a central gay character in a prime time network show (a landmark in LGBT representation that Vice President Joe Biden once suggested "did more to educate the American public than almost anything anybody has ever done") and, understandably, focused on the best friendship dynamic between the two putative leads.

After the show settled into a groove with the main characters, the exploits of Karen and Jack developed into a little bit more than two-dimensional, cartoonish B plots they'd previously inhabited (although they never *stopped* being that as well), but to this viewer the foursome never coalesced into a fully functioning engine. As a comparison, I have always found that episodes of *Friends* that feature all six characters in the same room are some of the most satisfying (consider the Thanksgiving episodes), whereas I cannot think of a case where I felt the same about the cast of *Will & Grace*.

Sex and the City 2001, 2003

For my money, *Sex and the City* suffered from the opposite problem that *Will & Grace* did. While it accurately captured the *event-followed-by-encapsulation-the-next-day-at-brunch* rhythm of many friendships, I always felt as if the characters' individual storylines fell flat when contrasted with the four of them together, commiserating over cosmopolitans. It would be hard to imagine a television series that consisted *solely* of four white girls sitting around chatting, but that was always when the series truly clicked.

Everybody Loves Raymond 2002

Another series that was created to feature a stand-up comedian and his existing work, *Everybody Loves Raymond* had a throw-back, *All in the Family* feel to it, the type of show where the surrounding characters orbit around the lead and capture (sometimes with uncomfortable accuracy) the subtle fluctuations in the web of familial relations.

Given that Ray Romano was not known as an actor, the creative forces behind the show wisely surrounded him with talented and seasoned veterans, from television stalwarts like Patricia Heaton and Brad Garrett (himself a road-tested stand-up comedian and talented mimic) to legendary character actors Doris Roberts (who seasoned her talents onstage in plays such as Neil Simon's *The Last of the Red Hot Lovers* and Terrence McNally's *Bad Habits*, and with recurring roles in TV shows *Alice* and *Remington Steele*) and the amazing Peter Boyle (who slipped between comedy and drama with ease, whether in *Young Frankenstein*, *Taxi Driver*, *Yellowbeard*, or *Monster's Ball*).

As such, it seems a shame that the Screen Actors Guild only gave the ensemble award to this cast once, but they were nominated a number of times.

Desperate Housewives 2004, 2005

I'd like to recuse myself from weighing in on this particular show. In all honesty, I never liked it; I thought it failed as satire and had a smugness in its execution (specifically in the incongruently chipper score) that always drove me bananas. When we don't agree with such recognition, it helps to consider that such things can be a marker of the times. In hindsight, we can view this show's win as a testament to the power of popularity versus true merit. (I'm thinking of Isaac Hayes winning the Best Original Song Oscar for "Theme from *Shaft*.")

The Office 2006, 2007

As with *Everybody Loves Raymond*, it is surprising that the Screen Actors Guild didn't think to bestow this honor on *The Office* more than twice during its nine-season run. Perhaps the sheer size of the cast, along with its shifting roster, might have played a part. But this remains the quintessential example of the workplace ensemble comedy. *The Office* always ran like a Swiss watch, in large part due to the fact that a number of the actors also served on the writing staff, which could only have added to the sense of community. The show also survived a long run by taking a page from the *Friends* playbook and shifting the relationships between the characters in an effort to keep it fresh.

While there are many who feel that the show never recovered from the loss of original lead Steve Carell, I think that Ed Helms was an inspired choice as his "replacement." The showrunners always managed to use changing fortunes in the careers of those who moved on (Carell to film, Mindy Kaling to her own show, *The Mindy Project*) to great revitalizing effect, for instance with the addition of *Bridesmaids'* Ellie Kemper as receptionist Erin Hannon and British expat Catherine Tate as the cunning Nellie Bertram.

30 Rock 2008

Although the most important element of ensemble comedy may be how cast works together, *30 Rock* is an instance where I think that a wildly talented cast, in roles both big and small, can be cited across the board for their individual work beneath the umbrella of the show.

The writing on the show is sharp (although in some episodes heavily invested in current events, which doesn't always work very well in syndication), but the gut-busting exploits of characters played by Tracy Morgan, Jane Krakowski, and Jack McBrayer stand on their own and are not dependent on successful integration with surrounding players.

Glee 2009

Co-created by Ryan Murphy (*Nip/Tuck*, *American Horror Story*), *Glee* seemed to tap into an unrecognized desire for a musical-based show (other than TV movie *High School Musical*). Like *The O.C.* with choreography, this teen-set series hit a high level of popularity out of the gate and threatened to bottom out early on from an overreliance on stunt guest stars (including Neil Patrick Harris) and, later on, tragedy in the form of main cast member Corey Monteith's death.

A show that features musical numbers in every episode requires a certain level of interconnection among the cast, and that work was rightly rewarded in *Glee*'s first year on the air.

Modern Family 2010, 2011, 2012, 2013

A show that takes on the changing face of families in twenty-first-century America would have enough to do simply trying to keep track of the comings and goings of its large cast of characters. But *Modern Family* also manages to maintain a high level of sharp writing that never *quite* tips over into door-slamming farce — and certainly never at the sacrifice of character integrity.

Given that the show manages to include eleven characters, in all manner of familial configurations, in virtually every episode, with quick wit and believable family dynamics to boot, it's likely that *Modern Family* will continue to win this ensemble award for the foreseeable future.

Where does *How I Met Your Mother* fit into the pantheon of ensemble comedy? I think Carter Bays and Craig Thomas have learned lessons from *Friends* about the shifting dynamics between characters and the strength of keeping the core cast working together as often as possible. They've also created a world, like *Seinfeld*'s, that looks very much like ours but is also distinctly its own, and one that works with stories that revolve around individual characters but ties up together nicely by the end of each episode.

Sounds worthy of an ensemble award of its own, doesn't it?

season three (2007–2008)
THE HUMBLE JOYS OF SLAPSGIVING

Two steps forward . . .

suit up! LEGEN . . . DARY THOUGHTS ON THE SEASON

For a guy who bemoans the fact that his life isn't going anywhere — romantically, at least — Ted Mosby doesn't develop much in this season. He's on the rebound and putting himself on the Barney Stinson diet of pickup lines and one-night stands. But Ted is far too smart to fool himself into believing such behavior is a way of putting himself "out there," and as a result we are left to believe that what he's doing is a little selfish, even if he dresses it up as getting over his breakup with Robin. What he doesn't realize is that even when he's floundering around in a sea of flirtation and empty sex (if you can call that "floundering"), he is actively engaged in propelling himself to his hoped-for destination. Even if it *is* an ongoing case of two steps forward, one step back.

For those of you who are wondering, "two steps forward, one step back" isn't just a botched refrain from an awesome Paula Abdul song ("Opposites Attract"). In fact, it's not a lyric in that song at all (the actual line is "two steps back"). So why am I writing about it? Well, it reminds me of a time when Paula Abdul was more than just a talent show punchline, and I think that bears mentioning. Plus, the dancing in that video is pretty rad, and it puts me in mind of what it takes to be a "two-stepper."

As it relates to *How I Met Your Mother*, the idea of taking two steps forward and one step back indicates that the person doing the stepping understands the actions they are taking and has consciously made the decision to continue on this arduous path because, despite losing fifty percent of the distance made every time they move forward, the ultimate destination is worth the extra effort.

The gang at MacLaren's continue to suffer the whims of fate. This has much to do with the framing device of Future Ted narrating all the goings-on — like anyone recalling a story, Future Ted picks out all the necessary elements required to make a specific point, leaving the rest to the dustbin of history. But it also provides a sense of comfort: the overriding sense of nostalgia that pervades the series works precisely because of this framing device, looking back as we do from the safety of the other side of all this turmoil. At no point do we think that Ted *won't* meet the mother of his children, so we feel at ease with any hairpin turn that might appear in the road. But the characters don't know what choices are going to affect their lives and thus aren't able to recognize the whole "two steps forward, one step back" formula. From the outside, the pattern is clearly visible; as such, I propose that we adopt the term *two-steppers* to describe those people who are slowly progressing toward their ultimate goal without realizing the extra steps they are taking along the way.

See? That was worth the walk, right?

In a season shortened a little by the 2007–2008 writers' strike, we still manage to learn more about the characters we've come to love. Most striking is Lily's shopping addiction, which goes from being a *Honeymooners*-style punchline ("To the moon, Lily!") to addressing the genuine impact this kind of behavior can have on a relationship. The way Bays and Thomas take a real-world situation and wring it for both laughs and complications is the type of approach that endears the show to many people. It's not often in network television that characters wrestle with the financial implications of homeownership, and while no one would confuse *How I Met Your Mother* for a *Look Back in Anger*–type kitchen sink drama, it is satisfying to see this type of concern not only being addressed but playing out over the course of a number of episodes.

Also satisfying is the whole "Ted Mosby Porn Star" doppelganger bit in "I'm Not That Guy." It's funny enough to see a guy who grew up in Shaker Heights, Ohio, idolize *our* Ted Mosby and decide that the best way to honor his idol is to assume his name as a pornographic actor, but it's even funnier when that event really resonates with the audience: in this case, me.

Now, I can't say that there is anyone using my name to labor in the adult industry (as far as I know), but I can report that I *do* share a name with another guy whose path I've crossed a number of times. And while this hasn't resulted in seeing my name next to a title like *Lance Hardwood: Sex Architect*, it has resulted in a newspaper headline erroneously attributed to me, to say nothing of almost paying my namesake's late fees at a Blockbuster in the late '90s. It would be a terrific button on the story if the charge had been for a pornographic film, but unfortunately it was for a much more sordid title: Tommy Lee Jones' epic *Volcano*. Despite his poor taste in movies, Bizarro Jesse has become a well-respected journalist, and, for anyone looking to know the difference between us, I generally say that he goes to places like Syria and Afghanistan and I go to bed at 9:30. But trying to make this delineation is often more trouble than it is worth, so I'll take credit for his work from the war-torn frontlines because, hey, I'm nothing if not cordial in conversation. Any other tack would be the very epitome of two steps forward, one step back.

Perhaps the greatest example of this overriding theme comes in a very meta-textual manner, in the form of Britney Spears. (I can only imagine that, outside of academic circles, I am the only person ever to have written that sentence.) Spears was well cast as the receptionist to Stella, Ted's late-season serious girlfriend. She played the well-meaning-if-eternally-puzzled character of Abby, and it is interesting to consider where this guest spot falls on the arc of her image rehab. We should note that the wig she sports in "Ten Sessions" disguises the short hair she wore at the time due to an unfortunate incident with a pair of hair clippers in early 2007.While she has since regained success and confirmed herself as a reliable commodity via a number of dance hits and her judging on *The X Factor*, the "Ten Sessions" episode came after a bad 2007, which saw her struggle with addiction, paparazzi, and an amateurish performance at that year's MTV Video Music Awards. Many thought her career was truly over, but high-charting singles like "Piece of Me" went a long way to re-establishing her musical credibility, while her appearance on *HIMYM* proved that she could be relied upon to deliver the comedic goods. But it is the gang whose forward momentum truly concerns us, specifically Ted's. And if the end of the season is any indication, he is ready for the next big stage of his life. Even if he's ready for it with the wrong woman.

remember the time . . .
HIGHLIGHTS, RUNNING GAGS, AND CATCHPHRASES

- The confidence of a returning third season is shown in the continuation from last season, finishing off one of Barney's catchphrases started from the previous season's ending episode. ". . . dary!" might seem like a strange way to inaugurate a season but in this case not only is it fitting but, after a dicey run in the ratings for the first two seasons, it feels well earned

- Also well earned is the *HIMYM* online presence, with websites such as theslapbetcountdown.com, tedmosby isajerk.com, lilyandmarshallselltheirstuff.com, and

guyforceshiswifetodressinagarbagebagforthenextthreeyears
.com, all active sites at the time the episodes aired

- This season also showed that Neil Patrick Harris had a
heretofore untouched talent for physical comedy; either
that or he can really take a slap, as we see him take out an
end table in "Slapsgiving"
- Perhaps even more amazing for NPH fans was the inclusion of a sweet callback to his Doogie Howser days in "The
Bracket." At the end of that episode, Harris re-enacts the
closing moments of almost every episode of his first series,
writing his thoughts in a computer journal while a plinky
synthesizer plays overtop
- "Everything Must Go" not only taught us that the most
important demographic in the art world is the G-CWOK
crowd (Gay Couples Without Kids) but also made another
reference to a well-respected show set in a bar. When the
gay couple buys a painting, they refer to it as an "original
Anton Kreitzer," a pseudonym that Norm used for his
nasty boss alter-ego on the *Cheers* episode "The Two Faces
of Norm"
- We also learned that in a desperate effort to "win" the
breakup with Robin, Ted allowed himself to get drunk
enough to get a tramp stamp tattoo ("Wait for It"), and
that he has a rather involved primping routine for his hair,
as witnessed in "The Platinum Rule"
- That last episode also gave the audience a clear view of
Lily's hair evolution through three scant seasons, from
orange, to dark red, to severe bangs. All very stylish but
hell for a makeup department on a show that features numerous flashbacks

taking life and turning it into a series of crazy stories
THE EPISODES

3.01 wait for it

The first episode of the season is full of two-steppers. Ted is on the rebound, and it looks like he is going to slither down the Barney Stinson waterslide of singledom as Barney's wingman. Nonetheless, in this episode we get a good view into Ted's interior world, confirming that he's so eager to become a player on the dating scene because he's still nursing a wounded heart after his otherwise "clean" breakup with Robin.

Josh Radnor has said that part of Neil Patrick Harris' talent is to say and do terrible things but still manage to appeal to the viewing audience without them wanting to "punch him in the face." It strikes me that efforts are made in this opening episode to provide a similar foundation for Ted, testing the limits of his inherent likability with some questionable (and possibly sleazy, at least in future episodes) behavior. The opening narration from Future Ted goes a long way to lay that groundwork, telling his kids that he had to "become the person" he needed to be to meet their mother. And that guy probably wouldn't include a butterfly tramp stamp on his romantic résumé.

Meanwhile, it appears that Robin is "winning" the breakup after her return from Argentina. But it's all a front. Sure, she has a gorgeous massage therapist boyfriend in tow — Gael, a man so handsome, free-spirited, and charming that both Lily *and* Marshall have crushes on him — but he's a rebound guy of the highest order. Ted

Lyndsy Fonseca

confronts her about this and tries to make up for the lack of yelling in their breakup by hollering at her in the hallway outside her apartment, but she admits to having been just as broken by the end of their relationship as he was. This helps Ted get through his anger at her apparent winning of the breakup, until she admits to one of Gael's, how should I say, shortcomings. Let's just say that Ted is the "bigger" man. So, you know, he definitely wins the breakup.

empire state building fun facts

- The appearance of Robin's exotic boyfriend Gael provides fuel for the unkillable *Friends* conspiracy, in particular by looking a whole lot like Rachel's new boyfriend Paolo, an Italian import that from season one who drove Ross crazy with jealousy.
- This episode is bookended with the first appearance of the yellow umbrella, which figures strongly in identifying the mother of Future Ted's kids.

3.07 dowisetrepla

The two-stepping continues, but it's primarily for Marshall and Lily in this episode. The idea of homeownership is one of the bigger steps into adulthood (and certainly the largest investment). It is generally looked at as a single step, and a forward one at that. But thanks to Lily's secret compulsive shopping habit and fifteen maxed-out credit cards, she and Marshall can only get a mortgage at eighteen percent, which, as anyone who has bought a house knows, means they can't *actually* afford the house — but the bank really likes those kids and wants to do a charitable thing. (Ha!)

The couple has a huge fight and goes through the painful work of thrashing their way through a messy secret. They learn that the crux of married life is not whether or not you have problems, but how you handle them when they inevitably arise. They also learn that a good marriage has *plenty* of secrets and that some things are better kept hidden. That only spices things up, right?

It is interesting that as much work as Carter Bays and Craig Thomas have done in the series to subvert the standard gender roles of romantic comedy, they revert to a *my-wife-can't-stop-shopping* storyline so prehistoric that it felt stale when Wilma Flintstone screamed "Charrrrrrge it!" Perhaps we can look at this thread as a different kind of subversion, one that is critical of a consumerist society that compels people to spend money in an effort to fill an existential hole that only deepens with each dollar they spend. People in the modern world can find themselves on a never-ending treadmill that leads inexorably to misery and debt.

Or, maybe it's just for the gags. Yeah, it's probably that. Women just can't control themselves in a shopping mall, am I right, fellas?

In an effort to get a decent lending rate (an absolutely unavoidable rite of passage for any potential homeowners), Marshall and Lily briefly consider an on-paper divorce. This brings up the question of who would get the friends in such a split. Robin avers that she would go with Lily and Marshall would get Ted and Barney. This seems like a fair and equitable split of platonic assets, except I can imagine that Ted and Barney would see Lily on the side for lunch and gossiping. Marshall would find out, but he'd be cool with it because, hey, he understands how great she is. He married her, after all. Then Ted and Barney would arrange for a "chance" meeting between Marshall and Lily, at which point they'd fall back in love and get remarried, with Robin as the maid of honor and Ted and Barney as co-best men.

What I'm saying is that there is no future in which Marshall and Lily aren't married. Not in a world I want to live in, at least.

To that end, the couple stay together and get the apartment of their dreams. They will find themselves two steps down the financial ladder but, in the end, they'll find that creating a home in the long run is worth the immediate pain.

empire state building fun facts

- The realtor who shows Marshall and Lily their dream apartment is played by Maggie Wheeler, who played none other than Chandler's nasal-voiced on-again, off-again girlfriend Janice on *Friends* . . . so the conspiracy thickens.
- Robin suggests that Mount Waddington, at 4,019 metres, is the tallest mountain in Canada, when in fact it is only the highest peak in the Coast Mountains of British Columbia; the title of tallest in the country goes to Yukon's Mount Logan at a height of 5,959 meters, a difference of 1,940 meters.
- If you are looking to live in a neighborhood that has a nickname — especially a portmanteau like SoHo (made up of South of Houston) — then you'd better make sure you can afford it; and if you have to think about it, then you probably can't (even if the name does stand for down-wind of the sewage treatment plant). But don't worry, the bank will still lend you the money! They *totally* have your back, dude.

3.09 slapsgiving

The genesis of the whole *two steps forward, one step back* saying begins with an old fable about a frog trying to climb out of a well. For every two steps the frog climbs, he slips back one, which means that although he makes progress, it is double the effort, and a good lesson for a frog never to jump down a well. A good lesson to anyone, for that matter.

Similarly, Ted and Robin are quite froggy in this episode. They are making a good show of being over each other and good friends, and Robin even has a new boyfriend named Bob (an older forty-one, but envisioned by Ted as *much* older — like, grandpa old), but they both know very well that they are only pretending to be friends. They can't think of anything to talk about and, as a result, avoid being alone together at all costs. There's no word from the world of herpetology (that is, the study of amphibians) on whether or not romantics on four legs are as likely to slip up and have sex with their exes as those of the two-legged variety, but if so, then Ted and Robin sure as hell pull a "frog step" around this Thanksgiving.

This leads to an uncomfortable Thanksgiving dinner. Well, a *Slapsgiving* dinner if Marshall has his way. While Lily is trying to initiate a new tradition now that they are married, Marshall creates a website called slapcountdown.com that does exactly as its name suggests. Barney tries to play it cool, claiming that all the suspense is removed by nailing down the date, but he still fears the wrath of Marshall's meaty paw. In fact, worrying about the red-faced encounter deprives him of sleep — and ten pounds. If anticipation can make a thing sweeter, it can also make it more dreadful.

Much the same can be said about Ted and Robin. They feared that their friendship would never survive the turmoil of having once been intimate. Oddly, it seems that having sex somehow helps clear the air and allows them to start rebuilding again, if only for them to realize that reconstruction was necessary. Their ability to revive the "Major Buzzkill" joke is a good indication that there is a strong foundation still there to support a friendship.

I'm sure being a frog isn't nearly as complicated. At least their slap bets can't be *nearly* as sadistic as Marshall's.

empire state building fun facts

- The "Major Buzzkill" joke and salute re-emerge in later seasons.
- Neil Patrick Harris is a consummate physical comedian, given his ability to take a slap and flatten a side table without putting a wrinkle in his suit.
- Robin suggests that Canadian Thanksgiving is to celebrate

a failed attempt by Martin Frobisher to discover the Northwest Passage: it goes back this far, sure, but it's meant as more of a liturgical festival to celebrate the harvest.

3.12 no tomorrow

Things can get slanted in your late twenties. Whether it comes to how you see yourself in the present compared to the person you wanted to become, or a symbolically slanted floor in an apartment you just bought near a sewage treatment plant, it's often tough to keep your feet underneath you.

Finally, after a season of acting like an alcohol-poisoned frat boy, Ted is taken to task in this episode for his caddish behavior, even if he doesn't want to hear it. For a while, he thinks that the universe is playing tricks on him by rewarding his bad behavior with bad-boy riches. He makes the mistake (again, as he has for most of the season) of tagging along with Barney. Given the downward spiral Ted's evening takes — making out with a married woman, putting bottles of Dom Pérignon on someone else's tab, getting socked in the eye — it's no surprise that the bar Barney has dragged him to is called The Low Point.

Good thing he doesn't meet Future Ted's wife, even though she's at the bar that night. He can't imagine she would have liked him, given how much he realizes he doesn't like himself. The mysterious yellow umbrella shows up at the end of the episode, with Ted picking it up at the bar as he searches for his lost cell phone. In the hands of other writers, this might have come across as a shallow tease, but Carter Bays and Craig Thomas (who wrote this episode), make it feel perfectly placed. The audience feels like they are in good hands with grace notes like this, reminding us that the creators are keeping an eye on the final prize as they entertain us along the way.

While Ted is having what he thinks is a profound "no tomorrow"–type evening, Marshall and Lily have Robin over to the new apartment for game night. It becomes clear that the floor of their apartment is noticeably slanted, and while they both think the situation is hopeless (Marshall frets about not being able to get a pinball machine), it's singleton Robin who shows them the inherent fun offered by the canted floor by introducing the sport known as Apartment Roller Luge. They learn how to make the best of a bad situation, as does Ted, who realizes that finding out who he is and correcting course is as close a single guy can get to turning lemons to lemonade.

Ted has taken *way* more than two steps back, so he's certainly earned the next step forward his romantic life takes.

empire state building fun facts

- Barney can't believe the poor ratio of guys to women in the bar, suggesting that there hasn't been such a lack of dudes in New York City clubs ever, even in the Great Dude Shortage of 1883. What could have led to such a shortage of dudes? Perhaps that it coincided with the first season of baseball's New York Gothams playing in the National League. It wasn't a great season — they finished sixth with a 46–50 record — but they did go on to become the New York Giants who, in turn, became the San Francisco Giants. That's *got* to be why there were so few dudes in NYC nightclubs in 1883, right?

3.16 sandcastles in the sand

There is a lot of two-stepping going on in this season, but who knew that it had its own psychological term? Well, probably anyone with a passing knowledge of the field, but it still took me by surprise. Hey, I took English lit in university, leave me alone.

Marshall is convinced that his term "revertigo" is the clinical name for the phenomenon of people regressing to previous versions of themselves when in the company of certain individuals from their pasts. Lily is susceptible to a particularly funny version of this with her friend Michelle, whose appearance is enough to turn her into a finger-snapping, head-bobbing round-the-way girl.

It is this friend of Lily's — who is in the process of finishing her dissertation on behavioral psychology — who confirms that there *is* a term for it, but it's actually known as "associative regression" (which sounds more clinical but isn't nearly as much fun to say as "revertigo").

Robin endures this phenomenon when her first boyfriend from Canada visits New York. Despite the fact that Simon dumped her back when she was sixteen — for a girl who had a pool — Robin wants to prove herself to be the clear "winner" when they reunite. Everyone can tell that she is the winner — except Robin, that is, who revertigos (revertigoes? revertiwent?) all the way back to her adolescence and once again falls for the failed musician, who lives with his mother and works at an Ottawa waterslide park.

This can only end badly, another fact that only Robin can't see. Barney would have likely seen it coming a mile off if he hadn't been blinded by his search for the Robin Sparkles video that gives this episode its title. It's funny to note that while this episode aired in the not-too-distant past of 2008, there are a few things that curiously age the show. Characters using flip phones instead of smartphones is a great indicator of the era, but the idea that YouTube hadn't yet blossomed to the point that nearly *every* recorded image in the known world is searchable within seconds certainly makes us realize how quickly time and technology march on by. Good thing, too, because it would have made the search for this long-lost Canadian pop video (on *VHS*, for God's sake) a lot less interesting — and taken up roughly sixty seconds of plot.

We eventually see the cameo-studded video, and revealing it to Barney is a moment of big vulnerability for Robin, which also leads to the biggest step forward of the episode: the two of them locked in a kiss. It's almost worth going through a breakup with the loser bassist of a band called The Foreskins a *second* time just to get back on the path you were meant to follow.

empire state building fun facts

- The inclusion of Canadian hero Alan Thicke makes sense in Robin's video (filmed during the week-and-a-half of summer available to those hearty Canucks), and the addition of American teen pop sensation Tiffany as a Robin Sparkles backup singer is a nod to the fact that Robin Sparkles' original mall-based success was based on Tiffany's career-making mall tour of 1987.
- It's strange that James Van Der Beek was chosen to play Robin's Canadian ex-boyfriend, given that he's not Canadian. If the creators had wanted to continue the Alanis Morissette correlation, they should have cast Matt LeBlanc, who played a similar beefcake role in one of Alanis' early dance-diva videos, "Walk Away" . . . but maybe they didn't want to add fuel to the bonfire of *Friends* comparisons.

3.17 the goat

After the tumult of "Sandcastles in the Sand," Robin is in a very vulnerable place and takes what likely feels less like a step back and more like a jump into the mouth of a volcano: she sleeps with Barney.

And so we have the start of — Robarney. Wait . . . Barbin? Brobney? Rarnobin? Sue me, I don't write for *Us Weekly*.

What at first plays like an episode that will explore Robin's difficulties quickly refocuses to Barncy as the official campaign to humanize him continues. We still don't see much much regarding his feelings for Robin, but the guilty conscience that is churned up after he sleeps with his bro Ted's ex-girlfriend, a clear violation of the letter and the spirit of The Bro Code (in particular, Article 150 of said code) is new territory for Barney.

Barney hires Marshall as his lawyer not only for privilege of confidence but in the hope of finding a loophole in The Bro Code, so he can stop feeling bad and buying increasingly meaningless devices from Sharper Image. This marks the first appearance of Barney's leather-bound, gilt-edged volume that governs all things about and between bros, a tome that he has now violated. As he wrestles with the idea of a confrontation with Ted, both the viewer and Barney himself realize that he has a conscience after all.

Ted looks like he's ready to let it all go, but saves his kindness for Robin. He forgives *her* but rides Barney pretty hard (not devil's threeway hard, but hard nonetheless) which seems a little unfair. She's just as much to blame as Barney is for the tryst, but Ted inexplicably holds Barney to a higher standard when, frankly, he should expect more from Robin and almost *nothing* from Barney in the ethics department. Maybe the fact the Ted is turning thirty skews his own moral compass — or, it could be a sign of early-onset dementia. I mean, come on. Barney would try to sleep with anything in a skirt. Why *wouldn't* he try to nail Robin?

I guess that's why Ted's proclamation that his friendship with Barney is over rings false. It could be that there is a whole lot of season to get through as well, but his reaction is a good reminder that friendships go through the two-step tango as well.

Plus, if Ted knew how well matched Barney and Robin were, he'd likely have been easier on his bro in the first place.

3.20 miracles

Growing up is a difficult thing to do, and the forces that sculpt you can come from unexpected places. For some, it's the friendships we make or the surrogate families that sprout around us. For others, it's getting T-boned in a taxi by a jackass on a cell phone.

Different metaphysical strokes, I suppose?

It says a lot that the very epitome of the two-step is saved for this, the final episode of the season. A near-death experience could be seen as the ultimate version of that phenomenon, especially if you take one step back into the great yawning void of the afterlife. Not that Ted goes *quite* that far back, but the serendipitous forces that put him in that particular cab, in the path of that particular jackass, and the resulting brain-rattling that ensues, are enough to convince him that he is a changed man.

He's very much a stereotypical guy at the beginning of the episode, expressing alarm at the idea of making plans with his girlfriend Stella six months in the future. Not that he's all that worried about the actual date, but it feels like an alarming commitment considering Stella's young daughter and the kind of guy that both women will expect him to be by that point.

This is the very picture of late-twenties dread for a guy, at least in TV land — that he'll have other people's concerns to put ahead of his own. At least Ted is the sort of guy who acknowledges that he has fears about it, but that isn't enough for the single mom — and who can blame her? Ted tries to talk it out and Stella leaves him with a shrug and a "we're good."

Here we get to the very crux of male-female communications (again, in the world of TV drama). Ted is convinced that her parting remarks mean that she has received his information about wanting to break up (because it's the "good guy" thing to do) and is moving on. Stella, on the other hand, thinks it's nothing but a small fight and that "we're good" means that they're going to put a pin in the conversation and cover it later. Given this kind of profound disconnection between the sexes, it's a wonder the species has continued at all.

Things wind up nicely at the end of this truncated season, with Ted and Barney making up (after the latter's ostensibly unforgivable contravention of The Bro Code) and Barney realizing what matters to him: Robin. Even more promising is Ted's final-scene proposal to Stella. The real miracle is that after years of fretting about never meeting the woman of his dreams, he is finally able to picture himself settling down with someone . . . even if she doesn't own a yellow umbrella.

That's a pretty grown-up corner to turn.

empire state building fun facts

- Barney offers up the Date-Time Continuum: you never make plans with a person further into the future than the amount of time you have currently spent together — out of all of Barney's cockamamie advice, this piece seems the most sensible, not only from an emotional standpoint but from a mathematical one.
- Robin's disbelief in miracles (which causes Marshall great consternation) stems from a childhood incident in which her parents tried to smooth over putting down a family dog by convincing her that Sir Scratchewan had received a cutting-edge surgical technique that turned him into a turtle. In other words, Robin's parents thought she was stupid.
- The music chosen for the series is usually of the bland, indie pop variety that underscores the emotion of a scene without getting in the way: in "Miracles," Marshall, Lily, and Robin all rush to the hospital in slow motion while a Radiohead song ("Nice Dreams" from *The Bends*) plays.

mother herrings
THOSE WHO WOULD BE MOM

- Cathy (Lindsay Price) in "Spoiler Alert": Ted thinks he's found the perfect girl but is blind to the fact that she *never* stops talking.
- The Woman in "No Tomorrow" (Nicole Muirbrook): she had very little to say to Ted as they brushed past each other at a club, but fans buzzed online that she might wind up being the woman Ted ultimately winds up with, due to her otherwise unmotivated exchange with him.
- Stella (Sarah Chalke): the tattoo remover who captivates Ted and prompts him to propose marriage. On paper this looks like a "Mother" lock, but there are too many pieces of evidence that point in another direction. By season's end, however, it does look like they're seriously headed to the altar.

house guests

- Enrique Iglesias as Robin's Argentinian boyfriend, Gael, in "Wait for It"
- Mandy Moore (*Tangled*, *A Walk to Remember*) as Ted's impromptu fling Amy in "Wait for It"
- Danica McKellar reprises her role as Trudy from season one's "The Pineapple Incident" in this season's "Third Wheel"
- Busy Phillips (*Freaks and Geeks*, *Cougar Town*, *Dawson's Creek*) as Trudy's sorority sister Rachel in "Third Wheel"
- John Cho (Neil Patrick Harris' co-star in the *Harold and Kumar* films) as the devilish lawyer in "I'm Not That Guy"
- Abigail Spencer (*Oz the Great and Powerful*, *Mad Men*) as Blah Blah (though she prefers to be called "Blah") in "How I Met Everyone Else"
- Lindsay Price (*Lipstick Jungle*, *Eastwick*, *Hawaii Five-O*) as Cathy in "Spoiler Alert"

- Orson Bean (*Being John Malkovich*, *Desperate Housewives*, *The Phil Silvers Show*, *Anatomy of a Murder*) as Robin's boyfriend Bob in "Slapsgiving"
- Heidi Klum (supermodel and *Project Runway* host) as herself in "The Yips"
- Kristen Schaal (*The Daily Show*, *Bob's Burgers*, *Flight of the Conchords*) as Laura Girard in "The Platinum Rule"
- Vanessa Minnillo (*The Bold and the Beautiful*, *30 Rock*, *Dads*, *Entertainment Tonight*) as Ashlee in "No Tomorrow"
- Britney Spears as Abby in "Ten Sessions" and "Everything Must Go"
- Bob Odenkirk (*Mr. Show*, *Breaking Bad*) as Arthur Hobbs in "The Chain of Screaming"
- Taran Killam returns as Gary Blauman, who tries to go out in a pee of glory but can't get the stream going in "The Chain of Screaming"
- James Van Der Beek (*Dawson's Creek*, *Rules of Attraction*) as Simon in "Sandcastles in the Sand"
- Alan Thicke (*Growing Pains*) as himself in "Sandcastles in the Sand"
- '80s pop star Tiffany as herself in "Sandcastles in the Sand"
- Will Forte (*Saturday Night Live*, *The Cleveland Show*, *30 Rock*, *Nebraska*) as Randy Wharmpess in "Rebound Bro"
- Larry Wilmore (*The Daily Show*, creator of *The Bernie Mac Show*) as veterinarian Dr. Greer in "Everything Must Go"
- John Getz (*The Fly*, *Blood Simple*) as Bob Hewitt in "Miracles"

maybe it's the booze talking
REACTIONS TO THE SEASON

Ratings for the third season continued to hover around the seven-to nine-million mark, which was a drop from the ten million or so viewers the show enjoyed weekly in season one and a second season that rarely dropped below nine million. "Ten Sessions" was the most-watched episode of the season with over ten million viewers, likely due in large part to the highly advertised guest appearance of Britney Spears.

The general consensus from the fan base was that this season was a solid entry. Of course, most fans were still concerned that the show might be canceled by the network for less-than-blockbuster ratings, but they did seem to enjoy Ted swinging so broadly from newly-broken-up-with sad sack, to douchey club guy ("No Tomorrow"), to his headfirst dive into the relationship with Stella. Many fans found that the long list of guest stars, in many cases stunt casting, detracted from the proceedings, but then again, the Britney Spears episode *was* the highest-rated of the year.

As for awards, the show received Emmy nominations for Outstanding Supporting Actor in a Comedy Series (for Neil Patrick Harris) and Art Direction for a Multi-Camera Series, the latter of which it won.

season four (2008–2009)
A "GIN AND TONIC" KIND OF INTERVENTION

The gang suffers a number of false starts

suit up! LEGEN . . . DARY THOUGHTS ON THE SEASON

Despite being a season about false starts, this is the one where the show really settles into a groove. The audience is now comfortable enough with the characters to start exploring and reworking the connections between the friends without worrying about hurting our relationship with them. Interestingly enough, the season that puts Ted's hunt for his kids' mother on the back burner is also the one where the show truly flourishes.

This is likely due to the mileage extracted from Ted's marriage plans with Stella. Not only does the lead-up to this momentous day get a lot of play (as do the gang's concerns about the union), but the eventual unhappy ending leaves Ted wounded for the balance of the season. I don't feel like I'm giving much away here because Stella is clearly not the Mother of the title — but that doesn't mean the guy can't have a failed first marriage, right?

In fact, the show's creators might have had a little more fun seeing these two get married and Ted realize (too late) that he's made a terrible mistake. But I suppose that would have undercut his place as the romantic underdog and would have left him without much to pine over, or overcome, over the course of the fourth season.

Instead, they give him a huge dollop of heartbreak and taunt him with what could possibly be the biggest job of his young architectural career. He works on designing the new Goliath National Bank headquarters (thanks in part to Barney) but the crush of the economic collapse of 2008 hinders his progress in that regard as well.

In the end, this is quite fair. Your thirties aren't necessarily about finding yourself as much as they are about finding yourself happy wherever you find yourself. Plans for relationships and careers are all fine and good, but the universe cares little for your blueprint and has a way of pushing you in directions you never thought you'd go, even if you don't think you want to be there.

Speaking of unexpected twists, both Alyson Hannigan and Cobie Smulders became pregnant while filming this season, and you can see the set design in the second half of the year suddenly became obstructionist, with classroom globes and potted plants jutting out into the frame to hide swelling bellies. Earlier work on "The Naked Man" episode, which required similar sleight of hand to cover up the titular birthday-suited suitor, proved a good training ground for this kind of blocking. Although, the flashback of Lily winning a hot-dog-eating contest proved a more satisfying angle to play. Maybe Robin could have developed a fondness for Ben & Jerry's instead of diaphanous blouses?

In the end, despite all the lurches forward and awkward resets, we still feel like we're in good hands this season. The overall aim for Ted to meet his soul mate is pushed off to the side but never forgotten, and we get to know the characters even better as they redefine their own relationships, while the talent behind the cameras locks into its own rhythm. This could be why it is, to date, the only season of the show to be nominated for an Emmy Award for Outstanding Comedy Series.

remember the time . . .
HIGHLIGHTS, RUNNING GAGS, AND CATCHPHRASES

- The "underpants radius," or the distance that a man can comfortably walk, starting from his bed, without wearing pants: as Marshall's unemployment gets longer, this radius become worryingly wider ("The Best Burger in New York")
- The *24* parody in "I Heart NJ" when Robin steals a girl's bike in an effort to make it from New Jersey to New York in time for the news broadcast
- Another callback to Neil Patrick Harris' *Doogie Howser* days in "The Stinsons," when Barney declares that child actors were "better in the '80s"
- *A Beautiful Mind* is parodied in "Shelter Island" as Barney tries to mathematically plot out how he can "bang Robin again"
- The Cheerleader Effect in "Not a Father's Day": a phenomenon that Barney points out in MacLaren's, The Cheerleader Effect (also known as The Bridesmaid Paradox, The Sorority Girl Syndrome, and, "for a brief window in the mid-'90s," The Spice Girl Conspiracy) occurs when a group of women looks "hot" when together in a group, but not individually
- Notafathersday.com, the website Barney created to sell a variety of "Who's NOT Your Daddy?" merchandise: better still, we see Barney at the end of the episode, despite championing childlessness, drunkenly singing "Cat's in the Cradle" while holding a little baby sock
- The constant recurrence of Ranjit (Marshall Manesh): is he the only limo driver in New York?
- Barneysvideoresume.com, a website that hosts the "awesome" video that Barney shows the gang in "The Possimpible": the over-the-top video résumé was inspired by "Impossible Is Nothing" by Aleksey Vayner, a Yale student who applied for a job with the investment bank

UBS with a profound piece of self-importance that became an Internet meme when it was passed around between other investment banks and wound up online. Items in the résumé include Aleksey's advice on how to overcome adversity, how much he could bench press (495 lbs), his downhill skiing prowess, his 140 mph tennis serve, his sultry ballroom dancing moves, and a karate chop that could break seven bricks. The only thing that hampers our full enjoyment of this meme is to learn that Vayner died in January 2013, of an apparent heart attack

- Canadiansexacts.org, yet another active site, one that features plentiful pictures of Alan Thicke, although not in demonstration of the acts listed thereon
- A surprise cameo from Teen Wolf (the movie version) playing basketball against Marshall's kindergarten team — in one of his increasingly outlandish retellings of the story — in "Murtaugh"
- A stunning theological revelation! Jesus invented both the Three Days Rule and the high five ("The Three Days Rule")
- Barney highlighting the dangers of skimming an e-vite when he brings a bottle of gin to a friend's intervention for alcoholism, which is poor planning on one hand but great if you're hoping to pass by an intake team at a rehab clinic without the tell-tale aroma of booze on your breath

taking life and turning it
into a series of crazy stories
THE EPISODES

4.01 do i know you?

Any relationship is full of false starts — those little bumps in the road that make you question whether or not the two of you are meant to be together. What it often comes down to is clear verbal communication, the knack for picking up on subtle non-verbal cues, and an ability to fake-love a Space Western with talking robots and growling Wookiees.

You know, just like it says in the Bible.

It becomes clear that Ted doesn't know that much about Stella. (When Marshall asks about her hobbies, Ted avers that yes, she is very likely the kind of person to *have* hobbies.) Marshall is worried the two of them are rushing into things, dancing on the sort of romantic ether that a couple can only derive from a marriage proposal offered and accepted at a kid's arcade (if my few times at Chuck E. Cheese's are indicative of anything, their proposal memories are redolent of hyperactive child sweat and vomit).

The tipping point comes when Stella admits that she's never seen the original *Star Wars*. Ted isn't too worried until Marshall rightly suggests that the only people who haven't seen *Star Wars* are the characters *in Star Wars*. I would add to this the Sentinelese, the uncontacted indigenous people of the Andaman Islands of India.

Not only must Stella watch the original film, Ted needs her to love it, which might be a heavy burden for some women to bear. Perhaps the only gesture more endearing would be swearing to love the film in sickness and in health, till death do you part. It seems like Stella fits well into the latter camp, but when Marshall finds out that she's faking, he isn't in a hurry to spill the secret to Ted. It would be a bad way to start their engagement, though it certainly provides excellent fodder for a late-relationship argument in which Stella can claim to have been "faking it" for years, only to have Ted clamp down on his ears and make "la la la la la" noises on his way to the movie room for yet another viewing of the sci-fi classic.

Another possible false start is in store for Barney, who tells Lily that he is in love with Robin. He tries to act like his normal, suave self but he finds that when emotions enter into the equation it makes *long division* that much *harder* (heh heh). By the end of the episode, Barney gives up on Robin, instead pledging his fidelity to the true love of his life, "bimbos." But it's hard to believe him as we find Barney so much more likable when he's showing his vulnerable side to Lily.

In the end, it becomes clear that the search for The One is about more than the sense of accomplishment at having found that person or even just having a warm body next to you at night. It's about really knowing someone, and being known in return. And that's the kind of thing worth enduring every kind of false start for — even if that false start might claim to prefer the new *Star Wars* films over the originals.

No, sorry. That would be a dealbreaker.

4.03 i heart NJ

The true difficulty of a long-distance relationship isn't in the number of miles between you but in the fact that you have to count that distance in miles at all. (Think about communicating your romantic intentions to your significant other — if the mental picture involves a "save the date" reminder on your smartphone, you are likely having a long distance affair. Or you live in a really big house.)

In this case, the gulf is between New York and New Jersey, and the geographical distance is nothing compared to the psychological one.

This emotional distance — and a miscommunication that is easily classified as a false start — are at the core of "I Heart NJ." Ted thinks the issue of where the newly united family will live has already been sorted, with New York the clear winner. That Ted has mistaken Stella's irony for sincerity (especially when she suggests that her daughter could make friends with that guy who sleeps on that couch in the alley) is a signal not only that Ted has a knack for missing cues, but also that he is seemingly impervious to sarcasm.

Ted and Stella are in the "growing pains" phase of their relationship, but with a wedding approaching fast, they are cramming a few years' worth of fights and cold realizations about each other into a short time span. Kind of like how Marshall feels when he tries to squeeze into a tiny subway seat in New York.

Just as bad in the misunderstandings arena is Robin, who quits her soul-crushing job at Metro News One in favor of an anchor position at a global news network that, as it turns out, is only an offer of an audition and not a guaranteed job. She even leaves her current post with a pretentious speech (ghostwritten by Ted), wherein she likens herself to a butterfly emerging from a cocoon. Once she realizes that she doesn't have a lock on the new job (especially when she sees that she's competing against an African-American woman with blue eyes), Robin likely feels more like a garden slug than a butterfly.

Both Ted and Robin learn that there is nobility in compromise. Ted reads a bedtime story to Stella's daughter and vows to move to New Jersey; Robin takes a reporter job in Japan. If Saint Josemaría Escrivá is right, and "compromise is a word found only in the vocabulary of those who have no will to fight," let it be said that both Ted and Robin have gone twelve rounds and only hope that giving in to the fight is enough to win them the stamina to fight again another day.

Fighting butterflies. There's something in that, I think.

Sarah Chalke

empire state building fun facts

- Robin quits after hitting her limit on terrible news puns (". . . and that's the tooth!"). It's nice to see someone take on this horrible yet pervasive affliction of modern journalism — because nothing makes me want to read a story about a serial killer with high SAT scores more than knowing he's a "cut above the rest."

4.04 intervention

This is an episode notable not only for a number of firsts for the *How I Met Your Mother* canon, but also for swan songs. Or what appear to be, anyway.

Big changes are in the wind, and everyone is doubting their choices. Ted doesn't think he's ready for the move to New Jersey and all the responsibilities it brings. Marshall doesn't want to move into the new apartment, not because it's downwind from a sewage treatment plant, but because of all the good memories stored up in the old apartment, a belief that Lily is quick to take up as well. Robin doesn't think she has what it takes to report the news in Japan. And Barney — get this — will do *anything* in an effort to get laid!

OK, so some things aren't changing.

The interesting element of this episode is not so much the story — everybody changes their mind, everybody changes their mind back — but the way it takes on the idea of aging. Barney pulls another of his crazy schemes, pretending to be an old man (complete with liver spots and a hand tremor) in hopes of convincing a bimbo that he has traveled from the future to persuade her that she must sleep with a man named Barney Stinson if she wants to save the world. It's not enough that this scheme appears to work; Barney has to prove to the gang that he will still be as "awesome" as he is currently when he actually *is* in his eighties, so he plans to don his elderly disguise to try to pick up a girl. The very idea of old man Barney leering at a

at the party instead of exiting it immediately after the Hedbanz box comes out. Or maybe that was just me. Sorry, honey.

Don't Hang around a Jilted Bride if You're Trying to Stay Pure for an Old Flame: Barney is a man of strong beliefs, none stronger than his desire to have sex with a desperate woman or, if luck is smiling on him, *two* desperate women. As much as he makes plans to "bang Robin" at the wedding like it is a quest worthy of Indiana Jones, we all know he really is in love with her and expressing it the only way he knows how . . . with nipple clamps. But for all his desire to be with Robin, he just can't pass up an opportunity to tie a woman to his headboard. Sub-moral for this one: don't forget to practice your zip snare knot before tramping off to a yoga retreat in Long Island for a shotgun wedding. This might be *too* specific to qualify as a moral, but if it helps a person in need, then it's worth it.

Don't Go to an Ex's Wedding, Even if Everyone Says "It's Cool": You know why? Because it might *not* be cool. The job you left your life in New York for might not be the step up the career ladder you hoped for (chimpanzee co-anchor notwithstanding) and watching a "safety school" ex getting hitched might churn up old feelings and lead to bad decisions. Like telling your ex not to get married and rush into "someone else's wedding, someone else's house, someone else's life." Even if you're right, that doesn't make it sting any less.

If You're Going to Ditch Your Guy at the Altar For the Father of Your Child, Make Sure the Child Is With You on the Ferry Back to New York: When Robin sees Stella cuddled up with Tony on the bow of the ferry, the only thing I could think is *where is Lucy?* And more to that, when Ted lists the reasons he wants to get married in the confrontation with Robin, he doesn't list Lucy as one of the motivations to wed. While Stella being a single mom is a key aspect of her character, this is one of those times where the kid isn't factored into the story as much as she would have to be in real life, which is a misstep by the writers.

Don't Look for Real Life in a Network Situation Comedy: Fair enough. A close approximation is a lot to hope for, and we get it watching the jilted Ted surrounded by his friends. You can't help but feel bad for the poor, lovesick dope. And haven't we all been that dope at one point or another?

empire state building fun facts

- Despite Marshall being "ninety percent sure" that the juice bartender is the lead singer of The Spin Doctors, he isn't — the actor is Aaron Hendry, who has also appeared in *Glee* and *Teen Wolf* . . . although the famous Spin Doctors song "Two Princes" *does* appear in Jason Segel's 2011 film *Jeff, Who Lives at Home*.

4.06 happily ever after

We know there is a happily ever after waiting for Ted — and both Present Ted and Future Ted know it, too. And *we* know it can't be with Stella. But does Ted?

The gang was aware that things were moving too fast and that Ted was rushing into a family life more out of his love of the very idea of being married than anything else. Their aborted intervention showed how they truly felt, but you don't railroad a friend with I-told-you-sos right after he's been ditched at the altar. You wait at least a day to do that.

Ted seems to think that one day after his abandoned wedding is enough time to heal and put back together the pieces of his life. Instead of dealing with the maelstrom of emotions such an event would cause, he addresses it "Ohio-style" — pushing it down and, when it threatens to burst through the surface, smothering it with more pain. That's healthy, right?

I have to admit something here: like Robin Scherbatsky, I am Canadian. As such, I am continuously amused at the Canadian jokes that pervade the series. But what surprises me is how much more "Canadian" — you know, staid, remote, and rigid — Ted is than Robin. Canucks are generally a reserved lot, and the sandwich of pain, suffering, and more pain that Ted describes as "Ohio-style" sounds just about as Canadian as poutine and maple syrup.

Regardless, I suppose that it's a common tactic to avoid problems instead of facing them. When the gang finally finds a restaurant they can patronize that is not on Ted's "Avoid Stella Map of Manhattan," and they see her getting takeout, they follow Ted under the table not only in a group show of solidarity for their friend Ted but also out of a similar inclination to avoid certain people from their own pasts. In the end, doesn't everyone have a person they'd go to great lengths to avoid? If not, congratulations! You're a perfectly well-adjusted human being — and I don't have any time for you.

While reminiscing about who they'd each like to avoid, we learn that Robin hasn't spoken to her father in three years. We also start to get a glimpse into the rearing that resulted in Robin emerging into womanhood as a gun-totin', Scotch-swillin', cigar-smokin' swapper of gender traits. Of course, it doesn't hurt that her dad wanted a son, and so he raised as her as one. As happy as she might be with her present self, she still has a particular kind of "daddy issue" that everyone under the table can empathize with. Except for Barney who, naturally, finds it "hot."

In the end, Ted quickly gets in touch with and lets go of his anger toward Stella. He knows that she's meant to be with Tony (the father of her child) and that as much as his imagined version of their confrontation results in Stella admitting her mistake in not choosing Ted, it is our boy who would have been mired in regret had the marriage gone through.

If for no other reason than having to live in New Jersey.

empire state building fun facts

- Eric Braeden from *Young and the Restless* is cast as Robin's father in a flashback: more on the controversy surrounding his return later, but did you notice the trademark soap opera organ swell when he walked in on "R.J." kissing one of her hockey teammates? A nice touch.

4.18 old king clancy

More and more, it seems like Ted's life is designed to fall apart in the fourth season. He seems to handle it all admirably, but still — you'd think a guy who has been jilted in love could at least find some solace in his work. But there are already hints that his career isn't going to work out as he'd hoped, and, in a clear demonstration of the two-step-one-step pattern, Ted keeps trying to roll with each slippery patch on the floor.

He's been commissioned to redesign the Manhattan headquarters of Goliath National Bank (where Barney and Marshall work) and he is doing some of the best work of his career, sculpting light and natural wood in interior spaces to make the workplace feel as welcoming as home. It's no surprise that a guy whose personal life has crumbled would try to make the workplace an inviting alternative to the warm hearth of the household. And you'd think the bank executives responsible for punishing work hours and sacrificed home life would celebrate an effort to keep their employees as comfortable as possible while they work their way to divorce and early heart attacks.

Well, think again! You don't know anything about high finance or the corporate world at all. Aren't you darling? Here, have a lollipop.

The project is scrapped, but Barney and Marshall go to great, dysfunctional lengths to provide Ted with the sense that he is still gainfully employed and has a purpose in life. Whether it requires hiring a phantom task force (comprised of GNB's custodial staff) or an entire softball team, Ted's friends make George and Martha from *Who's Afraid of Virginia Woolf?* look like the pinnacle of healthy interpersonal relationships.

When Ted finds out about the headquarters plans being scuttled, he's liable to swirl around the emotional drain. And he certainly doesn't let his friends off easy at first as he tortures himself with the notion that he will likely be fired from his job. But, in a marvelous display of chutzpah, Ted decides not to back down from life and opts instead to open his own shop. While it is possible that *chutzpah* in this case means not only "audaciousness" but "blind ignorance" (I mean, who tries to start a business in the post-2008 economic meltdown era?), Ted will not be cowed by heartless corporations and their bottomless pits of money and disregard for the people they employ.

What could be a better display of Ted's never-give-up attitude than turning unemployment into an opportunity? Some people foist the two-step-one-step on themselves, but it is the ones who soldier on in the face of life doling it out who deserve our true respect.

Although, when it comes to Ted's idea of "wood beams bathed in natural light" for the GNB atrium — what is this, 1979? Were there going to be exposed-brick accents and macramé plant holders?

empire state building fun facts

- The Canadian jokes keep coming, this time in the form of Canadian Sex Acts: now, I may be a bit of a prude, but not only have I never heard of the "Old King Clancy," I think it sounds like a whole lot of cleanup for what is ultimately a waste of perfectly good maple syrup.

4.20 mosbius designs

Here are a few of the opening lines I considered to start the recap of this episode, in which Ted bravely sets out to start life anew with his own architecture design firm, possibly the quintessential false start of the season:

"Ted tries to strike out on his own, but when he can't decide on the official Mosbius Designs pen, he just might strike out entirely." (Too harsh.)

"When there are layoffs looming at GNB, Marshall struggles to find the persona that will render him essential. And, like a thoroughbred breaking through the starting gate, Marshall tries a few different guises while champing at his bit." (Horseracing? Who cares?)

"Barney can't come to grips with his feelings for Robin, and after he tells an especially dirty joke about the difference between peanut butter and jam that offends Lily, his standard *consigliere* abandons him and he has to turn to Marshall in his time of need. Now, that is an offer no one could refuse." (So, Jesse, are you really sure about this whole writing thing?)

"There comes an hour in every person's life when the leaf clings but tightly to the tree, fearful of the fall but ever anxious to be free. Ted is that leaf. Mosbius Designs is that tree. Or, in another light, it's the other way around." (Seriously, I'm going to go make a sandwich.)

No matter how you start, betting on yourself is a scary wager. If you don't try, then you'll feel as if fear has ruled you and strapped you in for a life of mediocrity. If you try and fail, well, you're a failure. Ted can't shake his apprehension, best displayed in his retelling of the old architectural fable about a guy who designed the perfect library but couldn't understand why it kept sinking a few inches each year, only to eventually realize that he hadn't accounted for the weight of the books.

There is no better way to start than to just get to it, which Marshall learns when he becomes "Sports Guy," running a fantasy baseball league in an effort to dodge the executioner's blade at the GNB offices. Now, I don't know anything about fantasy sports leagues, so I'm not certain how realistic it is for the guy running one to wind up carrying eighteen thousand dollars as Marshall does, but if that's even close, then I'm considering getting into it as a sideline business.

Marshall can't handle it and has to bring in extra help, but he somehow manages to remain Sports Guy at the office. Ted, on the other hand, still can't cold call a potential client by episode's end, and it leaves us wondering if his luck is going to change or if this whole season is meant as his own personal Waterloo. We know that great things are in the offing for Ted, but it seems like he's going to be torn down to the studs before he can rebuild into anything resembling a success.

That's how I should have started the recap: a Napoleon reference. Is it too late to connect Mosbius Designs with "the playing fields of Eton"?

I wonder how that sandwich is coming.

empire state building fun facts

- The peanut butter and jam joke (reminiscent of Monty Python's "Funniest Joke in the World"), along with Lily's revulsion (she stalks off in disgust, not to be seen for four weeks), was introduced to keep Alyson Hannigan off set as she entered the final weeks of her pregnancy.
- We can tell that Cobie Smulders is also clearly pregnant in this episode despite efforts to hide it with billowing blouses and cheating angles.
- Not sure if you noticed, but there are posters for *Wolverine: Origins* all over the place in this episode, and Wolverine claws are even mentioned in a scene with Toy Guy at the GNB office. An allusion to a character who also has trouble fitting in and finding his place in a group or in the world? No, just a healthy bit of corporate synergy as the movie was opening at the time this episode aired and it was produced by 20th Century Fox, the same company behind *How I Met Your Mother*.

4.24 the leap

Oh, these guys. They've all got the leaps they face: for Marshall, it's toward the wood-paneled promised land of the neighboring rooftop; for Barney, it's the feelings for Robin that he fears; for Robin, it's the feelings she wants to avoid; and for Lily, it's her apparently genetic inability to keep a secret.

After a season of false starts, Ted finally gets his feet into the starting blocks and seems ready to run for real . . . only it's not the race he thought he was meant to run.

All things considered, it has been a terrible year for Ted. The benchmark of turning thirty is a tough one for most people, even if they don't find themselves left at the altar, fired, bested in a fight with a goat, and grasping onto their last chance at career validation by designing a rib joint to look exactly like a ten-gallon hat.

After three straight days of labor, Ted produces his brilliant work (which, as requested, looks very much like a cowboy hat) only to have his hopes dashed once again by the Swedish architecture collective "Sven" (who first appeared in this season's "Woooo!" episode). It's hard to blame the owners of the proposed restaurant for falling in love with Sven's proposed design for the building, shaped like a *Tyrannosaurus rex* (wearing a cowboy hat!). But it's the last thing Ted needs and he's left reeling, wondering what to do with the shambles that his life has become.

Meanwhile, we discover that Marshall has been eyeing the rooftop patio of the building next to theirs, sleek and wood-paneled, complete with a hot tub. He has considered trying to make the leap from his building ledge to the neighboring one for the better part of a year. But it becomes fraught with metaphorical meaning for the rest of the gang. Barney struggles to tell Robin how he really feels about her. It's funny to watch two characters who are *both* allergic to commitment try to come to terms with it in a back-and-forth that contains so many false starts that a person could get whiplash from watching it.

The metaphor rings truest for Ted, especially when Lily

suggests that he consider other career options, like the professorship that has been offered to him.

Ted falters at the thought of it. Who is he if not the architect of a building that dots the New York City skyline? There is something about taking a teaching job that smells like failure to him, and to us as well. But is he really letting himself down or simply off the hook? As we get older, we realize that compromise is an ugly fact of life and that we can't design our lives to fit our preconceived notions.

After a season of downs for Ted, it is fair to say that any triumph — even one so closely associated with failure as this one — is worth celebrating. It ultimately leads him in the direction he was meant to go, and, even though he can't see it at the time, we find some solace in the fact that he's running the race he's supposed to.

How that explains losing a fight to a goat, I don't know.

empire state building fun facts

- This episode was filmed out of sequence so that Alyson Hannigan could appear in the season finale while still on maternity leave: she gave birth to Satyana Marie Denisof on March 24, 2009 (the finale aired in May).

mother herrings
THOSE WHO WOULD BE MOM

- Vicky (Courtney Ford) in "The Naked Man": an elevator flirt who at first appears to be the perfect woman (see the Pablo Neruda poetry collection on her table) only to have her open her mouth and prove otherwise (the book was a gift from some "lame" guy). It's pretty clear she's not going to be the Mother when she becomes the target of the Naked Man gambit.
- Betty (Kimberly Pfeffer) in "The Stinsons": Barney's "stage wife," she has a brief fling with Ted, throwing off Barney's fake family plan.
- Stella (Sarah Chalke): . . . again, but then not so much.

house guests

- Regis Philbin as himself in "The Best Burger in New York"
- Jason Jones (*The Daily Show*) as Stella's ex Tony in a number of episodes
- Eric Braeden (Victor on *The Young and the Restless*) as Robin's father in "Happily Ever After"
- Dan Lauria (the father from *The Wonder Years*, yet another *guy-looks-back-and-narrates-his-past* show) as Nolan, a boss at Goliath National Bank in "Not a Father's Day"
- Jamie-Lynn Sigler (Tony's daughter, Meadow, on *The Sopranos*) as Jillian, otherwise known as the "Woooo!" girl in the episode of the same name
- Will Sasso (*MADtv*, *Shit My Dad Says*, Curly in the 2012 film version of *The Three Stooges*, all-time winner of Vine) as crazy bartender Doug in "The Fight"
- Reality TV mainstays Heidi Montag, Spencer Pratt, Kendra Wilkinson, and Kim Kardashian all play

themselves, coming to life on the covers of gossip magazines in "Benefits"

- Frances Conroy (*Six Feet Under, American Horror* Story) as Barney's mom in "The Stinsons"
- Laura Prepon (*That '70s Show, Orange Is the New Black*) as Ted's ex-girlfriend Karen in "Sorry, Bro"
- Kevin Michael Richardson (the gravelly *basso profundo* whose voice has appeared in *Family Guy, American Dad!, The Cleveland Show, The Simpsons, Gravity Falls*, and a hundred other animated shows) as Stan, the security guard with the most romantic texting abilities (via Pablo Neruda) in "The Three Days Rule"
- Dan Castellaneta (voice of Homer Simpson) as Milt the Homeless Guy in "Right Place, Right Time"

maybe it's the booze talking
REACTIONS TO THE SEASON

Ratings rebounded in the show's fourth year, generally trending between eight and eleven million viewers per episode. The highest-rated episode of the year was "Benefits," an unremarkable entry that featured roommates Ted and Robin embarking on a "friends with benefits" approach to conflict resolution in the apartment. Otherwise, a cavalcade of reality star famewhores (and I mean no disrespect to sex workers) featured in this episode, demonstrating that despite fans' protestations of *HIMYM*'s stunt casting, it clearly drew more viewers' eyeballs to the screens, be they TV, tablet, or 3D holographic displays like the monster-themed stop-motion chess game from *Star Wars Episode IV: A New Hope.*

The lowest-rated of the season? "Old King Clancy," which featured zero guest stars but did include the launch of canadiansexacts.com. Make of that what you will.

Michelle Zoromski of IGN noted that while the search for Ted's romantic soul mate (I make the distinction because isn't

Marshall really his platonic soul mate?) never left the stage, it did step out of the spotlight a bit, allowing the other characters room to spread their wings and keep us entertained, between "tracking down the best burger in NY, changing jobs, and spending plenty of time hanging out at their favorite bar."

I can only agree, and if it leads to bigger, better episodes for other characters — like the Barney-focused "The Stinsons" (where he is revealed to have created a fake family to please his mother), or a Robin and Marshall–centric story like "Little Minnesota" (Marshall takes her to the Walleye Saloon, a Minnesota-themed bar that reminds a homesick Robin of her native Canada), then so much the better.

The fourth season garnered another Emmy Award nomination for Neil Patrick Harris, for Outstanding Supporting Actor in a Comedy Series, and one for Outstanding Art Direction for a Multi-Camera Series, the latter of which the series won.

season five (2009–2010)
ROBOT DOPPELGANGERS STILL FART, DON'T THEY?

The gang starts to grow up. Maybe.

suit up! LEGEN . . . DARY THOUGHTS ON THE SEASON

How much of growing up is actually about settling?

This is a difficult question to broach, and one that you tend to avoid thinking about in your twenties. During that third decade of your life, you are still full of grandiose notions about the type of person you are going to become. Likely you will think less about *how* to get to being that person and more about how being that person is going to be *awesome*.

The kicker is that it isn't entirely up to us. There is a great deal of luck involved, an idea that flusters most twentysomethings, with their self-deterministic inclinations. The idea of compromise is abhorrent to us when we're young, and fidelity to an ideal is nearly divine, surely enough to light the path already laid out for us even if we don't know that it needs lighting.

Maybe that was just me. But I don't think so.

Perhaps Maya Angelou is right (well, isn't she always?) when she says that "most people don't grow up. Most people age." It's one thing to shuffle from decade to decade in a job that pays the mortgage and credit card bills and puts braces on the kid's teeth — it's entirely another to follow your heart's desire. The mere assumption of responsibility isn't growing up. It's when you put your mind to it and allow yourself to develop as a person that you get closer to true maturity.

At the end of the fourth season, Lily asks Ted why he wants to be an architect, in essence wondering what it has ever done for him other than wrack him with frustration and doubt. His answer is telling — if he isn't an architect, then who is he? By the end of the fifth season, Ted is a little more hopeful and finds solace in the fact that he and the rest of his friends resemble the five-years-prior versions of themselves in looks only. He is less concerned with the idea of who he was meant to be than who he already is. This might seem like a hopeless compromise, but concrete setbacks in life can quickly take a black-and-white view of the world and turn it into a series of shades of grey.

If Ted hadn't "settled" for a teaching job, how many great experiences would he have been deprived of? If Marshall hadn't "settled" for the big corporate job instead of working as an environmental lawyer, would he have missed out on owning his first place with Lily? Does Robin "settle" for Barney when they become romantically involved? Does Barney "settle" when he goes back to his single ways?

OK, bringing up Barney in a conversation about maturity is always a losing battle (at least so far), but you get my point.

Perhaps the question of settling is best explored in the "Jenkins" episode, when Robin and Ted explain to Marshall the idea that all relationships are made up of the Reacher and the Settler. In this theory, in every relationship one person has reached for a partner who's out of their league, while the other has settled for someone below their own. Naturally, Marshall is shocked to discover that he is considered the Reacher, but would he want to be a Settler if it meant not having Lily?

The idea of keeping up the appearances of maturity abounds, and in this the series is very true to life. Marshall and Lily haven't yet arrived at the "having kids" portion of their growing up, but they are desperately searching for a set of best couple friends ("The Sexless Innkeeper," "Perfect Week"). They try with Robin and Barney, and when that doesn't work, they run through a series of couple dates in an effort to find that perfect, urbane couple with whom they can do couple things. Apparently, this pretty much exclusively involves new risotto recipes and playing board games. They seem so frantic to find a perfect couple match (The Two instead of The One?) that they take out a Missed Connections ad on Craigslist for the couple they shared an awkward laugh with over an empty seat on the subway. And make an embarrassing video asking for a second couple date (itwasthebestnightever.com — yet another actual live website).

The only peace they seem to find in their quest to be grown-ups is their love of a quaint bed-and-breakfast ("Duel Citizenship"). And who wouldn't find tranquility in an atmosphere of oatmeal body scrubs and hot rock therapy sessions?

Well, Robin and Barney probably wouldn't. They seemed like such a promising couple at the beginning of this season, but the things that bring them together (a love of Scotch, laser tag, and cigars) can't vault them over their own immaturities, especially a fear of real commitment. In these types of pairings, we usually believe that the woman will help the guy settle down — I know that sounds hopelessly archaic, but I think people still believe it to be true. Carter Bays and Craig Thomas keep Robin as the least "girly" female in the cast, and her fear of commitment is played out as even more all-consuming than the terror Barney seems to feel at the thought of getting close to another person, another way in which the show creators subvert our romantic-comedy expectations. And while there is some comfort in seeing a familiar character revert back to familiar ways (for example, Barney breaking out the Playbook after his breakup with Robin in "The Playbook"), we still hope to see further growth in people we like to hang around.

In this season, we hope to see the gang mature and not just age. And for the most part, we get just that.

We also get hand-farts and a board game that spurts horse bile all over a Thanksgiving dinner. So, you know, we're talking about maturity in increments.

remember the time . . .
HIGHLIGHTS, RUNNING GAGS, AND CATCHPHRASES

- When Ted can't figure out how to spell "professor" on his first day of teaching ("Definitions")
- *Slape diem*: how this did *not* become a universal catchphrase is beyond me ("Slapsgiving 2: Revenge of the Slap")
- Marshall as "Vanilla Thunder" in "The Window": even more than the nickname "Big Fudge," this sobriquet bestowed upon current-day Marshall by his fifteen-year-old self must be a direct riff on Jason Segel's high school nickname, "Doctor Dunk"
- The Broadway-style musical number in "Girls Versus Suits": given the length of the series and the clear showmanship of a cast member like Neil Patrick Harris, is it any wonder that we finally received a full-blown musical number in "Nothing Suits Me Like a Suit"? Maybe we should have expected this, but I don't think we could have known that the number would be supported by a fifty-piece orchestra and sixty-five back-up dancers. A great way to celebrate the show's one hundredth episode
- "Why is *Ulee's Gold* in *every* crossword puzzle?" ("Rabbit or Duck"): a question asked by any crossword puzzle devotee and ultimately answered by the *New York Times'* own Will Shortz in "Robots Versus Wrestlers" — as we suspected, it's because of all the vowels
- Barney's "relationship gut" in "The Rough Patch": the fat

suit NPH wears is eerily reminiscent of the one Courtney Cox donned to play Alternate Universe Monica in the *Friends* two-parter "The One That Could Have Been" and in flashback episodes

- The inability of Barney to take a bad picture: no matter what the circumstances, he always presents himself perfectly for the camera ("Say Cheese")

taking life and turning it into a series of crazy stories
THE EPISODES

5.01 definitions

The first episode of the season sees Ted, Robin, and Barney taking the first few tentative steps toward growing up. And, exactly like a baby's first steps, they are shaky, lacking confidence, and punctuated by poopy pants.

Well, maybe not *exactly* like a baby.

Ted starts his new life as a professor, still unsure of what kind of teacher he wants to be (ruler-snapping disciplinarian or hacky-sack-playing *bro*fessor). In a nightmare he has before his first class, one of his students asks what he can teach them about architecture when he's failed in his bid to become an architect himself. It's funny how the perception of failure can haunt even successful people, and how people measure success, for that matter. If the only yardstick for a young professional is success on the scale of designing a building that marks the Manhattan skyline, then almost everyone is a failure. But that's how much failure can sting — even if you haven't experienced it, you fear it lurking around every corner.

Ultimately, it is the fear of failure that prompts new couple Robin and Barney to keep their burgeoning relationship a secret from the rest of the gang. When it is finally revealed, they resist having The Talk, the conversation that defines a relationship. They are both emotionally stunted and profess to not being good at the "relationship thing." It is precisely this kind of similarity that could lead to a very successful coupling, which might be the first time in recorded history that emotionally stunted psyches actually *resulted* in a long-term relationship.

For the most part Marshall and Lily remain on the sidelines in this episode, other than Lily and her evil scheme to lock Barney and Robin in a room until they land on a definition for their union (seriously, she's an evil puppeteer — a few tweaks to her life story and she wouldn't be a kindergarten teacher, she'd be the *capo di tutti capi* of an East Coast crime syndicate). On the personal growth front, both Marshall and Lily have all the outward appearances of having grown up much faster than their friends. They're married and own their own place, and yet they still hang around with these knuckleheads who can't say the words "boyfriend" or "girlfriend" without stuttering like Fonzie trying to say "I'm sorry."

It would be nice to think that Lily's machinations are about trying to pull two of her friends into the world of grown-ups and not merely a flexing of her Machiavellian muscles. There's nothing lonelier than being the only adult in a room full of kids (and God knows Lily gets enough of that at work), but you stick with your friends even if it takes them a little while to catch up. That's almost the most grown-up thing you can do.

Other than not crapping your pants.

empire state building fun facts

- There are a battery of '80s movie references in this episode, from how the rules of *Gremlins* apply to dating girls, to what *Predator* can teach you about choosing the right necktie, to a reminder that Indiana Jones was a college professor in his off time, when he wasn't scaling the high seas of adventure.

5.05 duel citizenship

For all his erudition and high-minded cultural pursuits, Ted is the juvenile one this time around, taking time out from all his book-learning to guzzle caffeine-laced sugar juice and convince Marshall to hit the road for a college-style road trip to Gazola's in Chicago for a slice of legendarily bad pizza. And then Marshall goes and ruins it by inviting a *girl*.

Well, his wife. But it's funny to see Ted so heartbroken at the prospect of having to include Lily on the mythic road trip (including numerous stops for her to pee). Ted's sensitivity goes out the window with a crushed can of Tantrum, the favored fuel of their Wesleyan-era quests, and maybe his uncharacteristically dudelike demeanor can be blamed on the energy drink that has the most caffeine legally allowed over the counter. Wouldn't he normally be the kind of guy who would love to hear an endless audiobook memoir about a boy and his dog read by Kenny Rogers? Given how much of a "girl" he can be, shouldn't he be *charmed* by the bed-and-breakfast they stop at instead of pushing straight through the twenty-two hours of driving required to hit their destination? And when the idea of listening to something in the car comes up, Ted suggests . . . the Jerky Boys?

There are many different sides to people and, frankly, we don't know Ted all that well from his Wesleyan days. Sure, in flashbacks he's shown to be hopelessly pretentious, but that doesn't mean he avoids all the trappings of *bro*dom — especially with his good friend Marshall. In fact, he can let that side of himself, the one that likely pushes aside a copy of Celine's *Journey to the End of the Night* in the original French to engage in a high-stakes fart contest, loose around his roommate.

Ted takes it hard when Marshall tries to convince him that they've left all that behind ("We're not in college anymore. We don't have to drive all night."). Ted likely isn't that worried about it, but is possibly jealous that Marshall met The One in Lily at such a young age and that the two of them have everything that he desperately wants. He doesn't come right out with this envy — protesting that he misses spending time with Marshall since he and Lily have morphed into an indivisible "we" — but I think we can all agree that Ted wouldn't get worked up enough to kidnap a short-short-housecoated Marshall to eat marginal pizza just because he misses "the good old days."

In the end, aging isn't for the faint of heart, especially when you have to watch your friends live what is, in many ways, the life you wanted. Ted needs to keep that in mind, and he also needs to realize that you can't go back again. Or, as Marshall puts it when he first bites into the Gazola's slice: "I feel so young . . . except for the chest pains."

empire state building fun facts

- Gazola's is supposed to be at 316 Kinzie Street in Chicago; the intersection actually hosts a parking lot, William J. Cassidy Tire Company, and the *Chicago Sun-Times* building.
- Robin goes through a crisis regarding her citizenship, thinking she'll have to forgo her Canadian passport for an American one: the Canadian jokes are getting a little stale by this time, but they are nicely offset by Barney's ugly American routine. Although, it *is* pretty cool that Canadians have Elton John on their money.
- Yes, Tim Hortons is a real coffee chain, and it's just as Canadian as hockey and curling.

5.09 slapsgiving 2: revenge of the slap

Slapsgiving is a wonderful time of year, the kind of holiday that can bring together bickering friends, heal familial wounds, and really kick off the holiday season — with the chance to slap a guy right in his face.

Why, I can remember the first Slapsgiving I ever attended.

There was turkey and stuffing and jokes and then, when the parents had sipped enough of their "grown-up soda," we all started slapping each other. Heck, the slapping got so spirited that I must have fallen asleep from exhuastion because I don't even remember the drive to the hospital. Slaps are what made this country great. They build character!

Lily's dad, Mickey, sure could use a psychological growth spurt. He shows up at the first Slapsgiving his daughter and Marshall are hosting at their new apartment, unannounced and proudly holding the latest in his long line of failed, and frankly terrible, board game ideas ("I've got *Diseases!*"). Mickey's been dead to Lily for a few years now, after a lifetime of missing dance recitals and spending college money on dubious backroom deals at board game conventions in the hospitality suite at a Hav A Nap underneath a highway off-ramp.

It's no surprise when we find out that Marshall is behind Mickey's unexpected drop-in. He's a guy whose family is so close that they continue Sunday dinner prayers via Skype. Of course he would try to concoct a reconciliation that Lily doesn't want and that Mickey, despite his suggestions otherwise, has done little to earn.

Mickey (as played by the terrific Chris Elliott) is a classic Peter Pan who arouses Lily's *you're-dead-to-me* look when he moves back in with *his* parents and forces his retired father back to work so that he can try to get Aldrin Games Unlimited off the ground. As angry as that made Lily, seeing him at her doorstep on Slapsgiving is enough to rip the whole group apart. It is enough that as we get older we have to worry about parenting our own parents, but it's compounded when you realize that even as a child you had more horse sense than your own father. It's enough to make anyone grow up far ahead of schedule.

Luckily, the gang hasn't matured enough to forgo the Slap Bet. When it comes to Slapsgiving, slaps are the reason for the season. In a stunning display of selflessness, Marshall gives away his slap to Robin and Ted, leaving them to work out who gets to slap Barney

Chris Elliott

in the face. Sadly, when the two bicker over who should get the right, they nearly spoil the whole damn holiday, letting a beautiful gift like the slap tear them apart instead of bringing them closer together.

But that's the thing about Slapsgiving — it's about giving as much as receiving. Whether that's giving love to a fellow human being or cuffing that human being right across the jaw, Slapsgiving can not only reach across great divides, but also provide a soothing salve for a broken heart.

That salve can also be applied directly to the slap site. Let it sit for twenty minutes, then alternate with an ice pack. Trust me, it'll keep the swelling down.

empire state building fun facts

- Not only is Chris Elliott the perfect choice to play Lily's dad, with dreamy-eyed lunacy being one of the finest arrows in his quiver; he also shares a David Letterman–related pedigree with show creators Carter Bays and Craig Thomas. Elliott was a writer and performer on Letterman's original late-night show, where he created memorable characters such as The Panicky Guy, The Conspiracy Guy, and The Guy Under the Seats (a guy who lived under the seats in the studio where Letterman's show was taped). Interestingly, Chris Elliott is part of what could only be called a show-business dynasty: his father Bob Elliott was one half of the comedy team Bob and Ray, and his daughter Abby Elliott was a cast member of *Saturday Night Live* for four years (and would later appear on *HIMYM*). Chris spent a year on *SNL* from 1994 to 1995, and his father Bob appeared on an *SNL* Christmas special in 1978, making for the only three-generations-deep appearance by a family on the long-running sketch comedy show.

top ten rejected marshall eriksen nicknames

Marshall has had a few nicknames ("Marshmallow," "Vanilla Thunder," "Beercules," and, most memorably, "Big Fudge"), but any of these would do in a pinch. According to me, the guy who came up with them.

10. Lukewarm Fudge

9. The Hairless Sasquatch

8. Mookie Eriksen

7. The Norwegian Nightmare

6. Here Comes the Fudge

5. AGuyWhoSays"What?"GetsHitInTheNutsack (older brothers only)

4. Zitch Dog Millionaire

3. Vanilla Fudge (not affiliated with the late-'60s psychedelic rock group or any of its *many* reunited line-ups)

2. Boozechilles (guess what his greatest weakness is?)

1. Slapsy Russell

5.11 last cigarette ever

Kids, there was a time when people could smoke just about anywhere they wanted. It wasn't all that long ago that it was fair game to light up in certain sections of restaurants, airplanes, and, if I'm not mistaken, operating rooms. For all the demonization of smoking that has occurred in recent decades, it wasn't so far into the past that it was as prevalent as second-hand smoker's cough.

I guess that's why seeing anyone smoke on TV is a shock these days. I'm sure we all know people who smoke, but they generally have the decency to treat it as the dirty, disgusting, filthy habit it is. You know, the kind best suited to dingy alleyways crowded with trash or a lightless vault buried a hundred feet below ground, with exhaust vents that lead directly back into the homes of other smokers — a snake pit of a place where there is naught to listen to but polka music and the wet, chest-rattling coughs of fellow smokers.

But I digress. Clearly I am not a smoker, and as such, I was glad to see in this episode (via Future Ted's kids) a commensurate level of dismay at the notion that the main characters of the show all smoked at one time or another. A smoker once told me that it is a singularly selfish habit and I'd agree — it provides a momentary fulfillment of yearning for the practitioner and a lifetime of health debits for everyone subjected to it. Who wants to see five characters we've come to know and love act in such a selfish way?

Marshall has the right idea when he steps into a flashback of thirteen-year-old Marshall smoking and beats the snot out of him. Maybe he should have done the same to his friends.

I suppose you have to face these things in order to move on, to walk through the fire, so to speak. But even the episode title is a misnomer as the final cigarette of the episode, the one that they each claim will be their last ever, is revealed to not be so via Future Ted's voiceover. Funny how the show can get away with that, given its future vantage point that allows us to see the fits and starts, successes and setbacks we all face, but at a remove that allows for the eventual truth to seep in. Future Ted tells us the later dates that will *actually* see each friend smoke for the last time, so we don't feel cheated when the title turns out to be a big fat lie.

empire state building fun facts

- There is a sneaky Canadian element in this episode: the song "Cigarettes and Chocolate Milk" by singer-songwriter Rufus Wainwright is featured, although Wainwright is really only half-Canadian (on his mother's side).

5.14 perfect week

Worried that he might get fired, Barney tries to go for a Perfect Week — that is, to sleep with seven different women on seven consecutive nights with zero rejections. Lily suggests this is a "cry for help" but if Ted is right, and Barney's entire life is just such a cry, then should we be surprised that he would try to resolve a crisis at work with an unbroken marathon of sex?

If you'll allow, I'd like to take a quick diversion into Greek mythology (the author said, channeling his inner Poindexter). Once upon a time there was a minor god known as Priapus. He was a chill guy, known as a protector of livestock, fruit plants, gardens, bees, and one other thing — male genitalia. He possessed a comically oversized member that was constantly erect and (if various frescoes are to be believed) could easily have been mistaken for a third leg.

I guess there are worse problems to have. But he'd likely be bummed to discover what his name now signifies: the medical condition known as priapism. It's a possible side effect from the use of Viagra, and we all know that if a man maintains an erection for more than four hours, he should trundle off to the emergency room. In fact, Marshall exhibits this very trouble in a flashback to his use of the wonder drug, one that leaves Lily contentedly humming to herself and Marshall hunched over with a strategically placed throw pillow.

Why do I mention this? Obviously, Barney is a son of Priapus (one of his alter egos, Lorenzo Von Matterhorn, even suffers from the same genital affliction as the rustic god, although it is now apparently named "phallumegaly"). His constant hunt for meaningless sex would have made the minor fertility god burst with pride (forgive the imagery). But both the god and the man have their curses to endure. Priapus, despite his prodigious gifts, was jinxed by Hera to be forever impotent. Barney's impotence is more emotional. What self-respecting grown man would try to score the so-called Perfect Week?

A guy who was raised by a single parental figure who had a

variegated number of sexual partners, *that's* who. And he succeeds, despite Lily's inability to understand the nature of a jinx.

The sex-as-baseball theme that runs throughout the episode makes sense in that, as Future Ted notes, sports are a way for people to escape the problems of their lives, if only for a short time. For Barney, sex is *exactly* that, a refuge from the cold realities of a harsh and unforgiving world. If you were working in an environment where a botched billion-dollar merger was laid at your feet, wouldn't you try to lose yourself in a bout of sexual aerobics?

The gang's ability to handle Barney's wanton proclivities morphs in this episode, turning them from nauseous bystanders to active participants. It's a strange shift, especially to see Lily literally throw herself in the way of Barney's potential seventh conquest as she makes her way toward a New York Yankee visiting MacLaren's, the kind of competition no man in New York could vanquish. But it makes sense: they know the kind of week he's been having at work, fretting about his future employment and, despite a problem with a gag reflex, they are willing to help out their friend.

Now if only they could befriend poor Priapus.

empire state building fun facts

- Ted tries to be a grown-up professor but mistakes the genuine student's name "Cook Pu" as a practical joke: am I the only one who found this running gag a little off-putting? I mean, I get the poop-joke angle, but wouldn't you think Ted would be a little more culturally sensitive?
- It comes to light that Marshall and Lily share a toothbrush (yuck) but in season one's "Zip Zip Zip," they are clearly seen with their own toothbrushes. Maybe their relationship has evolved. No, wait . . . that's not the word I'm looking for.

5.22 robots versus wrestlers

Given the main conflict in this episode, I will present two opening paragraphs: One high-minded, the other more down-to-earth:

The pitched battle between high art and mass culture is on full display in the dryly titled "Robots Versus Wrestlers," with the distinctly American thread of anti-intellectualism sewn throughout and pulled tight in a manner that makes Ted both the distilled essence of the horn-rimmed educator and, given his third-act about-face, the epitome of America's ascendant trucker-cap culture. How else to explain his abandonment of Dante's indelible *Divine Comedy* in the original Italian for the transient, neuron-crushing spectacle of unitard-sporting troglodytes beating robotic foes into shards of twisted metal?

Or:

In the episode "Robots Versus Wrestlers," these robots fight wrestlers. Why hasn't somebody done that for real? Who *wouldn't* pay to see that?

Aren't they both right?

Barney is worried that the gang is going to split apart, what with Robin having recently moved in with her boyfriend, Don. He's worried that Marshall and Lily will have a baby and Ted will be found alone in his apartment, devoured by cats — and then where will Barney be?

He should be worried. Barney knows that as the threat of growing up encroaches, he is likely to be left behind by the rest of the gang. Everyone but him is poised to take the next step into adulthood. Not that it stops them from making farting noises every time Ted tries to quote poetry, but there are different levels of maturity. Right?

Given the choice between attending the aforementioned cybernetic gladiatorial skirmish and the lofty Jefferson Van Smoot Annual Spring Social in the Alberta Building penthouse, Ted can't help but lean toward the latter. He's tired of people interrupting his recitations with bodily noises, and he's not likely to have that problem in a crowd that features award-winning filmmaker Peter

Bogdanovich, *New York Times* crossword puzzle editor Will Shortz and, for some reason, Arianna Huffington.

He quickly realizes that his preening pretentiousness is just as childish as blowing raspberries and that despite the inevitability of growing up and drifting apart, stiffing your real friends for a roomful of monocles and ascots is not worth the effort.

For one thing, you'll miss the beautiful irony of a discussion about growing up that takes place between Lily and Barney . . . while seated front row at Robots Versus Wrestlers. You're also liable to miss seeing your own doppelganger, which is worth going to any number of Mexican-themed wrestling nights. And *that*, my friends, is as good a collision of high and low art as you are ever likely to see.

empire state building fun facts

- While the architect that Ted mentions is fake ("Lewis Lamar Skolnick" is a composite of names taken from characters in *Revenge of the Nerds*), there *is* an Alberta Building in New York. It's a luxury apartment building at Riverside Drive and 620 W 143rd Street, and it's nice but nowhere near the "best building in Manhattan" that Ted rapturously describes in this episode.
- The social is thrown by Jefferson Van Smoot: that last name will return in coming seasons when it comes to a certain *Captain* of industry.

5.24 doppelgangers

It probably isn't wise to start with the end, but Ted utters a few wise words near the close of season five's final episode. He says that we all wind up as doppelgangers of ourselves — you may look the same, but if you compare your current self to the you of five years ago, you'll likely discover a whole range of changes.

They say history doesn't repeat itself, but it sure does rhyme, and we get that here with Robin's job offer in Chicago for a position as lead anchor. She has just moved in with Don, and when she has to decide between a life with him and furthering her career, she chooses love over career for possibly the first time in her life. The threat of Robin leaving her circle of friends has happened before, only that time she actually took the job and moved overseas. This time around it plays more into Barney's fears about the group growing up and moving on without him, and ultimately winds up in heartbreak for Robin — when Don, the scumbag she gave up the job for, takes the job himself and moves out.

Marshall and Lily are still grappling with the decision to have kids. They've left it up to the universe, agreeing to wait for the reveal of the fifth and final doppelganger (Barney's) before starting a family. This seems like a surprisingly immature display for these two, especially with regard to such a grown-up move as having a family. But in the end it's more about gauging their readiness for that next step than about relying on the cosmos to deal them the appropriate hand.

We also get to see Barney come to terms with his abandonment issues a little, learning bit by bit to put the feelings of other people ahead of his own, although his sexual proclivities take a turn for the weird when he dons disguises to better his chances of sleeping with a woman from every country in the world. Between the brunette taxi driver and the red-haired street performer, I'm starting to wonder if Barney has multiple personality disorder. If he does, it must pay to have a high-paying job to go along with that malady — all the better to pay for an endless clothing rack of costumes.

In a season where every character (except Barney, natch) has undergone an amazing amount of growth — Ted lost everything, Robin lost in love, and Marshall and Lily are ready to have children — they all seem poised to take the next big steps in their lives.

Now, if only someone could address their clear drinking problem. Would the show be as much fun if the gang congregated at AA meetings instead of MacLaren's?

mother herrings
THOSE WHO WOULD BE MOM

- Judy (Molly Prather) in "Double Date": the date who didn't remember Ted, she probably wouldn't make much of a potential Mrs. Mosby given that she finds him so forgettable.
- Shelly (Eva Amurri Martino) in "The Playbook": Lily's colleague who she's kept on hold for three years, waiting until Ted was ready. The ease with which a certain Lorenzo Von Matterhorn seduces her suggests that she's a poor match for Ted.
- Maggie Wilks (Joanna García) in "The Window": the "ultimate girl next door" with a small window of availability between relationships; unfortunately, she inevitably meets her "boy next door" soul mate before Ted can seal the deal.
- Natalia (Bar Paly) in "Rabbit or Duck": she is likely the perfect woman, a concert violinist who can quote every line from *Caddyshack*, so it's extra tragic when Ted blows it by holding on to Barney's cell phone with the Super Bowl–advertised phone number and answering it every time another woman calls.
- Royce (Judy Greer) in "The Wedding Bride": she's OK with Ted's history of being left at the altar; Ted isn't so understanding about Royce's gambling addiction or habit of sharing a bed with her brother.

house guests

As the show became a bigger presence in the public eye, it managed to attract more and bigger guest stars. In fact, season five had the most celebrity cameos and guest stars of any season yet.

- Kenny Rogers as the narrator of the audiobook Lily forces Ted and Marshall to listen to on their road trip in "Duel Citizenship"
- Alan Thicke as himself in "The Rough Patch"
- Matt Jones (Badger in *Breaking Bad*) as the guy who tries to deliver a pizza in "The Rough Patch"
- Chris Elliott (*Get a Life*, *Cabin Boy*, *Late Night with David Letterman*) as Lily's estranged dad, Mickey, in "Slapsgiving 2: Revenge of the Slap"
- Harvey Fierstein (*Torch Song Trilogy*, *Bullets Over Broadway*) as Lily's smoking voice in "The Last Cigarette"
- Stacy Keibler (one-time model and retired professional wrestler with the WCW and WWE) as Karina, the new MacLaren's bartender who Barney attempts to seduce (even though it means retiring his beloved suits) in "Girls Versus Suits"
- Tim Gunn (*Project Runway*) as himself — and also Barney's emergency tailor — in "Girls Versus Suits"
- Rachel Bilson (*The O.C.*, *Hart of Dixie*) as Cindy, a PhD student who Ted goes on a date with — and, he reveals, the roommate of the Mother — in "Girls Versus Suits"
- Amanda Peet (*Studio 60 on the Sunset Strip*, *The Whole Nine Yards*) as Jenkins in "Jenkins"
- Jim Nantz (sports broadcaster) as himself in "Perfect Week"
- Carrie Underwood as Tiffany in "Hooked"
- Jennifer Lopez as Anita in "Of Course"
- Laura Prepon returns as Karen, Ted's worst ex-girlfriend, in "Say Cheese"
- Anne Dudek returns as Natalie in "Say Cheese"
- Director Peter Bogdanovich, *New York Times* crossword editor Will Shortz, Arianna Huffington, and Michael York, an industry veteran who has been in everything from *Logan's Run* to the Austin Powers movies, all appear in "Robots Versus Wrestlers"

- Chris Kattan (*SNL*, *A Night at the Roxbury*) as "Jed Moseley," an evil New York architect in "The Wedding Bride"
- Malin Akerman (*Trophy Wife*, *Watchmen*) as Stella in "The Wedding Bride"
- Jason Lewis (*Sex and the City*) as Tony in "The Wedding Bride"
- Christina Pickles (Mama Geller on *Friends*) as Lily's grandmother in "Slapsgiving 2: Revenge of the Slap" (Rumor alert: Marion Ross from *Happy Days* was originally slated for this role, which would have had a bigger impact as a pop culture reference but would have disappointed the *Friends*-versus-*HIMYM* conspiracy theorists.)
- Ben Koldyke as Robin's morning show co-host and future boyfriend, Don Frank, first appearing in "The Playbook"

maybe it's the booze talking
REACTIONS TO THE SEASON

Season five saw a return to season three numbers, which were not terrific, again hovering between the seven- and nine-million marks. The most-watched episode of the season was "Jenkins," which should have made Neil Patrick Harris proud as it was his directorial debut. The lowest-rated was "Zoo or False," which might have struggled to find viewers when it first aired since it had been three weeks since a fresh episode had been broadcast.

The growing pains of a series now well into its run were remarked on by some fans, who complained that while the others were evolving, Ted was regressing. While I agree that Ted has come surprisingly close to jettisoning his likability in the run of the series, I think that his emotional state in this season is fair for a guy who knows exactly what he wants but just can't seem to get it.

The Academy took more notice of the show this season, with nominations for Art Direction, Hair-Styling, and Music and Lyrics

Rachel Bilson
EMILEY SCHWEICH / PR PHOTOS

for Carter Bays and Craig Thomas for "Nothing Suits Me Like a Suit." Neil Patrick Harris was nominated again for Supporting Actor and the show managed to take home the Art Direction statuette.

a quick refreshment
BARNEY STINSON'S PLACE IN THE PANTHEON OF TV WOMANIZERS

We could easily see Barney Stinson as television's greatest womanizer. But, to be fair, there have been a number of characters who have slept their way to stardom at the expense of women with broken hearts and low self-esteem. Barney is a descendant of a fine TV tradition, a *bro*genitor, if you will.

First off, we should wonder why we make room for serial womanizers in our viewing habits in the first place, given that we rarely find them anything but contemptible in real life. By his own admission (after running through a number of his skirt-chasing "plays"), Barney Stinson is "a monster."

For the most part, though, the attempts made by these loveless Lotharios are so outrageous and over-the-top that only an idiot would consider them long enough to snap at their flashy lures, let alone be hooked long enough to make it back to an apartment for meaningless, bone-bending sex. Angles like Lorenzo Von Matterhorn's or the free "consultation" offered by Dr. Stinson's Breast Reduction get points for creativity, but Barney's beloved "bimbos" are the only ones who fall for it. I suppose we feel that the exploits are so cartoonish as to defy believability, but I also think the women in question need to be portrayed as dim bulbs so that, as an audience, we don't feel terribly bad for them and can continue the friendship we've struck up with a sleazebag we wouldn't even acknowledge in real life.

There is also the question of what motivates a person to act in such a destructive manner, treating sex as either a simple callisthenic routine or flat-out revenge on an entire gender. Often, we'll get some reference to a past heartbreak as a motivating factor, but in the best cases (and we get this with Barney), we'll be party to the revelation of other areas of interest that broaden our knowledge of the character. If we're really lucky, we'll get to see that character act in a selfless manner that reinforces our faith in humanity just a little bit.

Perhaps the prototype of the television womanizer is Jack Tripper's best friend Larry Dallas (played by Richard Kline) on the sitcom *Three's Company*. In an era like the 1970s, Larry's comfort in leisure suits and lie-fueled casual sex could easily have come across as gutter-level charm. A used-car salesman by trade, Larry often lied about his actual profession in an effort to impress suitable candidates for his bedroom exploits, and although he never created the sort of elaborate stratagems favored by Barney Stinson, he must have been a good talker if pretending to be "*Playboy's* best photographer" worked as an aphrodisiac.

Not all of TV's womanizers have made efforts to hide their unsavory nature. As portrayed by Charlie Sheen, Charlie Harper on *Two and a Half Men* is a fine example of the type of person who confirms all our worst fears about humanity. Skeevy and manipulative, with a dreadful sense of style, he has almost nothing in common with Barney Stinson other than a near-sociopathic pursuit of sexual conquests and a love of cigars. We get to see Barney put the well-being of others before his own whereas Charlie has been known to give his paramours herpes. If the two men were cigars, Barney would be a Montecristo No. 2 (known as "The Torpedo") and Charlie would be a Century Sam (known as "machine-rolled factory floor sweepings").

Perhaps a forgotten figure in this panting pantheon is Kirk Morris (as played by Jere Burns) in *Dear John*. An adaptation of a British series, this stateside version starred Judd Hirsch as a member of a lonely hearts club for the divorced and widowed. Kirk laid it on quite thick, ostensibly attending the group meetings not for consolation and healing but as a prime place to fish for fresh tail. This is a gambit that Barney would likely not only approve of but add to his list of Bimbo Delivery Systems. When it comes down to it, Kirk turns out to be full of bluster, more of a frightened little boy than a suave lady-killer; in this he is a true brother of Barney Stinson, motivated by a profound fear of being alone after the loss of his wife, who left him for another woman. (Remember the woman who left the hippie version of Barney, an act that ultimately turned him to suits and the Dark Side?)

We certainly can't forget fellow horndog Dan Fielding (John Larroquette) from *Night Court*. Dan was an Assistant District Attorney, though he rarely seemed to do any work. His job seemed more an excuse to meet any number of ditzy and desperate women who traipsed through Judge Harry T. Stone's court. First introduced as a stuffy, three-piece suit conservative, Fielding's penchant for kinky sexual encounters only started to emerge late in the first season. While he and Barney share a lack of discrimination when it comes to placing women in their horny crosshairs, the human side of Dan was hinted at only occasionally. Other than a love of compromising positions, Dan and Barney clearly share a deep affection for the glory and wonder of a well-tailored suit.

If Barney learned anything from Joey Tribbiani (Matt LeBlanc) in *Friends*, it's that charm can go a long way. Perhaps the most likable of all these Casanovas, Joey showed that a guy didn't have to connive to make his way into a woman's pants. In fact, this is the key to Joey's likability (other than his inherent daffiness): he seems to put little effort into his pickup attempts, opting instead for a cool approach and a lack of self-awareness that is easily misread as confidence. While women don't *throw* themselves at him, he seems to walk into a room and immediately have the strongest chance of bedding the most women within a ten-foot radius. While Barney might not choose to show his sensitive side as quickly as Joey does, he can pull back the curtain to reveal a snapshot of his soul now and again, which works just as well as a cocked eyebrow and a "How *you* doin'?"

Perhaps the finest embodiment of the TV womanizer is Sam Malone, played by Ted Danson on *Cheers*. Unlike most of the characters on this list, women actually *do* throw themselves at the ex–Boston Red Sox pitcher, but he also likes to have his reach exceed his grasp and often tries to woo women who are clearly out his league (isn't that the crux of the whole Sam and Diane relationship?). He often flames out, but his indelible belief in himself allows him to shrug it off the way he might shrug off throwing into a Grand Slam. What can you do but dust yourself off and focus on the next conquest . . . er, batter.

The depth of Sam's character is shown in his battle with alcoholism. He is clearly shown to have an addictive personality and, in the absence of booze, it is no surprise that he would try to lose himself in sex. It is important to note that in an episode late in the series' run, Frasier suggests that Sam is a sexual addict and should attend group therapy to help with this disorder.

Barney would probably never admit to having a problem with sexual compulsion (well, maybe in a moment of weakness), but it wouldn't take Sigmund Freud to suggest that he is trying to screw away a deep and profound pain. Other than that, Sam and Barney share lists of sexual conquest that reach into the triple digits. In season three, Barney celebrates his two-hundredth sexual encounter, and Sam once admitted to Diane that the number of women he'd bedded was around the four hundred mark (well, he starts to say four hundred, but when Diane reacts with shock he tries to cover by saying ". . . four *honeys*").

In this light, Barney does have a long way to bang in order to catch up with the granddaddy of all philanderers, but Sam *did* have the benefit of traveling the country as a professional athlete. How can a guy restricted to a single Greatest City on Earth™ possibly compete with that?

season six (2010–2011)
EVERYTHING IS BETTER IN THE HOSER HUT

*What to expect when your expectations
are more than you expected*

suit up! LEGEN . . . DARY THOUGHTS ON THE SEASON

If the previous season was about settling, this season is about how tough it is to deal with the events that life throws your way, from the ones you never want to encounter to the ones you desperately hope will happen.

The sixth season of *How I Met Your Mother* is the best representation of the series as a whole: funny but studded with moments of real-life drama, with an eye to the bigger picture. The viewer will be rewarded for paying attention to each episode, not only for all the callbacks and recurring gags from previous years but for the echoes that resonate from one episode to another. Not many sitcoms have themes and running gags that play out from the first entry to the last, but *How I Met Your Mother* certainly does, from the music to peripheral characters to a seemingly throwaway remark about sundresses.

Yes, it is worth it to pay attention to that kind of detail.

Season six straddles comedy and drama more than any other up to this point in the run of the series and satisfies due to the successful negotiation of both (never going too far into farce or sliding down the slippery slope of schmaltz). The series has a strong sense of itself as an entire dramatic unit, with each episode marking a chapter in the story of all the characters' lives. Everyone has a solid arc this season — there isn't a manufactured crisis or an easy reversion to old character traits in the bunch. You get the sense that Carter Bays and Craig Thomas may have been enduring some growing pains of their own when they were drafting season six; but maybe they were just concerned with pushing their creations through their own maturation process, facing the expectations they've had for themselves and examining whether or not they have met them.

During the course of this season, everyone has to make a decision that could either dash their expectations or surpass their wildest hopes. Robin comes close to going down a perilously vacuous career route ("False Positive"); Ted broaches the possibility of fulfilling his dream of putting a mark on the New York skyline, only to consider abandoning it for a woman ("Architect of Destruction"); Marshall and Lily continue their efforts to start a family while gratifying their own personal goals ("False Positive," "Bad News"); and Barney has to address the emptiness left in his life by an absent father ("Cleaning House"). Their own expectations of where they would be by this age and how the people in their lives would fit into those plans change throughout the season in much the same way that they do in real life.

Second only to the expectations we have for ourselves are those our parents have for us. In particular, the expectations placed on the characters by their respective fathers play out across this season in ways both large and small. Whether tossed-off jokes about how terribly disappointed Robin's father will *always* be in her due to the fact that she wasn't born a boy, or Ted's post-divorce dad sporting a fedora and soul-patch while on the hunt for age-inappropriate action (well, that's more a case of Ted being disappointed in his father than the other way around), or the more serious storylines involving

Marshall's and Barney's fathers, it is clear that the group members all suffer from trying to measure up to their dads' expectations.

The specter of the past haunts this season, best embodied in the storyline around the new GNB headquarters and the plan to demolish the historic Arcadian building to make way for it. This is a perfect example of Barney's "New is always better" mantra, and the ultimate fate of that old building leads us to believe that the show's creators are on his side. But maybe that isn't too surprising in a series where a future version of one of the characters looks back over everything with a godlike wisdom (and if God doesn't sound like Bob Saget, then I don't want to know the deity). But perhaps the various characters' struggles with the marks their fathers have left on their lives is the antidote to this future-is-best position: by acknowledging the effects of their upbringing on how they act now, they come to see that the past has a value of its own. Perhaps old is almost as good as new after all. Especially seeing as Barney's "New is always better" rule is his oldest and, by his own definition, best guide for living.

remember the time . . .
HIGHLIGHTS, RUNNING GAGS, AND CATCHPHRASES

- Captain Galactic President Superstar McAwesomeville, the alias Ted opts for in "Natural History" after the Captain tells him that a real man chooses his own nickname
- Jorge Garcia as The Blitz in "Blitzgiving" reciting Hurley's lottery numbers from *Lost* . . . except this time in the form of a phone number when Marshall must fulfill a bet to send a snapshot of his junk to a random stranger. In fact, all the *Lost* references from this episode
- "Barney's Favorite Things," a play on Oprah's gift-giving extravaganzas — although Oprah never gave away remote control helicopters and velour track suits ("False Positive")

- Barney's diamond-striped suit, named after the wrestler Ted "The Million Dollar Man" DiBiase, who wore a gold-studded suit with a diamond-encrusted belt ("False Positive")
- The countdown from fifty to one in "Bad News": this is a reference — and an arty one at that — to the 1988 film *Drowning by Numbers*, a puzzle-piece film by British filmmaker Peter Greenaway (*The Cook, The Thief, His Wife & Her Lover, Prospero's Books*) which features a progression of numbers from one to one hundred in the form of numbers appearing in scenes or in dialogue spoken by the characters
- Ranjit as an angel, swooping in to help Barney in "Subway Wars" and helping Barney and Robin stop Ted from making a huge mistake in "Challenge Accepted"
- Marshall and Lily's Valentine's Day tradition of watching that most romantic of movies . . . *Predator* ("Desperation Day")
- Robin's declaration in "Last Words" that she's "been known to locate certain objects from time to time," à la Morgan Freeman in *The Shawshank Redemption*
- The Exploding Meatball Sandwich in the episode of the same name
- The "Who's on First" roundelay with New York club names in "Hopeless"
- Barney's dad, played by John Lithgow, asking, "Hey, small-town preacher from the Midwest. Is there a law against dancing?" in "Hopeless." Lithgow played the small town preacher in *Footloose*, the 1984 Kevin Bacon film about a town that outlawed dancing
- The Return of the Cockamouse in "Natural History"
- The baby talk thing that Robin's *Come On, Get Up New York!* co-host, Becky, does with the crew from "Baby Talk": this featured echoes of *30 Rock*, with a certain potential *HIMYM* cast member having worked the same angle

taking life and turning it into a series of crazy stories
THE EPISODES

6.02 cleaning house

The finer episodes of *How I Met Your Mother* combine broad comedy with a poignancy that, on paper, shouldn't mix well but do. This episode could stand as one of the best examples of that uneasy, unexpected combination.

Growing up without a father has clearly had an effect on Barney, leaving him searching for an identity, first as the soul patch–sporting hair shirt–wearing teen we see in the occasional flashback and then, after a serious heartbreak, as the prowling predator of New York's dankest bars. Growing up without a strong male influence can have a definite impact on a boy's future relationship with women and, in Barney's case, serves as a dire warning.

His brother, James, has turned out just fine. He's met a nice guy and settled down, even had a kid. He's also keenly aware of all the fictions their mother Loretta doled out in an effort to shield her boys from the harsh realities of the world. Sadly, Barney is not so wise. As a child, it was easier for him to believe that the Postmaster General would write to apologize for losing all the birthday invitations his mother sent out than to admit that none of the kids in school wanted to be his friend.

Actually, if we consider the kind of punishing childhood Barney appears to have endured, it's a good thing he didn't turn out to be a sociopath with a meat cleaver instead of merely a pervert with a never-ending supply of prophylactics.

Frances Conroy

Barney is so desperate to fill that sense of incompleteness that when his brother finds his father, the younger Stinson tries to appropriate that man as his father, too. Never mind that James and his dad are black — after a lifetime of Loretta's dysfunctional white lies, Barney is adept at believing the most outrageous stories (and also perpetrating them, as we saw in season four's "The Stinsons," in which he presents an entirely fictitious family for his mother's benefit — the fruit doesn't fall far from the dysfunctional tree).

But Loretta tried her best to be both parents for her boys, and it is in this realization that we get to the heartfelt aspect of the episode. Given the chance to know his real father, Barney refuses and says that she did enough to fill both roles. It's difficult to straddle the line between comedy and drama, but seasoned pros like NPH and Patricia Conroy nail it and leave us laughing while we tear up.

During the course of this episode, Ted also has to deal with the fear of expectations when Robin oversells him to a colleague in an effort to arrange a blind date. It's a fine B story for this entry, but the episode belongs entirely to Barney and his tangled family

the married Zoey to deal with, and judging from the eggs she uses to pelt his windows, she will prove to be quite a handful. As for Robin, well, maybe her problems are a little *less* than a handful.

empire state building fun facts

- This is the first time we hear Barney's "New is always better" mantra, which may apply to architecture but not so much to Jumbo Jim's Grape Scotch ("Don't let it touch your skin").
- The specter of towering '80s rock 'n' roll giants Guns N' Roses looms throughout this entry, from the episode's title (which is a play on their *Appetite for Destruction* album), to a *Chinese Democracy* joke (that definitively contravenes Barney's assertion that new is always better), to the mention of Zoey's past arrest record, which included her being detained after a 2009 GN'R concert.
- Robin blithely mentions that either Ted or Barney has a penis that resembles Winston Churchill. Great, now I can't look either of those guys in the eye again.

6.12 false positive

Marshall and Lily think they're pregnant and, over a thirty-six-hour period, suffer through the highs and lows of that granddaddy of all expectations. Not that they're worried *about* being granddaddies — that's still decades off for Marshall and, come on, Lily is a woman. Are you even paying attention?

There is a big difference between "expectations" and "expecting." One is the belief in what will happen in the face of uncertainty while the other involves bloating, weight gain, and, if I know anything about birthing, a quick and painless end to the seventeen-month gestation period.

While Marshall and Lily are "expecting," the gang tussles with their own expectations of where their lives would wind up. As Future Ted notes, when you hear good news from your friends, you are happy for them for roughly a second, at which point you immediately start to review how this happy bulletin impacts your own life. This is a common psychological occurrence that doesn't really have a decent name, although my therapist suggests that "classic compensatory narcissism" is a good fit, and that it is paired "with all the standard feelings of inadequacy and poor self-esteem." But what does my therapist know about the ongoing rivalry I have with my dog? I mean, he seems to just *wake up* and be in a good mood — and what am I supposed to do with that?

Robin is dealing with her own career mess, as she seriously considers taking the job of Currency Rotation Specialist (aka Coin-Flip Bimbo) on *Million Dollar Heads or Tails* instead of a low-paying research position at Worldwide News Network. Her drunken New Year's resolution is that she will wear the ID badge of the news network of her dreams, but she has trouble coming to terms with the hard work and low pay of the research job. Her expectations of a storied journalism career stalled, she contemplates taking the coin-flipping job: it won't challenge her but, hey, it'll allow her to capitalize on her prettiness and allow her to avoid facing her career crisis head-on.

What stops her? At first, it's the pregnancy news. It's the sort of development that naturally makes a person re-evaluate their place in the world (narcissism notwithstanding). But when the pregancy turns out to be the false positive of the episode's title, Robin wavers. Suddenly, she's less worried about her legacy (no longer concerned with being "cool Aunt Robin"). Funny how a sudden lack of concern for how your life looks to others can put you in a place to make *terrible* decisions. What turns her back from the precipice, from diving into the kind of abyss that would seriously impair her own sense of self — to say nothing of a possible neck injury?

The least harsh person you would expect: Ted. He's often the softest touch of the group but after watching Robin toy with her own destiny, he snaps and bullies her into making the tough choice. He does the same with Marshall and Lily (ordering them to have more sex because, you know, he's such a disciplinarian) and Barney (threatening him with physical violence if he doesn't return the douchiest of pinstripe suits and instead donate the money to charity), but it is his interaction with Robin that is especially passionate. After taking the professorship and broaching the notion of giving up on his architectural ambitions, Ted is sensitive to those who might give up their big dreams — even if those dreams do allow you to wear shiny dresses and flip coins for Alex Trebek.

Oh, and Alex Trebek shows up in this episode. I didn't expect that.

empire state building fun facts

- Sneaky Canadian alert: the woman who Barney tries to pick up at the end of the episode with a PSA-style *One to Grow On* appeal ("We've had a lot fun here tonight . . .") is Canadian actress/singer Melissa Molinaro, who is otherwise known for her role as "Nooki" in the sublimely titled *Jersey Shore Shark Attack*.

6.13 & 6.14 bad news & last words

The death of Marshall's father is one of those powerful life events that, true to real life, come when we least expect it. Many viewers assumed that the titular bad news would have to do with Marshall and Lily's attempts to have a baby. There is a countdown built into the episode, with numbers appearing in every scene and working their way down from fifty to one. The idea was to build in a sense of a big event on the horizon, and not a happy one at that (as Carter Bays said at the time, "You talk about a difficult assignment . . . it's hard to add a sense of foreboding to a sitcom").

Much could have been lost in the use of the countdown gimmick in "Bad News," but the ending is so powerful (shot in one take, with Jason Segel not knowing what news he would have to react to before hearing it spoken by Alyson Hannigan) and has such a lasting impact on Marshall's character (and the series) that the jerry-rigged time clock is quickly forgotten.

While the news delivered at the end of the episode packs a wallop, it is the following episode, "Last Words," that really allows the full breadth of comedy and drama to flourish. Jason Segel in particular has to shoulder a heavy load, working through the shock of Marshall's recent loss believably and still delivering a few jokes along the way (specifically, about the reverend who is to lead the memorial service for his father being the toughest bully Marshall ever had to deal with, a joke that packs its punch when we see that the bully in question is easily two feet shorter than the towering youngest Eriksen).

Much of what makes the series so endearing is the mixture of broad comedy and specific observation. In "Last Words," we can easily understand the pain Marshall endures (as Bays has noted, they've marked many major events in young adulthood and the death of a close loved one is, sadly, "another one of those mile-posts") along with the helplessness his friends feel while standing by his side at the memorial. Robin designates herself "Vice Girl" and holds a magical purse that contains any item she thinks Marshall might require during this hard time (from liquor to cigarettes to firecrackers), while Ted and Barney try to make Marshall laugh by finding the quintessential *guy-getting-hit-in-the-nuts* video. It's hard in this instance not to see Ted and Barney as Carter Bays and Craig Thomas, two sweet and heartfelt guys trying to make you laugh at a time when it's the hardest thing imaginable. Along the way, we come to grips with the overwhelming demand we place on parting words to be profound and meaningful — along with the demand we place on a guy getting hit in the nuts to be hysterical and life-affirming.

Even more central, and less expected, is the theme of fatherhood and the long shadow it can cast across a person's life. Marshall's dad was his hero; Lily's dad is a hapless dreamer; Ted's dad, post-divorce, is a bit of a douche; and Robin . . . well, poor Robin may have the worst daddy issues of them all. But by episode's end, they all call their fathers in an effort to have more meaningful conversations than the ones they last had. More importantly, Barney calls his mother and tells her that he's ready to meet his father. It's this kind of nested dramatic pivot, where one character's journey fishtails into another's, that makes watching this series so rewarding.

empire state building fun facts

- The role of Robin's father was recast when Eric Braeden was not available for shooting the few lines required of Robin's father for this episode. A little online kerfuffle was kicked up when Neil Patrick Harris tweeted that Braeden was a "D-bag" for backing out the night before the shoot because the role wasn't "substantial" enough; Braeden countered that he had just come back to work on *Young and the Restless* after hip surgery and was exhausted. NPH apologized for the rare outburst.

6.19 legendaddy

The sixth season is where show creators Carter Bays and Craig Thomas truly hit their stride with the desire to blend broad comedy and poignant drama. We have the events of "Last Words" to prove it, along with the commitment to reference those events throughout the rest of the season and not conveniently forget about them to make way for wacky shenanigans, as some sitcoms might. But like "Last Words" before it, this episode stands as a watermark of Bays and Thomas' lifelike merging of the funny and the sad, and is particularly memorable because of the way it broadens Barney's character. So much so that I will refrain from making a "broad" joke here.

Which is too bad, because I had a *doozy* locked and loaded.

The key to a series like *How I Met Your Mother* lasting as long as it has rests not only in the constant reworking of the nature of the relationships between the core characters, but also in investing depth into an ostensibly shallow character such as Barney. What started on the page as a "John Belushi type" morphed into a more urbane flavor of sleazebag when Neil Patrick Harris was cast in the role. The added bonus of casting an actor of Harris' talents was that when the creators were ready to fully render the character's background and motivations, they had an actor in place who was more than up to the task (it's hard to imagine David Spade providing the same sort of depth — not that he was up for the role, but you see what I'm saying).

Casting is key for a long-running series, and not just for the central roles. Guest stars of all stripes have shown up on the series, often seemingly for the extra ink their appearances will generate (Jennifer Lopez, anyone?). In casting Barney's long-lost, delinquent father, the producers could not have chosen a better actor than John Lithgow. As performers, he and Harris are cut from the same cloth: equally at home in comedy or drama, veterans of other successful TV series, and seasoned Broadway actors always up for a song and dance.

When Barney's dad, Jerry, answers a letter his son has written, he winds up disappointing Barney. At first blush, Barney is embarrassed by the suburban vanilla life his dad has created (especially after his partying days as a rock 'n' roll roadie when Barney was a kid and knew him as "Uncle Jerry"), but more than that, Barney is naturally upset at not having had a dad to teach him things like how to use a screwdriver — or, say, treat women with respect and dignity.

That said, the absence of a father goes a long way to explain Barney's womanizing. The show's creators could have taken an easier, more "comical" route, perhaps casting Barney's dad as a tour-hardened roadie and skirt-chaser who could drink his young son under the table. Instead, they opted for a subtler route, one that allowed for a greater understanding of a character who, as played by Harris, manages to get away with some truly horrible behavior while still charming the audience. And even though the creators could have coasted on that wave through to the end of the series, they chose a heartfelt route. This is best summed up by the final scene of the episode, which presents not a grand resolution between father and son but one less final, with Barney mourning the childhood he could have had.

empire state building fun facts

- Before playing Barney's dad, John Lithgow had most recently acted on television as a serial killer on *Dexter*, prompting Carter Bays to suggest that one reason Mr. Lithgow was happy to take this role is that it featured "a way lower body count" than his previous TV appearance.

6.24 challenge accepted

Season six is bookended by two things: the gang at a wedding and a George Harrison song. We find out a little more about the wedding at the very end of the season, and the song will have a different feel by the end as well. At the beginning, it is curious and unexpected, but by the end it is light and hopeful.

"Ballad of Sir Frankie Crisp (Let It Roll)" is from George Harrison's first solo album after the breakup of The Beatles. *All Things Must Pass* was a massive triple album filled with material released after the crack in his creative dam burst wide open. The song that features at the start and finish of season six is a cinematic ode to Friar Park, the estate that Harrison bought in early 1970. As you might imagine, Sir Frankie Crisp was a previous owner, and the song is a catalogue of the different rooms within the Victorian Gothic mansion, including odd little homilies that Crisp inscribed throughout the house.

I bring all of this up because a review of the song by Scott Janovitz on allmusic.com could easily serve as a fine description of this whole season of the show. Janovitz suggests that the song "offers a glimpse of the true George Harrison — at once mystical, humorous, solitary, playful, and serious."

This calls to mind the films of Cameron Crowe (*Almost Famous, Jerry Maguire, Elizabethtown*), which manage to make classic rock songs feel contemporary and fresh by coupling them with scenes that reward the investment we've made into the story and the characters within.

Ted has broken up with Zoey. He appears to be handling life after the breakup well, but when he's faced with the prospect of choosing light fixtures for the new GNB building, he freaks out. Echoing the story he previously told about the architect who built a library but forgot to take into account the weight of the books, Ted frets that the choice of lightbulb (which there will be *fifty thousand* of once the building is complete) will have a disastrous result that he cannot foresee. Vulnerable, he considers getting back together with Zoey, despite the GNB building being the very reason they broke up in the first place.

The allure, and expectation, of returning to the past is understandable: comfort. Despite Barney's long-standing rule that new is always better, even he would have to admit that familiar terrain is occasionally preferable to uncharted ground. He and Robin look back on the good times in their relationship and flirt with the idea of getting back together (despite things having ended for them as they did, with Robin turning into a hunchbacked hag and Barney growing kind of adorably tubby). Surely even he has to admit that his oldest standing rule (which kind of defeats its own existence) is up for debate if he considers how well he and Robin could work together if they could just iron out their communication issues.

Ted is saved from getting back together with Zoey, surely a disastrous idea if he hopes to continue designing the new GNB building in peace. As the old Arcadian building is demolished in a scene intercut with Lily's news that she is pregnant, we realize that this season has been about how making peace with the past is required in order to move forward.

Jennifer Morrison
BOB CHARLOTTE / PR PHOTOS

Also — the cliff-hanger at the end with Ted as best man at Barney's wedding? *Wow*.

empire state building fun facts

- While we may not have considered it, we certainly can't be too surprised that anyone who immediately bores Barney would sound like the muted horn voice of Miss Othmar from the *Peanuts* cartoons.
- Other than the bookending scene of the wedding and the George Harrison song, the first episode of the year starts with Barney bemoaning the end of sundress season: at the end of the last episode, he bumps into Nora, his ex-girlfriend from earlier this season ("Desperation Day") and comments on how beautiful she looks, stating that he thought it was "too late for sundresses."

mother herrings
THOSE WHO WOULD BE MOM

The only serious girlfriend that Ted has in this season is Zoey (Jennifer Morrison), although Future Ted does psych us out in "Challenge Accepted," at first claiming that the woman who mistakenly receives the orchid intended for Zoey is the kids' mother . . . . the jerk.

house guests

- Rachel Bilson returns as Cindy (the Mother's roommate) in "Big Days"
- Frances Conroy reprises her role as Mrs. Stinson in "Cleaning House"
- Ben Vereen, the legendary entertainer known from his TV work in *Roots*, *Webster*, *The Fresh Prince of Bel-Air*, and the short-lived *Tenspeed and Brown Shoe* (with a young Jeff Goldblum) as Barney's brother James' father in "Cleaning House"
- Wayne Brady returns as James in "Cleaning House"
- Maury Povich as himself in "Subway Wars"
- Jennifer Morrison (*House M.D.*, *Once Upon a Time*) as Ted's girlfriend Zoey, who first appears in "Architect of Destruction"
- Will Forte returns as Randy Wharmpess in "Canning Randy"
- Kyle MacLachlan (*Blue Velvet*, *Twin Peaks*) as the Captain, Zoey's husband, in "Natural History"
- Dan Bakkedahl (*Veep*, *The Daily Show*) as Curtis the Natural History Museum security guard in "Natural History"
- Nicole Scherzinger (the Pussycat Dolls) as Jessica Glitter, Robin's former co-host on the Canadian children's TV show *Space Teens* in "Glitter"

- Alan Thicke returns as himself — who, it is revealed, was a co-star of *Space Teens*
- Bob Odenkirk returns as Arthur Hobbs
- Jorge Garcia (*Lost*) as The Blitz in "Blitzgiving"
- Alex Trebek as the host of *Million Dollar Heads or Tails* in "False Positive"
- Michael Gross returns as Ted's dad in "Last Words"
- Ray Wise (*Reaper*, *24*, *Robocop*, and most notably as Laura Palmer's father in *Twin Peaks*) as Robin's dad in "Last Words"
- Bill Fagerbakke returns as Marshall's late dad in a number of episodes
- Katy Perry as Honey in "Oh Honey"
- Artemis Pebdani (*It's Always Sunny in Philadelphia*) as Anna in "Desperation Day"
- Nazanin Boniadi (*Homeland*) as Nora, Barney's object of affection and well-matched laser tag opponent in "Desperation Day"
- John Lithgow (*Dexter*, *3rd Rock from the Sun*) as Barney's dad, Jerry Whittaker, in "Legendaddy"
- Nancy Travis (*So I Married an Axe Murderer*, *Becker*, *Last Man Standing*) as Jerry's wife in "Legendaddy"
- Chi McBride (*I, Robot*, *Boston Public*, *Gone in 60 Seconds*) as the foreman who insists on calling Ted "Hot Shot" in "Challenge Accepted"
- Dave Foley (*Kids in the Hall*, *NewsRadio*) as Mr. Bloom, the head of a prestigious New York environmental law firm, in "Challenge Accepted"

maybe it's the booze talking
REACTIONS TO THE SEASON

Ratings continued as they had the previous season, in the range of eight to ten million viewers per episode. The highest-ranked episode of the year was "Last Words," with ten-and-a-half million viewers, benefiting from the emotional wallop (and just slightly lower numbers) of the preceding episode, "Bad News." The lowest-rated was "Landmarks," which marked the end of Ted's relationship with Zoey and might have indicated how little the fans liked her. (Robert Canning of IGN complained of this season that "Ted, Zoey, and The Arcadian [are] a trio with the power to suck the life out of any given episode.")

Again, Emmy showed love to the show in nominations only, with the usual nods for Outstanding Art Direction for a Multi-Camera Series, Directing for a Comedy Series, Cinematography for a Multi-Camera Series, Make-Up for a Multi-Camera Series or Special (Non-Prosthetic), and Picture Editing for a Multi-Camera or Single-Camera Comedy Series.

season seven (2011–2012)
WAIT FOR IT . . .

It's all about timing

suit up! LEGEN . . . DARY THOUGHTS ON THE SEASON

According to Future Ted, if there is one overriding theme to his story (which he is "totally, almost, not really all that close to the end" of), it's timing. This is of course a necessary component in a story about all the matters of chance and tricks of fate required for two people who are destined for each other to meet. Patience is clearly another component, and Future Ted must be raising his kids right because they've displayed seven years of it so far.

Timing is an important aspect of any story of success. For a series that is concerned with elusive romantic success, it is even more so. It occurs to me that there is even more of a correlation between this show and the films of Cameron Crowe than I'd previously realized. The characters in Crowe's films are very concerned (you might even say obsessed) with the specter of failure. The funny thing is, Crowe had success from a very young age. His experiences as a teenage music journalist for *Rolling Stone* (which included interviews with the likes of Todd Rundgren and Bob Dylan) were the inspiration for his film *Almost Famous*. At the grand old age of twenty-two, he pitched a book project wherein he would enroll undercover at a high school and write about the tribulations of the modern American teenager. The book was a success and was adapted to the screen as the seminal high school adventure *Fast Times at Ridgemont High*. His first film as a director was the almost as important teenage romance *Say Anything . . .*

Not a bad start to a long career.

His characters, however, are a whole different story. Orlando Bloom's character in *Elizabethtown* is responsible for a belly flop of a running shoe launch that costs a company $900 million (and is so crushed by the failure that he attempts suicide by a grim Rube Goldberg arrangement of a butcher knife taped to an exercise bike that, naturally, fails); Tom Cruise's character in *Jerry Maguire* is plagued by failure when he foolishly writes a naïve mission state-ment that results in his dismissal from a powerful sports agency.

We might ascribe it to their ages (late twenties to early thirties), but the characters of *How I Met Your Mother* are likewise preoccu-pied with failure. Ted is driven a little mad not only by his search for The One but by his desire to leave a mark on the Manhattan skyline. In this season specifically, Marshall is terribly concerned that he will fail as a father (a likely scenario if he insists on com-paring himself to his own father, who he viewed as a superhero). Robin is convinced that her hopes for a career as a famous journalist are fizzling as she toils beneath piles of research at a global news network. Barney worries that he will be defeated in his attempts to screw every woman in New York.

Hey, who's to judge a person's goals, right?

I suppose it is a sign that these phenoms, while having enjoyed the spoils of early achievement, are haunted by the inevitability of failure. When a person endures a period of marginal success and countless rejections, it not only toughens the skin but makes later success an even sweeter fruit. Not only that, a halfway sensible person knows that unsuccessful efforts are inevitable and that the one who excels very early may experience failure down the road more bitterly than those who are accustomed to defeat.

Why do some people have so much success in youth? Talent is an obvious requirement, but luck is also needed. But what is luck other than timing in a shinier suit, with a top hat and cane? (No monocle — we're not talking about Mr. Peanut here.)

How long should a series run? This is an important question because as difficult as it is to create a successful show, it is even more difficult to end it in a satisfying way, especially any show that runs past five seasons (*The Office* is a prime example).

There are signs when a long-running series starts running out of breath. First, a show beyond its fifth season will often have a propensity for lampooning its own opening credit sequence (Exhibit A: Barney's lame attempt at a new gang of friends credited in "46 Minutes"). A perfect example of this is the juggernaut that is *The Simpsons*. That show has not only collapsed in on itself via inside jokes and references to its own past episodes, but even presented a mid-episode redo of the show's opening sequence when the family entered the Witness Protection Program and became "The Thompsons" (season five's "Cape Feare").

Another telltale sign of a creative team becoming restless is when a complicated approach to storytelling is applied to an otherwise straightforward tale. Now, *HIMYM* is known for fracturing the space-time continuum on the regular, but when the complications become the entire reason for the episode (see "The Burning Beekeeper"), the audience is left to wonder if the gas is running out on their beloved show. Again, we can look to *The Simpsons* and the "22 Short Films About Springfield" episode, which, in the end, was an excuse to use as many of the vast supporting characters on the show as possible in quick, stand-alone vignettes.

By the end of this season, we could be forgiven for wondering how much road there is left on the journey to meet the mother of Ted's children. The use of Barney's wedding as a framing device for the season, carried over from season six, teases out a little more information and seems to neatly set the table for a culminating and concluding season eight.

Looks like our timing was a little off on that one, too . . .

remember the time . . .
HIGHLIGHTS, RUNNING GAGS, AND CATCHPHRASES

- The Edward Fortyhands drinking game in "The Naked Truth," which is funny but, thankfully, never took off with fad-obsessed binge drinkers
- The gang moving with the times, not only switching from flip phones to smartphones but mastering the art of hashtags, like #stinsonrocks in "Ducky Tie"
- Groova Palooza, and Marshall and Ted's disastrous, epic attempt to get nachos while on "sandwiches" (the notorious code word Bays and Thomas created for "stoned to the eyes on weed")
- Barney's one-quarter Canadianness, revealed in "The Slutty Pumpkin Returns," which feels like sweet revenge for Robin
- Christmas lights synced to AC/DC's "Highway to Hell" in "Symphony of Illumination"
- Learning in "Tailgate" that Marshall's dad is the source of his son's conspiracy theory beliefs, especially that Roswell was covered up by selling alien carcasses as SPAM (Sliced Processed Alien Meat)
- Stinsonbreastreduction.com and linsonbreastlawsuit.com, two more onscreen jokes that were turned into active websites ("The Stinson Missile Crisis")
- The adaptation of the *Star Wars*–related sex fantasy from *Friends* (your standard Princess Leia fare) to one involving a Stormtrooper ("Trilogy Time")
- The reminder that if we don't "trill it up" (i.e., watch the

original *Star Wars* films) every three years, the Dark Side wins ("Trilogy Time")

- The return of the Ted and Barney's bar (which includes a banner in a font similar to *Cheers*, along with the show's theme song) in "Puzzles": also, puzzlesthebar.com is a functioning website (which sadly announces that the foam party is canceled, but confirms that they have booked DJ Pauly D for the 31st!)
- Marshall and Lily's long-term bets box under the bed ("No Pressure")
- Barney's stripper girlfriend's stage name being Karma: that's some sweet situational irony
- Lily's continuing inclusion of Robin in her sexual fantasy landscape ("The Rebound Girl," for one, but seriously, it's all over the place): is this a conscious callback to her role as Willow on *Buffy the Vampire Slayer*?
- The "condolence high-five," which Barney tries to make into a thing in "Good Crazy." He succeeds for the most part: however, if you feel like trying it out, don't make the mistake I did and debut it a funeral — people get all uptight at those things

taking life and turning it into a series of crazy stories
THE EPISODES

7.01 the best man

If timing is everything, from falling in love, to landing a pickup line, to telling a crowded room full of drunken wedding-goers that you're pregnant, then this episode is a master class in asynchronous behavior from everyone in the gang.

Many of their timing issues spring from how the gang handles announcements. Public speaking is tough for most people, but few necessarily have the same problems we see here. Ted has to provide a toast at the wedding of his old friend Punchy. There are a few handy rules that Ted should have followed in this situation, and I offer them up here for any budding best men in the audience:

1. Open with a joke (but keep it clean — there are likely elderly people in attendance)
2. Tell a few choice embarrassing stories about the groom (history dictates that this is where you can work blue, but maybe when it comes to the story of that time he couldn't "seal the deal" with a prostitute behind a seedy bar, rely more on the power of suggestion than the gritty details)
3. Close with a heartwarming toast to the love of the happy couple and the many years of wedded bliss ahead
4. DON'T reveal all the bad times you're going through and devolve into a blubbering mess of hot tears and runny snot

That last one is meant specifically for any Teds in the audience. I'm sure it doesn't feel good to have all the recorded versions of these breakdowns posted online for everyone to see even if Ted enjoys the auto-tuned fame he finds in Finland when the remix of one of his toasts goes viral. But still, it probably wasn't the best idea.

Marshall and Lily are still sitting on the news of their pregnancy from last season. Lily wants to wait the requisite three months before spilling the beans, but almost finds her news spilled for her when she has to avoid alcohol (more of a red flag in this group than if someone were to, say, drink a whole lot), but in the end a drunken Marshall unwittingly gives away more than just his and Lily's secret when he defends the teary-eyed Ted to a group of Finnish onlookers at the wedding, attributing Ted's breakdown to how happy he is that a certain lady is pregnant. Unfortunately, by not specifying which lady — and that he didn't mean the bride — he inadvertently causes a Montague vs. Capulet–style rumble in the wedding hall. But then again, Marshall's drinking for two, so it's hard to find fault with the guy.

Most heart-hurting of all is poor Robin. Her timing is *way* off when she suddenly becomes quite aware of her feelings for Barney and can't bring herself to tell him until he receives a call from Nora. How can we feel anything but empathy for her when she assists Barney in a gambit reminiscent of Cyrano de Bergerac, opening up to Barney without him knowing that she is spilling the deepest contents of her own heart. It shouldn't come as a surprise that Robin is out of touch with her own feelings — having been raised as a boy by her father didn't do her any favors in this department — but we can't help wondering why it's only when an option is taken away that a person suddenly realizes it's the option she wants.

As Robin later says to Ted, chemistry is great, but timing is a bitch.

empire state building fun facts

- Ted's old friend Punchy has figured in episodes before, but his Cleveland Browns–themed wedding is central to this episode and is as good a chance as any to introduce

Nazanin Boniadi

ourselves to the guy who play ed him: Chris Romano (credited on the show at Chris Romanski) is a long-time producer and occasional writer of the show (he penned this season's "Twelve Horny Women"), and has written episodes of *It's Always Sunny in Philadelphia* and *The Sarah Silverman Program*. He is also the co-creator and co-star of *Blue Mountain State*, an *Animal House*–style university football comedy that aired on the Spike channel.

7.03 ducky tie

There are a few things you should do when you run into an ex: make sure you look your best, open with a devastatingly witty line, and mention all the great things that have happened in your life since you and this loser went your separate ways (feel free to embellish your lateral move at the office into a meteoric career rise, but don't out-and-out lie — you're likely to be found out).

There are a few things you shouldn't do when you run into an ex: engage in any *Three Stooges*–related buffoonery (that includes all tripping and spilling of drinks, or uttering "Nyuk!" at any volume level), admit to how great the other person looks (particularly egregious would be to suggest that they can "really fill out" a suit or an evening gown), or crumble at the first silence and admit you've been as lost as an Alzheimer's patient since you broke up.

At least Ted was wearing a tux when he ran into Victoria.

We haven't seen Victoria in a little while, and Ted is still smarting from the end of their relationship. Not only is he very concerned that she might have been The One, he's also wracked with guilt over what prompted the breakup in the first place — his cheating.

Their timing is awful. While the old spark is clearly still there, and Robin is no longer an impediment to relationship happiness (as far as Ted is concerned), Victoria is about to get engaged. These kids can't seem to catch a break.

That doesn't stop them from kissing, mind you. It also doesn't stop a revelation or two along the way, specifically that Victoria might not be as much of the victim of Ted's cheating as he'd originally thought. As it turns out, her fiancé-to-be Klaus is the same Klaus from her culinary studies in Germany. And the mourning period between the end of her relationship with Ted and the start of one with Klaus was not what you'd call exhaustive, lasting exactly one-and-a-half days.

Still, Ted can't shake his feelings for Victoria, and the audience agrees. In an online poll asking viewers to choose their favorite out of all of Ted's girlfriends, Victoria won overwhelmingly. But that doesn't mean he's going to have an easy go of it. After seeing her once, he's already trying to convince her not to go to the Hamptons, where Klaus plans to propose. Among all the truth bombs evident in this episode — especially from Victoria about how Ted's relationships with Robin and Barney impede his search for real happiness — is that in any number of romantic situations, it is the guy who does the asking but the girl who does the deciding. And what goes for the real world is doubly true in the *HIMYM* universe, even if it is marred by the inopportunity encountered by the fan's favorite girlfriend. Ted and Victoria's poor timing isn't the only fumbling on display here. Barney enters into the famous Ducky Tie bet with Lily and Marshall. While the bet is best remembered for its end result (Barney wearing an awful duck-patterned tie for an entire year), it is easy to forget that it began out of Barney's unflagging effort to see Lily's breasts. This is understandable, given her recent pregnancy-related flourishing (i.e., pregnancy boobs), and Barney deserves our begrudging respect for the labyrinthine efforts he's put into place in order to win the bet. That it requires psychologically conditioning Marshall to associate sneezing with a Japanese hibachi restaurant, a six-month culinary course in Hoboken, New Jersey, and the adroit placement of an alley within said restaurant, makes us wonder if the much-talked-about *HIMYM* spin-off could actually exist as a kind of shadow series that runs parallel to this one, titled *How I Saw Your Boobs*.

For what it's worth, I'd watch that show.

7.04 the stinson missile crisis

Viewers are presented with a mixed bag in this episode, with the stresses of a long-running TV series starting to show. It *is* the 140th episode, after all.

Barney is committed to proving to Nora that he's good boyfriend material, but Robin is going crazy because she's realized that her feelings for Barney run deep and she's suddenly painfully aware of her bad timing. It doesn't help that Robin works with Nora and has to endure Barney's non-stop barrage of flowers, chocolates, and Percy Sledge impersonations (though to be fair, NPH does a mean rendition of "When a Man Loves a Woman"). Through the framing device of Robin seeing a therapist, we discover that she tried to break up Barney and Nora, and that her sessions are actually court-mandated.

There is a lot of fun had at poor Robin's expense, from her crying and drinking under her desk at work to her crying and drinking under the booth at MacLaren's. It is a fine testament to Cobie Smulders' talents that she is able to wring laughs out of her character's suffering, but at the same time, Robin starts to feel a little broadly painted. Sure, she continues her distaff Cyrano de Bergerac routine by helping Barney dismantle his long-standing plays (or Bimbo Delivery Systems), but the fact that she's willing to disrupt Barney's potential happiness for her own selfish ends, only to have a change of heart, feels a little forced. I'd hate to think of the episode without the comedic elements of Robin struggling through her, but perhaps a semi-serious grace note at the end with her therapist would have validated our affection for the character and allowed the audience to believe that she's come through a tough time with a brighter future ahead. Otherwise, the risk is that she comes across as a flat-out sad sack, which doesn't feel like the Robin we've come to know and love.

The sense of restlessness that pervades Robin's experience extends to the show's writing as well. When the B story of Ted trying to shoehorn himself into Marshall and Lily's child-bearing (the "Team Baby" T-shirts he's had made speak volumes) comes to an end, he explains to Robin that "sometimes love means taking a step back . . . even if you wind up being left out." Robin responds that "the lesson you learned with Lily and Marshall is directly applicable to my situation and is, therefore, a valid part of how I'll eventually tell this story." Maybe it's just me, but this feels like a writer bristling at the standard tropes of the sitcom rule book, where two divergent stories tie together thematically and the B story has a subtle impact on the A story. It's covered up as a joke about how Robin is grasping for a way to explain why she's telling her therapist such a convoluted story (which eventually ends with the summation "the point is, it all tied together, right?"), but it still feels like a comment on the requirements of TV writing itself.

Especially in an episode that sees the madcap shenanigans of Ted and Marshall attending a birthing class together. That's some *wacky* sitcom fodder, right?

I don't mean to sound snippy, but in a better episode, the emotional cost of letting go of the things that you love would have hit home with a bigger payoff.

empire state building fun facts

- For those wondering how Barney could have a seemingly never-ending kickline of women to choose from at MacLaren's, one of his secrets is revealed in the process of dismantling his plays: the Cold Call 5000 (loaded with numbers from the customer base of a company that sells "body glitter and high-end pasties") constantly dials the numbers of impressionable women with a desperate Missed Connection–type message and an invitation to meet at the bar if they "believe in destiny."

7.09 disaster averted

How does a show that is essentially one giant flashback manage to handle a flashback within that flashback? By giving us more information on the characters and deepening our understanding of them, that's how.

This episode unfolds as a single flashback, all starting with Robin's therapist boyfriend Kevin wondering why there is a sign outside MacLaren's that cautions that there is "ABSOLUTELY NO BOOGIE BOARDING" allowed. This leads the gang reminiscing about Hurricane Irene and, instead of multiple locations and cutaways, for the bulk of the episode we see them battened down in Barney's apartment, thrashing out their problems.

I hesitate to say that what we find out about the gang leads to deeper characterizations (i.e., motivations for these newly revealed behaviors) but it does provide fertile ground for fun, especially in a lockdown scenario such as we see in "Disaster Averted."

For instance: we've never seen Ted as an avid emergency preparedness fellow, and while it does make for fun at his expense (from Robin inquiring about his "safety boner" to his fuchsia-colored rain boots, which both Robin and Lily comment that they want to buy), we don't learn the reasons why he's so quick to draft an evacuation plan that includes his dear friends. I'm reminded of Ben Stiller's character in *The Royal Tenenbaums*, who was moved to neurotic hyperalertness to disaster due to the loss of his wife in a plane crash, and I can't help but wonder what deeper motivations Ted has for this particular quirk.

Not that I expect such stinging pathos in a sitcom, but you see the difference.

During the hurricane, Marshall is in a two-week lapse between health insurance coverages and becomes fearful that danger lurks behind every corner. We see that, to Lily's dismay, he becomes incredibly clingy in a time of crisis, and while this isn't much of a surprise, the fact that this now includes his trips to the bathroom (the most *dangerous* room in the house) displays a new level of codependence.

We also get to see Lily admit that once in a while (especially when he won't stop tugging at her pant leg), she needs to be apart from Marshall. Coming from a woman who willingly shares a toothbrush with her guy, this constitutes a shocking revelation.

When it comes to Robin and Barney, we don't learn nearly as much: Robin pooh-poohs all the fretting over the hurricane that winds up battering the East Coast and holding seventh spot in the Costliest Hurricane in United States History competition (despite Robin's claim that it is simply "bikini weather") and Barney is kind of a jerk, tricking everyone into staying in New York instead of fleeing to the Hamptons — and even worse, making a crank call to Robin pretending to be her inattentive dad.

We learn that the gang, despite their bickering, will always be there for one another. We also learn that Marshall and Lily conceived their child in Barney's bathroom and that boogie boarding on the lid of a garbage pail is a lousy way to celebrate the fleeting, flickering flame we call life.

It's no Doogie Howser diary entry, but it'll do.

empire state building fun facts

- This marks another of the rare episodes not directed by Pamela Fryman: this one was directed by Michael Shea.
- In the *Indiana Jones*–inspired opening scene, which is meant to explain the disappearance of Barney's hated Ducky Tie, there is an appearance in the alley of a sign reading, "DUK TAI TRADING COMPANY."

7.11 the rebound girl

When Marshall and Lily consider moving even further away from Manhattan (to the East Meadow home they've inherited from Lily's grandparents), we are left to wonder whether they are really ready for it, why Robin is taking the news so badly, and whether Long Island truly is "Brooklyn's fart trail." The NYCentricity of the show can occasionally get in the way of the fun, with addresses and area code references always running the risk of sounding a little "inside." But, as everyone knows, there is nothing quite as inclusive as a good, time-tested fart joke.

Everyone is on the edge of a decision, like the old riddle about the rooster on the roof. If it laid an egg, which side of the roof would it roll down?

Speaking of eggs, Marshall and Lily are in nesting mode as they await the birth of their first child. Their plan to sell the house in East Meadow evaporates once they see it staged and come to believe that it is the perfect family home.

Ted and Barney are having a rough time in the lady department (Barney having broken up with Nora for Robin, who has chosen Kevin instead and Ted having gone through both Zoey and Victoria . . . again). Proving that the most creative problem-solving is usually accompanied by three fingers of Scotch, the boys decide they should have a kid together and be "bro-parents." Proving that periods of emotional distress are poor times to make important life decisions, the guys still think it's a good idea once they're sober.

I'd make a point about these guys putting all their eggs in one basket, but that would be trite, no matter how apropos — and I kind of just did it anyway, didn't I?

And Robin? Well, she's acting like a crazy person, right up to locking herself in the bathroom until Marshall and Lily pledge to stay in Manhattan. Other than it being an excuse to hear Cobie Smulders scream (a fine source of laughs only discovered late in the run of the series — who can keep a straight face when she screeches at her sweet-faced work nemesis, Patrice?), it's not clear

Neil Patrick Harris and Kal Penn
TINA GILL / PR PHOTOS

up front why the writers have Robin behaving like a spoiled teenager.

Barney's obvious unsuitability for parenting finally makes Ted cave on their deal (pet cobras notwithstanding), but that doesn't help Robin much. She drops a bomb at the end of the episode by telling Barney that she's pregnant. This is just after Ted has broken the news that they can't have a kid together to Barney and the scene is a fine example of the elegant plotting that is often hatched by the show's writers. In fact, the whole story surprises: what first appears to be another New York–centric episode quickly locks the characters down again, this time in a Long Island home, but doing so allows them space to unfold in ways we might not have imagined.

The timing may not be right for Ted and Barney to have a child, but as far as Robin and Barney having one (the old-fashioned way) is concerned, they realize that life doesn't wait for the right timing. It has a way of *making* the time right — whether you want it to or not.

empire state building fun facts

- *Ghostbusters* references have haunted the show since the pilot episode, but when Marshall looks for a sign from the universe he sees, in quick succession, a Cadillac ambulance, a "prohibited" sign, and the firehouse from the movie, which is for sale. Sealing the deal in the flashback, he sees Ernie Hudson (Winston from the movie) and asks to borrow his phone — of course prompting the question "Who you gonna call?"

- When Barney "proudly" announces that he's single, he hollers, "It's what America's been clamoring for!" — perhaps the writers had noticed an online fan backlash to the idea of Barney settling down.
- As for which side of the roof the egg rolls down? . . . Roosters don't lay eggs, silly.

top ten collection of barney's other "guys"

Barney seems to have an inside track: whatever you need, he's got the perfect "guy" he can contact. Other than a fella who can lay his hands on a group of monks when required (and we've all been there), here is a speculative list regarding his heretofore unmentioned "guys."

10. Tickets to a Celebrity Funeral Guy
9. Origami Guy
8. *Star Wars* Guy (for any related trivia or prop acquisition authentication)
7. *Star Trek* Guy (who tries to convince Barney that Kirk is cooler than Luke, if only to allow himself an opposing viewpoint to rally against and win over)
6. Stanley Kubrickian Interior Designer Guy
5. Gay Guy Guy (to determine if a guy is gay and if that guy, or any of his other gay guy friends, might serve as a Gay Guy Wingman . . . Guy)
4. Ivory Shoehorn Guy
3. Ivory Girl Model Guy
2. Savory-Flavored Condom Guy (if he's looking for a rubber with a nice French onion tang)
(And . . . wait for it . . .)

1. Unresolved Rage Against Women That Is Rooted in Mommy-
Related Madonna/Whore Issues and That's Why I Act Like
Such a Bad, Bad Boy To Get as Much Female Attention as
I Can Possibly Obtain Guy

7.12 symphony of illumination

Christmas in New York, the peaks and valleys of child-rearing, and the nauseating properties of Mannheim Steamroller: this episode truly has it all.

First off, Mannheim Steamroller. I know that this peculiar brand of orchestra-led-by-screeching-electric-guitar Christmas music enjoys a certain popularity, but it's like those trays of bleached tripe at the grocery store: somebody must buy that crap, but I've yet to meet that person. And at least animal stomach can wind up making a delectable dish like *trippa alla romana*. Mannheim Steamroller has surely only resulted in the evacuation of such tasty food from a person's stomach.

Well, at least that's what Robin says to cover her possibly pregnancy-induced nausea. She and Barney are still hiding the news and Robin needs an excuse for her tummy gurgles when Marshall outlines the war he's about to enter with an East Meadow neighbor for bragging rights to the best-lit house at Christmastime.

Barney is excited at the possibility of being a parent — with Robin, no less — until he reckons with the damage it would have on his Lothario lifestyle (a fate foretold by his former friend "Insane Duane," who was once Barney's partner in lascivious crime but is now married with a gaggle of kids and unafraid to be seen in public wearing sweatpants — the *true* sign that you've given up and are just waiting for your friends to bury you and start making passes at your widow). Funny, but absolutely believable, that it would take the idea of fatherhood to have Barney re-evaluate his life as a ladies' man — you'd think he would have come up against these thoughts while in a long-term relationship with Robin, but then again, nothing says lifelong commitment like offspring.

Having kids changes everything, that's clear. If you're in a position to wait for the perfect moment, when you are emotionally prepared and financially set, then good on you. For most people it has to happen unexpectedly because if you were to sincerely consider the impact it would have on your life, you'd likely never get around to it. Which is a shame because there is a dearth of cool people having kids on this planet, and if there's one thing cool people can do, it's rationalize their way out of things. Provided they are "book" cool and not "binge-drinking" cool.

Robin would argue that when it comes to having kids, the timing is never right, but, as she says to Lily, there is a wide gap between choosing never to do something and being told you never can. Robin is one of the broadest characters on the show in the later seasons, and while avoiding deepening her character may result in solid comedic results (see "The Best Man"), it is important for the audience to see the subtler aspects of her psychological make-up. Finding out that she will never be able to have children, and her subsequent desire to keep that news exclusively to herself, explains a great deal about Robin as a person. And this is the type of information we don't see much of in the later seasons, so it is especially rewarding to watch it here.

The choice to have Robin take over narration for most of this episode, telling the story of her brush with parenthood to her "kids," (later revealed to be a heart-wrenching figment of her imagination) is not only a clever swap of the usual *HIMYM* approach, but allows for a truly bittersweet ending. There aren't many sitcoms that would allow a Christmas episode to end with a childless character sitting alone on a snow-dusted park bench in Manhattan, ruminating on the finality of never being able to have kids.

7.22 good crazy

Throughout her pregnancy, Lily has experienced everything from reduced cognitive abilities ("pregnancy brain") to hyperactive sexual dreams that include Robin dressed up as a police officer (ummm . . . "sexy brain"?). This time it is Marshall's chance to undergo a psychological sea change connected to the impending birth of their child, one that resists being summed up in a glib two-word phrase. (Lord knows I've tried.) We're not entirely sure why Marshall is suddenly freaking out, but it's clear that a complex network of biological and mental influences are conspiring to shake an otherwise easygoing guy and turn him into a hyperalert, overbearing parental preparedness type. ("Bossy brain?" No, that's not quite right.)

No matter what the reason for — or the difficulty in naming — this phenomenon, Marshall sees impending fatherhood as a crisis situation (like Ted with a natural disaster) and tries to train for it by swaddling a watermelon like a baby. While I understand that this specific behavior (much like Niles' decision to test drive fatherhood by cradling a bag of flour in *Frasier*) would result in a quick institutionalization in any other situation, Marshall gets a pass. Looming fatherhood is enough to drive anyone a little crazy, and besides, the gang needs a tall guy around to get things off the top shelf.

What remains a mystery is Marshall's sudden lack of confidence in Lily's nascent talents as a mother. Could this be a simple reaction to her refusal to board Marshall's Crazy Train? Does he actually think she's been coasting on the very fact that she's had to carry their child for nine months and that when the rubber nipple hits the road *he'll* be in charge of the parenting? Does he purposely put everyday household condiments on the top shelf in the kitchen just to feel wanted? (If he's anything like me, then the answer to that last one is a resounding "Yes!")

Fed up and looking for a little space (which she often needs when Marshall gets clingy and weird — see "Disaster Averted"), Lily arranges for Barney to take her tall, snooty husband off her hands, sending them on a road trip to Atlantic City so that Marshall can blow off some steam — and Lily can read a goddamn magazine in peace and quiet. This proves to be not so much the antidote to Marshall's cuckoo behavior ("Baby-daddy brain?" Nope, too Maury Povich.) as the platform he needs to transform this manic energy, going from the overconcerned father-to-be to the triumphantly returning "Beercules" (introduced in "The Naked Truth" from earlier this season). Downing one hundred shots of tequila will do that to a guy — if it doesn't fit him for a toe tag first.

Barney has his own problems, as he finally faces the fact that his serious girlfriend Quinn strips for a living. Ted is trying to get over Robin (again) after professing his love for her (again, in "The Drunk Train") on the rooftop of the apartment (*again . . . seriously,* this guy needs a new bag of tricks). But the engine with the most pull in this episode is Lily's pregnancy, when she goes into labor and can't get a hold of the guys in Atlantic City.

Childbirth on TV sitcoms is just like it is in real life — full of miscommunications, sprints down hospital hallways, tearful reunions, and a mother swearing she's going to have a natural birth until the pain hits and she caves and demands an epidural. In other words, a barrel of laughs!

Getting to the actual birth of the Eriksen baby is a great way to hurtle toward the two-parter that ends the season, though it also worried stalwart fans given the shift from the show's once-trademark ability to blend comedy and pathos to what seems like uninterrupted door-slamming farce. But as far as episode-ending cliff-hangers go, Lily going into birth while Beercules makes it rain chips on the casino floor is a humdinger.

empire state building fun facts

- I've got it! "Daddy brain." Right?
- Once again, we hear about Ted's favorite poet, Pablo Neruda, a man known for his lush and often erotic love poems, which nicely align with Ted's romantic leanings

Becki Newton

— but does Ted share Neruda's love of Marxism? I'm going to hazard a guess and say no.

7.23 & 7.24 the magician's code, parts 1 & 2

There are two things a magician needs to succeed: good timing and a talent for misdirection. A sexy assistant and a way with rabbits certainly can't hurt, but a sexy rabbit would be even better. Now, if you switch out rabbits for "Ted and his fan-favorite girlfriend, Victoria," you get one of the main plots of this two-part season finale — and this also means I've managed to pull off both timing and misdirection, while inadvertently admitting to a sexual attraction to rabbits.

So, this is a bit of a mixed bag for me.

"The Magician's Code" is a two-parter in name only: from what I can determine, the title doesn't apply to the first part *whatsoever*. Maybe we could make the case that the efforts Barney undertakes to get Marshall from Atlantic City to the New York hospital in time for the birth of his son are on an epic scale comparable with anything David Copperfield has pulled off, but that's a bit of a stretch. I'm not sure if the show's creators were obligated to produce an hour-long season finale, but this is ultimately two regular episodes spliced together with the barest of connective tissue.

The first part is primarily about Lily giving birth. There isn't a lot of new information here, although it is interesting that a series about telling stories features a subplot in which Lily demands that Ted and Robin tell her stories to take her mind off the pain of her contractions and the absence of Marshall. This leads to a series of flashbacks to stories we've never seen before but that have the appearance of ones that we should have witnessed. Whether it's testing to see if banana peels really are slippery (answer: yes) or finding out what is behind that otherwise undetected door at MacLaren's (answer: Narnia. Okay, fine, it's just a broom closet crammed with the gang, who are pulling a prank on Marshall), this is the kind of approach that provides a richer sense of the characters' lives, referring as it does to a time period we've witnessed but events we haven't actually seen. This lends a sense of verisimilitude to the proceedings, reassuring us that the characters have lives outside of the events presented for our viewing. Referring exclusively to events we've already witnessed would only have made the gang seem two-dimensional.

Lucky for us, there is less of a focus on the kind of giving-birth hijinks often ladled on in a comic setting. True, we have someone passing out at the sight of the mother about to give birth, but instead of the father or another ostensibly "strong" male character, it is arguably the most butch character out of the group — namely, Robin.

Instead, things unfold exactly how we would expect them to: Marshall makes it there in time for the birth, Ted and Robin make up, and Barney gets his wish to provide the Abbott and Costello–ready middle name for the newborn: Marvin *Wait-For-It* Eriksen. The matters of timing and misdirection are not all that evident, which is why I think this first part is just so much treading of the dramatic waters.

Greater developments await us in the second part of the finale, which contains an *actual* Magician's Code reference. Barney has been worried that he's blown it with Quinn over his jealousy at her continued stripping (despite her unwavering protest that she is not in need of saving) and is pleased that she is still in his apartment upon his return. They decide to take a trip to Hawaii but are snared at airport security when Barney will not open a mysterious black box because, he says, of the titular code. It's no surprise that Barney adheres to the Magician's Code beyond all reason, but what is a surprise is what the box is actually revealed to contain, after all the comic *Sturm und Drang*. An engagement ring is a definite surprise, despite the relief Barney experienced at finding Quinn still at the apartment. After all, they did start their romance in the most unconventional of ways — in a strip club with Quinn bilking Barney out of thousands of dollars. To say nothing of the episode's closing scene, which links back to the wedding opener with Ted visiting Barney's bride-to-be — who turns out to be Robin!

There's the misdirection part.

Given the chance, Marshall and Lily might have launched an intervention. But they're too busy caring for a newborn, with all the expected exhaustion and rapidly approaching hallucinations that brings with it. They are clear that things will have to change regarding Ted's panic mode of asking for advice on the smallest of concerns.

That's not all for Ted. At Robin's urging, he calls Victoria to talk, since she was clearly (to hear Robin tell it) the closest he's ever been to finding The One. We are left to ponder the wisdom of that decision when Victoria arrives for their meeting in a wedding dress.

That old beast timing rears its ugly (and I assume horned) head once again.

I can't decide if Ted has the best timing in the world or the worst. Victoria's spontaneous suggestion that she and Ted run off together could be put down to cold feet, and Ted thinks this is likely, but eventually he takes her up on the request, and the two of them drive off into the sunset together. At this point it seems like he called her at exactly the right time — well, notwithstanding the same heartbreak that visited Ted when Stella left him now being heaped upon her poor fiancé, Klaus.

Critics of this episode opined that it left little to consider about the characters between seasons, but I would have to disagree. The relatively small dilemma of Marshall and Lily trying to have the perfect photo taken with baby Marvin aside, each development leaves us wondering not about *what* might happen (as we are given all the endings ahead of time) but about *how* these events are going to unfold. And that's a better cliff-hanger than any standard issue *will-they-or-won't-they* trick pulled out of the TV writer's bag of tricks.

empire state building fun facts

- The flashbacks in part one go for broad laughs, and, for my money, the *Terminator* gambit that Barney tries to use to get laid is off-the-charts cartoony: fully naked in an alleyway saying, "Come with me if you want to bang"? Groan.

- Ted and Victoria grappling with their obvious compatibility and the ethical implications of leaving a person at the altar is much more relatable and a richer source of laughs and, honestly, I'm *not* attracted to rabbits in any way: I don't even like how they taste.

mother herrings
THOSE WHO WOULD BE MOM

- Naomi, better known as the Slutty Pumpkin (Katie Holmes) in "The Slutty Pumpkin Returns": she meets all the criteria of Ted's perfect woman (funny, romantic, spontaneous) but it doesn't work out due to one small problem — they don't really like each other.
- The return of Victoria (Ashley Williams): we can be told over and over that Victoria is not the Mother, but fans love her, and the reintroduction of her character (yet again) can make an audience dream . . . can't it?

house guests

- Martin Short (*SCTV*, *Saturday Night Live*) as Garrison Cootes, Marshall's new boss, in "The Naked Truth"
- Kal Penn (*Harold and Kumar*, *House*, Associate Director of the Office of Public Engagement in President Obama's White House) as Kevin, Robin's therapist (and later, her boyfriend) in "The Stinson Missile Crisis"
- Jeff Probst (*Survivor*) as himself in "The Stinson Missile Crisis"
- Ray Wise returns as Robin's dad
- Wayne Brady returns as Barney's brother, James
- Chris Elliott returns as Lily's dad
- Patricia Conroy returns as Barney's mom
- "Weird" Al Yankovic as himself in "Noretta"
- Katie Holmes (*Dawson's Creek*, *Batman Begins*, tabloid headlines) as Naomi the Slutty Pumpkin in "The Slutty Pumpkin Returns"
- Ernie Hudson (*Ghostbusters*) as himself in "The Rebound Girl"

- Jai Rodriguez (*Queer Eye for the Straight Guy*) as Barney's brother's partner in "The Rebound Girl"
- Vicki Lewis (*Newsradio*, *Finding Nemo*) as the gynecologist Dr. Sonya (". . . a *little* bit") in "The Stinson Missile Crisis," "Symphony of Illumination," and "The Magician's Code"
- Bill Fagerbakke returns (in spirit) as Marshall's dad in "Tailgate"
- Conan O'Brien as a background extra at MacLaren's in "No Pressure"
- Michael Gladis (Paul Kinsey from *Mad Men*) as Chester in "Trilogy Time"
- Becki Newton (*Ugly Betty*) as Quinn

maybe it's the booze talking
REACTIONS TO THE SEASON

Ratings for this year started very strong, with the second episode, "The Naked Truth," bringing in over twelve million viewers (although this dropped by two million for the following episode, the more *HIMYM*-mythology-building "Ducky Tie"). Numbers lagged in the second half of the season with "Now We're Even" corralling an audience of a little over seven million. In a more dubious honor, this season of *How I Met Your Mother* was the most pirated TV show of the 2011–2012 season, with roughly 2.8 million downloads per episode.

Emmy Award recognition came with nods for Art Direction, Makeup for a Multi-Camera Series or Special (Non-Prosthetic), and Cinematography, and a win for Picture Editing for a Comedy Series.

season eight (2012–2013)
FORCE MAJEURE AT THE SPLITSVILLE CAFE

You can't make an omelet without
breaking up a few relationships

suit up! LEGEN . . . DARY THOUGHTS ON THE SEASON

In this season's "The Pre-Nup," Ted is forced to watch a German sitcom called *Strange Compatriots* (where two clashing personality types, one neat and the other one *very* neat, are forced to live together). He's not a big fan at first, but he soon falls victim to the show's charms.

"It's big comedy," he squeaks between laughs. "But you really care about all the characters."

Très meta, wouldn't you say?

I'm not sure how many seasons *Strange Compatriots* lasted, but I imagine that if Ludwig and Wilhelm had made it to eight seasons, trying to wring laughs out of who polished the doorknobs would have become a chore at best (just as trying as figuring out who used the last of the doorknob polish . . . *Ludwig!!!!!!*).

Dramatically, this season is about breakups (the couples who survive them and the couples who don't), but emotionally, it is about facing the possibility of letting your dreams go in hopes that they'll return to you. Considering all the news flying around at the time that this could be the final season of the show (especially due to rumored last-minute holdout Jason Segel), it could just as likely have been about the audience's breakup with the show.

We see this return of a life's desire most clearly in Lily, who has all but given up on a career in the art world when she is presented with the opportunity to serve as an art consultant for a billionaire client (an unexpected return of The Captain, the husband of Ted's ex-girlfriend Zoey). Marshall has nabbed his dream job as an environmental lawyer, but finds that the reality of such an arrangement can often fall far short of the dream that inspired it. Robin and Barney both (at different times, naturally) let each other go, only to fall back into each other's arms.

Then there's Ted. Poor, hangdog Ted. He gets back together with Victoria, but when *that* doesn't work out, he hooks up with the less-than-stable Jeanette, the last girl he will date before meeting his future wife. When *that* ends in a firestorm of broken vinyl and roasted red cowboy boots, he's ready to give up on finding The One. In New York, at least. He's all set to leave for Chicago; he just has to get to Farhampton first, for Robin and Barney's wedding.

As a long-time fan of the show, for me a lot of this season was about almost giving up on it. That's not an easy thing to write, but here we run into the pitfalls of trying to keep a show running for a long period of time. I have a theory that most shows should run no more than five seasons because anything longer than that means you have to start introducing a new raft of characters, or airlift the existing cast to an entirely different locale, or, God forbid, introduce a talking alien that only one of the characters can see.

Carter Bays and Craig Thomas keep things nailed down to the existing characters, and, while I applaud that decision, I still worried this season about the gang's exploits turning into standard cartoonish sitcom wackiness.

We come very close to this in two episodes this year, the first being "Who Wants To Be a Godparent?" in which the desire to be named godparent of Marshall and Lily's child becomes such a competition between the friends that it's turned into a game show, right down to a glittery game show set in the apartment above MacLaren's.

What follows may seem like screaming the truth about Santa Claus at the mall in December, but I can't help it: *really?!* You want us to believe that, with a newborn, Marshall somehow found the time to build an entire game show set, complete with a podium and a spinning wheel? No.

A similar situation occurs in "The Stamp Tramp," when Barney is on the search for a new strip club now that his ex-girlfriend Quinn has returned to work at the Lusty Leopard. Sure, it's amusing that the various strip clubs vying for Barney's patronage plays out like a high-stakes NBA draft (right down to bribery charges leveled at the agent — in this case, Robin), but the wheeling out of a podium (again!) at MacLaren's for Barney to make his choice public feels like such a close brush with shark-jumping that you can almost smell the salt water.

This is a common occurrence in the TV landscape. Even a lion-ized comedy like *Cheers* navigated such choppy waters during its eleven-season run, first when Diane left, and Sam Malone not only reverted back to his drinking but, after drying out, continued to act like a shallow, one-dimensional Lothario — which wasn't nearly as interesting as a *reformed* Lothario trying to keep a lid on his libido for his girlfriend. The last season or two of the show's run brought even more foolishness, with hijinks overtaking character logic and otherwise sane people almost destroying the bar in search for a hidden treasure.

What keeps us watching? Surely not just the need to meet the Mother?

No, because there are grace notes within the brassy noise of the season. *Cheers* got away with its transgressions because the writing within those lame episodes was still so damn good. In this regard, *HIMYM* has a similar card up its sleeve.

The writing is still sharp and funny and occasionally poignant:

Ted's genuine fear of never finding love in "Something New"; the tense exchange that occurs when Ted oversteps his boundaries and lectures Barney on Robin's true feelings in "Romeward Bound"; Lily's very real desperation about being a mother in "Band or DJ?"

That all helps, but even more compelling is the steady hand of an overall sense of purpose. It's not just that we are destined (along with Ted) to meet the Mother and fall in love. Specifically, it's that there are deliberate hands at work: the importance of Farhampton from season eight to season nine; the episodic bookends of "Good Crazy" in season seven and "Bad Crazy" in season eight; and the threading of Ted's on-again, off-again love for Victoria throughout the series.

Not only do we *finally* get to see the Mother at the very end of this season, but we have a stage well set for a wild weekend in Farhampton.

remember the time . . .
HIGHLIGHTS, RUNNING GAGS, AND CATCHPHRASES

- Bangtoberfest, a festival Barney tries to organize in order to regain his power with women in "Nannies" — CBS sells Bangtoberfest shirts online
- The Pre-Schtup, another invention of Barney's (patent pending) from "The Pre-Nup"
- Ted's misbegotten puppet teaching aid, Professor Infosaurus ("Who Wants to Be a Godparent?")
- The *Underneath the Tunes* special about Robin Sparkles ("P.S. I Love You")
- The former Brandon Walsh cramming a Timbit into a strawberry-vanilla donut and calling it a "Priestley" ("P.S. I Love You")
- Finally, the end of the red cowboy boots in "Weekend at Barney's"

- A *Downton Abbey* parody in *Woodworthy Manor* ("The Fortress")
- Barney's floating Jor-El head in "The Fortress" — and his admission that the Superman films are "uneven"
- My nominee for saddest episode of the season, "The Time Travelers," which has Ted spending an entire evening alone with projected future versions of himself and Barney
- Robin's claim that she created Marshall's Minnesota Tidal Wave cocktail, which leads to Marshall accusing her of "Zuckerberging" him ("The Time Travelers")
- Ted's steadfast belief that fanny packs are, in fact, "hands-free belt satchels" ("Something Old")
- Marshall pointing out the flakiness of a leather wrist cuff on a grown man — or anyone for that matter — when he refers to Ted's bracelet as "Wonder Woman's magic wrist cuff" ("Ring Up!")
- The many mentions of the various *Real Housewives* shows as the ultimate TV guilty pleasure — well, those and *Weekend at Bernie's* (see "Weekend at Barney's")
- The parallels between *The Wire*'s Omar Little and Lily in "Twelve Horny Women"
- Brobibs.com: though not a functioning website as of this writing, BroBibs *are* available on amazon.com! ("Lobster Crawl")

taking life and turning it into a series of crazy stories
THE EPISODES

8.01 farhampton

It's always a storytelling risk when one character breaks up with another in a callous manner. Leaving someone at the altar certainly qualifies as potentially heartless but the problem lies in whether the audience is expected to still like the character after that hurtful act of spontaneity. Because who could feel kindly toward a person after they jilt another in such a public (not to mention screwball comedy) manner?

We certainly didn't like it when Stella ditched Ted moments before they were to wed. He took the high road after his cuckolding (well, aside from his admission in this episode that he wrapped the note Stella left him around a brick and hurled it through her "perfect bay window"), but that didn't make us forgive the woman who broke his heart.

The tricky bit in "Farhampton" is that Ted's seemingly perfect-for-him ex-girlfriend Victoria does the very same thing to her fiancé, Klaus. Not only that, she has failed to leave a note explaining her departure, which strikes me as displaying a lack of "common courtesy," as Ted mentions, but also fails to leave a handy Exhibit A for prosecution in any future Breach of Promise lawsuits.

Naturally, Ted, is more concerned with the note and its contents than Victoria. That he goes to great lengths to place the note where Klaus will find it is also not surprising, as the complications in this season reach a peak level of sitcom farce. What's interesting is that Ted almost collides with Victoria's jilted fiancé, who is making his way down the drainpipe as Ted climbs up.

Turns out, Klaus has had his own cold feet and is leaving Victoria at the altar — without knowing that it is becoming a trend at this particular wedding and that he is sadly number two out of the gate with this Runaway Betrothed Syndrome.

Ted overcomes his fear of lamb grease (see below) and climbs the pipe so that he can switch the notes and absolve Victoria of any guilt in the fizzled wedding plans. Other than taking the title for Greatest Effort Required for the Most Passive-Aggressive Act (the trophy is a guy shrugging while he says, "I think this is an honor if *you* think it's an honor"), it provides an opportunity for Ted to later have an exchange with Klaus on the Farhampton train station platform about the true nature of *lebenslangerschicksalsschatz*, the German term for the rush of instantaneous and all-encompassing true love. And while the speech that Klaus gives has the bittersweet tang that we've come to expect from the show, it hides one thing: from a storytelling perspective, Klaus running out on Victoria is the absolute *opposite* of legendary.

Why? It's lazy. It lets Victoria off the hook for a selfish act and was likely undertaken so that the audience could continue to love the character. It would have been a richer decision to have Klaus actually be devastated by Victoria's act and have the characters, along with the audience, wrestle with that for much of the season. Instead, the decks are cleared for Ted and Victoria to continue their romance in a way that is lazier than the person responsible for the unpardonable sin of texting abbreviations, especially ROTFLMAO.

Don't get me wrong — Ted and Victoria are cute together and a part of me wishes she was the Mother. But after seven seasons of exploding the expectations of a network television sitcom, this choice is a noticeable stumble, IMHO.

empire state building fun facts

- Do you like Farhampton? Sounds like a quaint little

Ashley Williams
TRAVIS JOURDAIN / PR PHOTOS

cottage town in upstate New York, right? Well get comfy, because we'll spend a whole lot of time here come season nine — and *only* in season nine as it happens to be fictional.

- Ted believes at first that he can't shimmy up the drainpipe to leave Victoria's note because he couldn't climb the rope in fourth grade (when he followed a Greek kid who had slicked the cable with lamb grease): did anyone else find this unsettling in its insinuations?
- One highlight is Barney working against a stopwatch to summarize almost the entire previous seven seasons in under a minute, which he does with skill.

8.05 the autumn of break-ups

Now, I'm no fount of sassy, finger-snapping life wisdom (not until my fourth cosmo, at least), but I think any time a relationship is resumed after a long break period is more like hitting the un-pause button than a reset.

There are exceptions, of course. If we were to examine the phenomenon of rekindled relationships in Hollywoodspeak, we might consider the difference between the continuing action of a sequel and the blank-slate do-over of a romantic reboot. For example:

A partner returns to a marriage after serving in the military: a clear sequel of the *Godfather* variety (i.e., perfect).

A partner who serves in the military is presumed dead until he resurfaces seven years later a changed man: I would argue this is a sequel also, but of the doomed variety like *Speed 2: Cruise Control* (or season two of *Homeland*).

A guy is about to leave his wife but gets hit on the head and develops retrograde amnesia. He meets his wife for what he thinks is the first time and starts to woo her: this is a romantic reboot (and heretofore known as *Love Me, Love My Hippocampus*, my forthcoming novel — to be released with a cover just close enough to look like a Nicholas Sparks novel without resulting in a lawsuit).

A buttoned-down woman mistakenly walks into an S&M trade show and runs into an ex-boyfriend now selling clamps for various appendages. They start things up again, but it's nothing like the love they experienced as teenagers at Holy Oak Bible Study and Orienteering Summer Camp: this too qualifies as a reboot (and a gritty one at that).

The point is (and there is a point here, I swear), Victoria is right in thinking that all the getting-to-know-you stuff was covered in the first time at bat with Ted six years ago. Ted thinks that enough time has passed that they are in a romantic reboot scenario, possibly out of a near-autistic inability to read social cues (another way of saying that he's a "hopeless romantic").

Like the lifeguard who can never remember to take his umbrella, it doesn't matter because whether it rained or not, the dude got wet all the same (note to self: title for sequel to amnesia novel will be *Dude Got Wet All the Same*). So Ted proposes. He's good at that kind of grand romantic gesture, so much so that we can rightly assume that he's been proposing to girls since the third grade — luckily he didn't grow up in the Deep South or else he'd have been married a few times already. (I kid!) The response Victoria delivers — that they can only get married if he ends his friendship with Robin — comes a little out of left field. All the couples have hung around together in previous episodes without Victoria having *much* of an issue with Robin (despite Robin's role in the cheating that ended their previous relationship), so this qualifies as a hell of a turn-around.

Which is strange because it transforms Victoria from an alarmingly cool girlfriend (seeming fine not only with hanging out with Robin but with Ted doing the same) to a jealous shrew who doles out ultimatums with a deadly accuracy not seen since Jason Bourne went up against the CIA.

Even though Ted and Victoria make a terrific couple, there is a certain comfort in watching Ted refuse to choose her over Robin. Robin is family, and Victoria asking him to stop seeing her would be the same as demanding that he no longer see Marshall or Barney. And we all know *that* isn't going to happen.

Speaking of, *The Bourne Ultimatum* was a nifty sequel, too.

empire state building fun facts

- The sage Sassy Black Woman figure is prevalent throughout the entire episode, from Marshall channeling Oprah (well, playing Gayle to Lily's Oprah) when giving advice, to the back-up singers on Robin's boyfriend Nick's public cable access show — tribute to a resonant pop culture archetype or cultural insensitivity? You could make an argument either way, based on the history of the show.
- The her-or-me dynamic is once again reminiscent of *Friends*, this time of the whole Ross/Rachel/Emily debacle — but at least on *HIMYM* this conflict played over only one episode, instead of half a season.

8.06 splitsville

As the Autumn of Breakups comes to a close, we see that Robin's time with Nick is running out, which is a good thing. Despite his handsomeness, Nick has never been a terribly interesting character, and his good looks seem to be the only thing that would keep the interest of a woman like Robin. Well, his good looks and the adroit application of the sexual arts.

Despite efforts to make Nick interesting, he has truly only served the role of a barrier between Robin and Barney. When we first meet Nick, he's an attractive fellow with nice abs that Robin would like to grate cheese on. Later, we see him as a patient guy willing to withstand Robin's friendship with two other guys, both of them ex-lovers, who pull her away with late-night phone calls. We even see him as a struggling public-access-channel TV cook, desperately trying to compose a great catchphrase (somehow "Come on and eat my meat!" doesn't look so good on a baseball cap).

In this episode, we suddenly learn that Nick is a doofus. This smacks of last-minute characterization to further the plot (see the Victoria-versus-Robin incident in "The Autumn of Break-Ups"), though it might be considered plausible in that his relationship with Robin seemed mostly based on sex. A groin injury playing for Marshall's lawyer basketball team, Force Majeure, puts Nick on the sexual sidelines for a while and means that he and Robin have to fill up their time with other pursuits. So while I guess it's possible that she wouldn't have realized that he's a dummy until then, Nick's unyielding dunderheadedness in this episode plays like an established character trait, when in fact it hasn't been previously set up. No one would have confused him for a Mensa candidate before now, but nothing we've seen from him would indicate that he is the type of guy to play an entire basketball game with his shoes on the wrong feet (although this *is* a testament to his excellent athletic abilities).

It is elements like this that make me feel as if the series is running on fumes this season: while there is still a constant eye to the overall arc of the series, and interesting new bits of information are revealed about the core cast (Ted likes to sew!), there are too many times when expediency is chosen over characterization or fidelity to the innovation we've seen in previous years (whether subverting expectations of the genre or playing with structure in an elegant fashion).

In a stronger season, an issue like new parents Marshall and Lily being unable to have sex would have been a solid subplot instead of half-hearted running gag that builds up to a throwaway punchline.

8.15 p.s. i love you

Part of the fun of seeing a series through to its conclusion (its *planned* conclusion, that is, and not an unceremonious cancelation), is watching as all the loose ends are tied up. This episode sees a gratifying conclusion to the Robin Sparkles story — and a compendium of Canadian jokes — all crammed into a show that also sees Ted meeting the last girlfriend he'll have before he meets the mother of his children.

The whole idea that light and dark are two sides of the same coin is a staple of everything from comic books (Batman's nemesis Two-Face comes to mind) to cop movies (*The Departed* is a good example of this dynamic, and also of how to confuse an audience with what I *think* amounted to a quintuple cross). It's no surprise, then, that Robin felt penned in by the goody-goody image of Robin Sparkles — as an artist, writing about going to the mall can't possibly fuel the creative engine for very long.

If there were any doubt up until now that Robin Sparkles was based on Alanis Morissette, this episode all but erases it. When Barney tries to track down the object of Robin's teenage obsession (and by obsession, we mean that she stalked him, ultimately ending up with a fifty-meter restraining order — which is not, as Barney suggests, "like four years"), he finds out that there was a *Behind the Music*–type documentary about Robin Sparkles' fall from grace (and re-emergence as grunge singer Robin Daggers).

Not only does *Underneath the Tunes* show part of her long-lost video, which sounds *exactly* like Ms. Morissette, but the parade of Canadian testimonials in the documentary points directly to the mythos surrounding Morissette's *Jagged Little Pill* album. Of particular interest is an appearance by Dave Coulier (of *Full House* fame) denying his role as the source of the heartbreak that led to the song — a charge that has dogged Coulier almost since the day *JPL* was released. (It's also great to see Coulier resurrecting his "Cut it out" line from *Full House*, which is then commented on by Future Ted Bob Saget, who of course starred alongside Dave in the

'80s sitcom . . . honestly, this episode is like a pop culture vortex that could be studied for a week at Carnegie Mellon University.)

Robin Sparkles/Daggers' meltdown occurs at a Grey Cup half-time show, and while I won't divulge the object of her obsession in case you've forgotten what the "P.S." in "P.S. I Love You" stands for (or have forgotten what the Grey Cup is, for that matter), it does dramatize the duality of obsession and just how easy it is to wind up suffering a complete mental breakdown while singing a tortured love song to a bald TV band leader in front of a full house at Ivor Wynne stadium.

As always, the show is best when it's relatable.

The allure of that light/dark dichotomy is revealed when Ted sees a woman on the train reading the same book he is, *One Hundred Years of Solitude* by Gabriel García Márquez. That she's attractive certainly helps, but he is truly pulled in by the idea of connecting with someone who enjoys a book that *some* people have found well-nigh unreadable despite the bucketloads of praise heaped upon it.

During the course of their early courtship, the Dobler/Dahmer Theory is in full effect: Ted's theory that's as solid as the Reacher/Settler Theory of relationships from season five. The idea that the same grand romantic gesture will be viewed differently depending on how the intended feels about the gesturer is a wise observation. If you like the person offering their affection, you see him like Lloyd Dobler from *Say Anything* . . . holding a boom box aloft and charming the pants off you. If you *don't* like the person, then he's Jeffrey Dahmer, the notable serial killer, sex offender, and all-around despicable representative of the human race.

Which side of the fence Ted's new girlfriend Jeanette sits on is up for grabs. Marshall and Lily think that setting a fire at the university to trigger the fire alarm just so she could talk to Ted puts her squarely in the Dahmer camp. But when her insistence that she "couldn't stand the idea of not meeting" Ted makes him all dewy-eyed, he thinks she's a Dobler. Or, as he puts it, "She's John Cusack, I'm Ione Skye, and there's nothing strange about that!"

He *wishes* he was Ione Skye. She's so beautiful and nearly a genius in that movie. Methinks the dude doth profess too much.

All of this, plus an opportunity to see Barney get the snot beaten out of him by a donut-eating Alan Thicke, makes this one of the most enjoyable episodes of the season.

empire state building fun facts

- While the network airing *Underneath the Tunes* does exist (and MuchMusic really is the Canadian MTV), sadly there is no such Canuck version of *Behind the Music*.

the best canadian stereotypes

The first Canadian reference in the series came at the expense of the United States. Carter Bays and Craig Thomas saw Robin's Canadian heritage as a great vehicle for pointing out all the flaws in the United States. But, as Cobie Smulders put it, "They initially liked the idea because it allowed them to reflect on the things that the States doesn't have: universal health care, a great school system, all the great stuff up there . . . ever since then it's been jokes about our accent and donuts." That is only part of the picture. *How I Met Your Mother* has trafficked in some interesting stereotypes about Canadians, most of which are possibly exaggerations:

- Canadians are nyctophobic (though as Robin protests, "We're not afraid of the dark. I mean we don't love it, but who does?")
- Canadians say "eh" a lot — not to mention "aboot"
- Canadians constantly apologize (I'm sorry, but that's just not true)
- Canadians have two religions: hockey and Tim Hortons (I have it on good authority this is accurate)

- Canadians are impervious to inclement weather (they may wear T-shirts in sub-zero temperatures, but few would consider a hurricane "bikini weather")
- Canadians are annoyingly friendly (tell that to anyone who has made her way through downtown Toronto)

Canadian stereotypes Carter Bays and Craig Thomas have missed:

- Canadians chew their food thirty-two times before swallowing . . . it's the law
- Canadians make large wagers only to back out of them at the last minute
- *At the last minute* is a Canadian-coined term
- While many speak English, and others speak French, they all speak a secret, high-pitched third language so Americans won't hear all the jokes at their expense
- Canadians know how to treat a woman like a lady, and a man like a foppish dandy
- Canadians rest safe in the knowledge that a French cruller is nothing but deep fried hot air

8.16 bad crazy

It's episodes like this that make me glad I'm writing a book about this show. Or that make me *crazy* for this show.

No, wait. I meant the first thing.

We've seen a few different types of crazy on the show. There was the "Good Crazy" of season seven, which covered Marshall's hysterical overpreparedness in the face of his forthcoming child. We also saw the "crazy eyes" — a telltale sign of future cuckoo behavior — in season two's "Swarley." Those wondering if guys ever get a case of crazy eyes need look no further than Ted's behavior in this episode.

First, the crazy girlfriend. In the voiceover, Future Ted

introduces Jeanette as the last girlfriend he had before meeting the mother of his kids. I was a little leery of the unhinged woman trope but was willing to give the show's writers leeway after having spent seven seasons watching them subvert the standard clichés of the romantic comedy genre and make the female characters the strongest in the cast.

At least this episode addresses the allure of crazy. We can talk around it politely all day long but, seriously, crazy in the head means crazy in the bed. When this type of story is told, very rarely is the guy's role in the dynamic explored at all, and, if it is, we usually see the spicy sexual aspect given full credit. But, as we hear from a wise old lady with a face tattoo, these flavors of crazy are generally triggered by mixed signals from a guy. The *go-away-come-here-don't-call-me-introduce-me-to-your-parents* thing is enough to make the steeliest of minds go rusty and snap. It takes a toll on her psychological well-being and quite naturally leads to razor-sliced underwear and bloody entrails sent in the mail.

. . . I suppose. I think there has to be a *little* crazy there to begin with, but Lily is right when she tells Ted that he should stay with his nutty girlfriend because he's just as nutty as she is . . . and she's certainly right about the last part at least. He doesn't know what he wants and, really, how else to explain how much he likes those stupid red cowboy boots?

I mean, they look good on Jeanette, but so does the purple lingerie. On Ted? Not so much.

The episode also works because we continue to learn about the characters, particularly Robin and the mortal dread she experiences when she thinks of holding baby Marvin. She goes to great lengths to avoid doing so, out of a fear not of cooties (as far as I can tell, although you can never be too careful — cooties are at their strongest when the baby is super cute) but that a terrible fate will befall the child once in her care.

This wrinkle in Robin's psychology is a perfect example of the reason I think people have grown to love the show. Holding a baby for the first time *is* a nerve-wracking proposition. Her anxiety feels even more endearing when we realize that it touches on her claim that she never wants children of her own. That feeling turns to sadness when we remember that she can't have them (season seven, "Symphony of Illumination"). The characters are like friends whose history we have come to know well, and, as such, we are invested in their happiness. The baby-handling aspect of this episode adroitly brings out that strength in the show and reminds us why we fell in love with the gang in the first place.

It also helps that the old lady with the face tattoo turns out to be Mike Tyson and that he holds a great deal of wisdom on the subject of relationships. You know, as he would.

empire state building fun facts

- Was I the only one to wonder if Ted bought the Boba Fett costume from this episode (which he wears during his showdown with Jeanette) at the same time Barney bought his Stormtrooper getup?

8.21 romeward bound

While it never seems possible that Marshall and Lily will break up (despite the fact that they *did* break up at the end of season one), Lily's new job as an art consultant for The Captain seems to threaten their happiness at every turn. Whether it is Lily not spending enough time at home ("The Fortress"), or being presented with the opportunity to move to Rome for a year, as in this episode, Lily is forced to make choices and to put herself in the unlikeliest of places — that is, at the front of the line.

Think about it: she gave up her hopes of a career as an artist and taught kindergarten while Marshall went to law school, looked for a job, got hired by a heartless corporation that hollowed out his very soul, looked for a job again, and finally found his dream job as an environmental lawyer . . . and that doesn't even count

Kyle MacLachlan

the sacrifices she's made as mother to Marvin. Granted, Marshall seems like a very involved father who is just as sleep-deprived and delirious as Lily, but if there's one thing moms do best, it's put everyone else's desires well ahead of their own.

Lily can't make up her mind about what to do, finding all sorts of excuses to avoid going to Rome. This has less to do with her mothering instincts or concern for Marshall's career (which has unbeknownst to Lily suffered after a big court loss for the firm) and more to do with her own self-admission that she's a "scaredy cat." High adventure is not her thing: she returned two weeks early from her teenaged backpacking trip to Paris, and she was never more depressed than when she broke up with Marshall and took off to San Francisco.

I feel like of all the characters on the show, we learn the least about Lily. Other than her talent for manipulation and evolving sexual fantasies that include Robin more often than not, we have her locked down as faithful wife, mother, and teacher for most of the series. When she gets her dream job as an art consultant, it's a nice shake-up for her character, but learning about her own fears and how they have possibly held her back fills a big hole in our understanding of her psychological makeup. Not only does it explain how she could be such a rock in the lives of Marshall and everyone else in the gang, but it also makes us feel for her and the life she might have had.

This subtle development of Lily's character is offset by some broadness, but most of it is reserved for dream sequences. Lily worries that Marshall will have an unfulfilling life in Rome, which is best expressed as an existentialist black-and-white film.

Meanwhile, the "redonkulous" body of Liddy, Barney and Robin's wedding planner, emits a heavenly glow every time she takes off her bulky coat (shades of the suitcase from *Pulp Fiction*). It's a B story that looks juvenile on paper, but I give it a pass seeing as Liddy is never shown without her jacket on, which manages the neat trick of objectifying a woman's body without *actually* showing her body.

Oh, Carter Bays and Craig Thomas . . . I just can't quit you guys.

empire state building fun facts

- The single line of Italian that Marshall knows and repeats with different inflections, meant to be a translation of "Come on, bro, don't bogart all the Funyuns," uses the name of another actor as a verb — "Mastroianni," as in Marcello Mastroianni, the legendary Italian actor who appeared in exactly the type of foreign films lampooned in this episode.

8.24 something new

If at the start of the season we weren't sure if this batch of episodes would signal a breakup with the show, then by the final episode we know that there is still more to the story. And after a season of ups and downs (in both the character's fortunes and the show's quality), "Something New" puts the series right back on track, with everything we'd hope for in a season-ender: it manages to be emotionally gratifying while still managing to give the audience a cliff-hanger ending to lead into the ninth and final season.

Marshall and Lily pack for their trip to Rome, but Marshall still hasn't told his mother, who is understandably upset when she finds out (although, with Lily unwittingly spilling the news, I was surprised there wasn't more invective of the "you dress like a Kansas City whore" variety from Marshall's mom). To placate his mom, Marshall visits Minnesota so that she can visit with baby Marvin before they leave, but while he's back home he receives the news that he's been offered a judgeship.

I know that we learned about Marshall's application to be a judge in "Twelve Horny Women," but did we ever find out if he told Lily about it? I don't think he did, which would make them nice and even for the time that Lily applied for an art fellowship in San Francisco behind Marshall's back. And we all know what happened after that — they broke up, Lily wound up depressed on

and, after eight years, we had better fall in love with her as much as Ted will.

I feel like we're in good hands.

empire state building fun facts

- When Lily relays the story about Robin's fruitless efforts digging for her locket in Central Park ("Something Old"), we find out that the locket is actually stored in a race car pencil case of Ted's, where it has been sitting for a few years: I was surprised it wasn't in a more iconic item in the apartment, like the red London-style miniature telephone box.

mother herrings
THOSE WHO WOULD BE MOM

- The Mother (Cristin Milioti) . . . *finally*: there is a lot riding on her very brief appearance in "Farhampton" but she manages to appear engaging and mysterious even with a single line of dialogue, a good indication that Bays and Thomas cast the part perfectly (they're good at that, aren't they?)

house guests

- Thomas Lennon (*Reno 911!*) as Klaus in "Farhampton" and "The Pre-Nup"
- Bob Odenkirk returns as Barney's boss, Arthur Hobbs
- Jane Carr (*Dear John*) as Mrs. Buckminster in "Nannies"
- Dennis Haskins (Mr. Belding from *Saved by the Bell*) as a member of the New York State Judiciary Committee in "Twelve Horny Women"
- Peter Gallagher (*Sex, Lies and Videotape*, *The O.C.*) as Ted's scholastic obsession, Professor Vinick, in "The Final Page — Part 1"
- Seth Green (*Robot Chicken*, *Family Guy*, *Buffy the Vampire Slayer*) as Daryl, lynchpin of the Three Hackmigos, in "The Final Page — Part 1" (it's interesting to see him guest star, as *HIMYM* has been taken down a few times on *Family Guy*, where he voices the character of Chris)
- Rachel Bilson returns as Ted's (now-lesbian) ex Cindy in "Band or DJ?"
- Famous Canadians Alex Trebek, NHL Hall of Famer Luc Robitaille, Paul Shaffer, Alan Thicke, Dave Thomas, kd lang, Geddy Lee, Jason Priestley, and Steven Page all appear in "P.S. I Love You"

- Mike Tyson as a baby-loving, wisdom-spouting angel in "Bad Crazy"
- Kyle MacLachlan returns as The Captain in "The Ashtray"
- Ralph Macchio and William Zabka (*The Karate Kid*) as themselves in "The Bro Mitzvah"
- Casey Wilson (*Happy Endings*) and Keegan-Michael Key (*Mad TV, Key and Peele*) as Barney and Robin's restaurant foes in "Something New"
- Joe Lo Truglio (*Superbad, Brooklyn Nine-Nine*) as Mr. Honeywell in "The Stamp Tramp" and "Twelve Horny Women"
- Abby Elliott (*SNL*) as Ted's love interest/stalker Jeanette in "P.S. I Love You," "Bad Crazy," and "Weekend at Barney's"

maybe it's the booze talking
REACTIONS TO THE SEASON

During what many fans considered the weakest season of the show so far, the ratings reflected this general sense of a drop in quality. Numbers ranged between six and eight million viewers for most of the season, with "P.S. I Love You" being the only entry to crack double digits, with over ten million viewers (likely due to the return of Robin Sparkles/Daggers). The lowest showing was six-and-a-half million viewers for "Romeward Bound," again a surprise given that episode's importance to the overall arc of Marshall and Lily's journey in a season that often felt like it was treading water.

Max Nicholson at IGN suggested that the show was "rough out of the gate" trying to deal with leftovers from season seven, such as Barney's relationship with Quinn and Ted's with Victoria. His suggestion that Victoria was "revved up to near-psychotic levels of crazy" may be a bit of an overstatement, but the unsavory send-off for one of the more beloved supporting characters was a good signal of the trouble the series was in this year.

More accurate is Nicholson's opinion that the broader episodes

("Who Wants to Be a Godparent?" and "Nannies") were "painful examples of . . . cartoony comedy; frequent slapstick and fourth-wall gags [that] made you think you weren't watching the same show from a year ago." We could blame the uneven quality of this season on the uncertainty that dogged the show, in that it wasn't clear to anyone (including the showrunners) whether a season nine would even happen. I think they were running on creative fumes after seven seasons, but opinions might vary.

a quick refreshment
HOW I MET YOUR DAD — NOT A SEQUEL . . .

When John Cleese decided to gather the same group of talent from *A Fish Called Wanda* nine years later to make another movie, he noted that his intention was to harness the same creativity and madcap fun to make a movie that wasn't a sequel but an "equal."

I bring this up not to remind people that the resulting film — *Fierce Creatures* — was a grand disappointment or to imply that we might expect the same from the spinoff to *How I Met Your Mother*. I do so to suggest that even the term "spin-off" is a stretch, given that there won't be any characters that bridge the two shows and that the new series will, in essence, be a "spiritual cousin" to the long-running series we all love and hold dear.

I also mention this for my own delight, primarily to note that the original title of John Cleese's "equal" was *Death Fish II*, which, I think you'll agree, is quite delightful.

In fact, some of the first cries of foul that the announcement of this series drew (other than resistance to the very idea of a spin-off), was the title of this new show. Many believed that *How I Met Your Father* would have been a better choice. But in opting for the familiar *Dad* instead, show co-creators Carter Bays and Craig Thomas managed to announce that while the show will have a similar format and approach, it is meant to stand on its own legs.

Historically, these new chapters of existing franchises take beloved characters and place them in new settings. *Cheers* provides arguments for and against the practice: when it works, you have *Frasier*; when it doesn't, you have *The Tortellis*.

The idea of building a house based on the specs from the last one only to fill it with new characters has long been the domain of hour-long drama, specifically of the procedural crime variety.

"If *CSI* gets to have spin-offs," Craig Thomas has said, "and if *Law & Order* gets to have spin-offs, and there's mileage in a show that does a criminal investigation in a certain way . . . couldn't there be that for a comedy?"

One (relatively) recent example of this approach is *That '80s Show*, a show that tried in 2002 to replicate the successful format of *That '70s Show* with different characters — only to end in cancellation after thirteen episodes. That might have been enough to scare off other writer-producers, but not our *HIMYM* creators.

"There's been a few other format spin-offs that haven't worked," Thomas said. "I think Carter and I always feel like Barney's line, 'Challenge Accepted!'"

Many people might have concluded that the idea of the show would be to provide the other side of Ted Mosby's search for his soul mate by building a show around the Mother's collision course with destiny. But the intention was to find new stories to tell in a now-familiar format and, after nine seasons of bro-centric laughs, it was time to tell them from a female perspective. But how could the creators pull this off since, as Thomas has wisely noted, "we're not women"?

The idea to have a woman co-create the new show was also a practical one. After working on *HIMYM* for so many years, Bays and Thomas wanted to be in a position to produce and consult on a new series and not get bogged down in the day-to-day operations of one.

They believed partnering up with the right person was key to their success and happiness and, luckily, they found a *Saturday Night Live* veteran who has "much cooler credits than Carter and Craig," according to Thomas.

Emily Spivey cut her teeth on sketch comedy, working on *MADtv* before *SNL*, and writing episodes of *King of the Hill* and *Parks and Recreation* before creating her own show *Up All Night*. The single-camera comedy for NBC starred Christina Applegate and Will Arnett as new parents. The show was a hit with critics but stumbled in the ratings. A second season hiatus was called, and the network announced that the show would undergo a change in format from a single-camera to a multi-camera setup. During this time-out, Spivey (along with Christina Applegate) departed from the series.

Add to that work as a staff writer for a season on *Modern Family* and contributions to *Portlandia* (co-created by fellow *SNL* alum Fred Armisen) and you have the type of "amazingly strong, funny, female voice to collaborate with" that Bays and Thomas felt they needed to embark upon this new journey.

It didn't hurt that Spivey was represented by the same agency as Bays and Thomas, so you can thank the good people at United Talent Agency along with the forces of kismet.

Once the script was completed, the next and possibly biggest hurdle was casting the roles. Before casting the female lead of Sally, the supporting roles were cast.

Krysta Rodriguez (*Smash*) will play Juliet, the best friend and high-energy party girl who is likely to serve as the distaff Barney Stinson in this group of friends. She runs the most successful fashion blog in the United States so she is likely to be just as concerned about her appearance as Barney, although it remains to be seen how much she'll lean toward suits.

Nicholas D. Agosto (guest spots on *E.R.* and *House, M.D.* along with featured roles on *Heroes* and Showtime's *Masters of Sex*) nabbed the role of Frank, the IT guru behind Juliet's blog. He nurses a crush on Sally that is described as "one-sided . . . for the moment."

Taking the role of Sally's "terminally boring" soon-to-be ex-husband, Gavin, is Anders Holm, best known as a co-creator and writer of *Workaholics*, in which he stars as Anders Holmvik. He also had a recurring role as Mindy's fiancé on *The Mindy Project* and has appeared in *Modern Family*, *Key and Peele*, and *Arrested Development*.

Playing the part of Danny, Sally's older brother — and soft landing once she leaves her husband — is Andrew Santino, a ginger-haired regular on ABC's *Mixology*. On the new series, he plays Danny as an uptight lawyer who enjoys a close relationship with Sally but finds it tested once she moves in with him and becomes the Oscar Madison to his Felix Unger.

The part of Danny's husband, the easygoing Todd, was nabbed by Drew Tarver, perhaps most recognizable from his appearances in *Big Time Rush* and the TV series incarnation of *CollegeHumor Originals*.

The show's creators describe the main character, Sally, as a female Peter Pan who struggles with growing up. To further distance her from Ted Mosby, Sally is recently married at the start of the series, although she quickly realizes that she has nothing in common with her new spouse. Early rumors suggested that Eliza Dushku (*Buffy the Vampire Slayer, Angel, Tru Calling, Dollhouse, Torchwood: Web of Lies*) was in contention for the lead, but that idea appears not to have gone past the stage of her reading the pilot script.

Surprisingly, the producers opted for indie cred versus nerd cache when it came to the role of Sally. The casting of Greta Gerwig in the lead came as a shock. After a few years as an indie film "It" girl, with roles in *Baghead* (from mumblecore godfathers Mark and Jay Duplass), *Greenberg* (opposite Ben Stiller), and *Frances Ha* (which she co-wrote with director Noah Baumbach), many saw her acceptance of the lead role on a network sitcom as something akin to betrayal. As Kevin Jagernauth wrote online for Indiewire's The Playlist, the Twitter reactions were so full of outrage, "you'd think this news was like when Nirvana signed to Geffen Records."

Perhaps sensing the heat from cinephile hipsters, along with the expectations of *HIMYM* fans, Gerwig reacted to her casting with unaffected honesty: "I'm terrified."

Despite any fears, she will add to the show's strong female voice in her roles as an executive producer and a member of the writing staff.

"I contributed a lot into the pilot," she told *E! Online*. "It's funny. It shares the heart and soul with the original show so it has the sweetness and the funniness."

This is good news for fans of the original series, who would like to find a similar oasis of warmth and hilarity amid the usual network fare — especially if it can fill the hole left by the end of *HIMYM*.

As for the true identity of the titular dad, we'll have to wait to the end of this series. Until then, we are in no position to confirm or deny John Cleese being cast in the role. But we remain hopeful.

season nine (2013-2014)
WAIT FOR IT . . .

How he met their mother.

suit up! LEGEN . . . DARY THOUGHTS ON THE SEASON

Much like life, the road we've taken with *How I Met Your Mother* has had its share of ups and downs, left turns, and every other type of unexpected directional tangent save for a "Detour" sign crudely made by a certain Wile E. Coyote.

Although, to be fair, he *is* a coyote so . . . any kind of writing is impressive, really.

This final season is meant to wrap everything up, but it is far from a straight line. In fact, given that Carter Bays and Craig Thomas weren't certain that they would get a ninth season to finish off their show, you could look at this last run as a detour in and of itself. The idea to frame an entire season around a single weekend could only result in a complex maze of flashbacks, flash-forwards, and flashes-sideways, but while it represents a narrative gamble it is, in spirit, consistent with the entire series: innovative, irreverent, and irrationally watchable. After a fumbling eighth season, it is pleasing to see the show get its feet back, even if they do lead it down some unexpected and even head-scratching diversions.

While the marriage is never truly in jeopardy, the end result of Robin and Barney's wedding often feels murky. Will it be ruined by Marshall and Lily's epic fight — one that will certainly result from him accepting a judgeship, a choice that would ruin their plans to live in Italy for a year while Lily does her dream job? Can Marshall and Marvin make the trek to Farhampton in one piece? Are Ted's secret plans to move to Chicago going to ruin the reception? Will William Zabka ever receive notoriety for his poetry? And most important, is Ted genuinely over Robin, or will he sabotage the proceedings with a grand romantic gesture dressed as platonic friendship?

The amount of time and energy given to this last question over the course of the season, as we follow Ted's epic struggle to find a simple gold locket, comes as a surprise. A season that is ostensibly about Ted meeting the love of his life and future mother of his children instead turns into a rehash of many seasons' worth of the friends-again, romantic-again pivots between him and Robin. This has a very specific payoff by the series finale, but we spend so much time fretting about Ted having moved Robin out of his heart ("The Locket," "Platonish," "Sunrise") that we don't spend *nearly* as much time getting to know the Mother. While I doubted the choices made along the way, by the end it all seemed to work as part of a much larger and more satisfying plan. We don't see a great deal of the Mother early on, but when we do have episodes that feature or revolve around her ("How Your Mother Met Me"), they pack an extra-strength wallop.

Given the weight placed on this season, perhaps it is best to break it down into three areas of examination:

the season as a whole

I think it's interesting that a season, and a finale in particular, that deals with the disappointment of growing up and moving on from the close-knit friendships of youth left so many fans feeling disappointed. Were the divisive Farhampton framing and shocking final episode nothing more than misguided artistic choices that made many in the audience cry foul, or were they the greatest meta-stroke of genius yet from Carter Bays and Craig Thomas? They've done it before, from slyly referencing their own show in the German sitcom *Strange Compatriots* to breaking the fourth wall in season seven's "Mystery vs. History" (with a conversation about Woody Allen addressing the camera in *Annie Hall* capped off with Robin addressing the camera, saying, "Can you believe this guy?").

I would like to believe that the emotional response by the fan base was part of Bays and Thomas' plan, but in the end nobody can ever deliver an artistic statement that satisfies everybody completely, and certainly not in television. While *HIMYM* is by no means the first show to inspire collective outrage or disappointment with its ending, it's certainly true that the immediate feedback loop of the internet has changed TV finales forever. Not everyone was happy with the elliptical ending of *Cheers* but people didn't have a ready-made platform from which to voice their outrage — we were left to wrestle with the murky final scene and ultimately focus on what we had enjoyed and what we had lost in the closing of Sam Malone's bar.

The same goes for a show like *Friends*. Certainly the internet was around, but Twitter hadn't yet been invented — much less become the media force it is now — when that series ended. The show's creative team didn't have to worry about tweeting backlashes fueled by snarky hashtags mid-finale, otherwise we would have been wading through a sea of sentiments like #RossandRachelAgainREALLY?

Truth is, the audience has more input these days and it is unavoidable. If *M*A*S*H* were around today, it would probably only take a couple of days before an alternate "happy ending" version was recut from existing footage and posted on YouTube. Would that show have ended on the same grace note if we'd had a flash-forward to Hawkeye and B.J. laughing as they clinked martini glasses in a Manhattan bar?

In fact, a lot has changed over the course of this show. As Marshall says in the penultimate episode, "The End of the Aisle," "It was all over Friendster and MySpace. . . wow, 2007 was a long time ago." (Speaking of, I just noticed what a time capsule the opening credits are — don't smartphones make Lily's disposable camera obsolete?) When the show began, the creators didn't have to contend with the real fear of negative criticism trending before the final credits rolled — but over the course of *HIMYM*'s run, things changed. This couldn't have been more pronounced than in the immediate Internet wrath inspired by the *Kill Bill*–inflected martial arts vibe of "Slapsgiving 3: Slapsgiving in Slapmarra." The only thing more offensive than this episode is the purple suit Barney wears for the first half of this season before changing for the rehearsal dinner. Are we supposed to believe he's the Joker? Because, for a guy with impeccable taste in bespoke clothing, that's the only rational explanation I can think of for that hideous eyesore. I don't recall anybody online kicking up a ruckus about *that* abomination.

The only internet chatter that I'm glad happened but *didn't* come to fruition on the show is the Ted-has-Alzheimer's theory that was floated online. I'm happy people put it out there — if only to remind people how horrible Alzheimer's is and how equally horrible a movie *The Notebook* was — but I'm happier still that it turned out to be false. People found justification for this theory in the Mother's hope in "Vesuvius" that Ted doesn't become the guy who "lives in his stories." Of all the possible sad endings that we might have come to expect from a show that heaped on bittersweet storylines, this one would have been too much to bear.

Which brings me to how the show's fans view the entire series. Their feelings have undoubtedly been clouded by the emotional roller coaster that was the actual finale, but I think there is a more deep-seated sense of fans having had their emotions toyed with over the whole run. Word got out early that the scenes with Ted's kids for the series finale had been shot between the first and second seasons. The fact that the grace note of the series had been set in stone so early may have had as much of an impact on how people viewed the series — especially considering the mileage squeezed out of the Ted-Robin-Barney back-and-forth — as did the heart-stopping final scene.

the final episode

"Last Forever" closely resembled the finale of *Will & Grace*, which similarly skipped over a long period of time. At least with *HIMYM* this was an organic occurrence, whereas with *Will & Grace* it felt like an effort to sum up an entire season in a Very Special One-Hour Episode™.

In addition to their resemblance in format, the two finales share thematic similarities. They both address the bittersweet nature of adult friendships, specifically the way that people who were in your life every single day can suddenly become marginalized or completely absent. Both are ultimately upbeat on the topic — steadfast in the belief that these connections are never fully severed — and both put forth the notion that true love, whether romantic or platonic, is patient and kind.

More than the actual ending (which we'll cover later), I'm interested in the reaction the final episode spurred. Let it be said that many of the long-time fans of the show were not quite so kind.

Many saw it as a sad ending considering the fate of the Mother, and I can't fault them for feeling betrayed. So much was riding on discovering who the Mother was and how she would finally cross paths with Ted that I understand how viewers could have felt cheated after not getting to see a parting shot of her in a pleasingly domestic tableau, perhaps with Ted and the kids over a Thanksgiving dinner.

It seems to me, however, that such a desire stems from a

misunderstanding of the entire series. Identifying the Mother was never anything more than an ornate, overly complicated narrative frame for the show's portrayal of friendship in your twenties and thirties. The beating heart of the series has always been the nature of the gang's relationships, and I have to say that I'm surprised that many of the *HIMYM* faithful felt such outrage at the Mother's tragic end when she was a character we'd only gotten to know over the course of this last season.

In the end, the final season answered the question "Who is the Mother?" and the final episode gave us a concrete reason why Ted would have been telling his children all about her, other than just misty-eyed nostalgia. And could we really hope for anything more than that?

the mother

Perhaps the sentiment that "all good things must come to an end" is best expressed through our relationship with the Mother. We've been given clues about her all the way along (what she reads, what instrument she plays, the fact that she creates heart-wrenching paintings of robots playing sports), and while that has made us feel like we are getting to know her as a person, it is no replacement for actually meeting and learning about her. It's a slow, roundabout friendship that we strike with the Mother over the course of the season, but it works — and I'd be hard pressed to think of this final season without thinking of the Mother as one of the core cast of the show.

Much of that has to do with the great casting of a talent like Cristin Milioti. Milioti may have been cast in large part due to her musical abilities and how they would inform the character of the Mother, but she played the comedic and dramatic turns required with such effortless charm that it feels like she could shoulder an entire series of her own, especially given the angle taken in the episode "How Your Mother Met Me."

Cristin Milioti
ANDREW EVANS / PR PHOTOS

There is a certain genius in having all of Ted's friends meet the Mother before he does, and I think this was largely responsible for the tumult that resulted from how she was handled in the finale episode. Milioti fit in so well with the gang individually that it feels like a true shame that we don't get to see much of the Mother interacting with the gang as a whole. Her quick wit and adventurous spirit would have been well suited to the shenanigans at MacLaren's Pub, justifying the idea of a tenth season dedicated to exactly that.

Maybe that's just me hoping to get another season out of the show. Although, if the cast ever reunites for a TV movie, I vote that they should cover the period from directly after Robin and Barney's wedding right up until Ted and Tracy get married. Wouldn't that be fun?

Well, a fella can dream, can't he?

remember the time . . .
HIGHLIGHTS, RUNNING GAGS, AND CATCHPHRASES

- The old-person clarion call of "Patinkin!" in "The Last Time in New York"
- "Thank you, Linus." If only we could *all* enjoy the "full Kennedy service" enjoyed by Lily over the weekend
- Marshpillow 2.0, a creepy new version of the body pillow Lily uses when Marshall is away, now complete with an iPad for a head
- More *Weekend at Bernie's* nods in "The Broken Code"
- The triumphant reopening of Gazzola's in "The Poker Game"
- The *Seinfeld*ian comedy of manners inherent in the giving of wedding gifts and sending of thank you notes in "The Poker Game"
- Marshall's legal eagle funk band, The Funk, The Whole Funk, and Nothing But the Funk
- Detective Ted Mosby's greatest failure: trying to figure out

The Pineapple Incident from season one, which is revisited in "Mom and Dad"

- The agony of poor Billy Zabka, showered with popcorn by angry moviegoers due to his role as the bad guy in *The Karate Kid* and destined never to be known for his poetry
- The return of the heroic folk song "Marshall Versus the Machines" in "Bass Player Wanted"
- Marshall's "slappetite for destruction" in "Slapsgiving 3: Slappointment in Slapmarra"
- The hot new "Ring Bear" wedding trend, courtesy of Barney Stinson
- Finally, an explanation of Barney's job: after years of answering questions about what he does with a dismissive "*Please*," it turns out that Barney's job actually *is* PLEASE — Provide Legal Exculpation And Sign Everything
- The sweet flourish of magical realism when Robin floats away at the end of "Sunrise"
- Stinson's Hangover Fixer Elixir in "Rally": a recipe developed by Dr. J. Barnert Stinsonheimer during FDR's top-secret Too Many Manhattans Project, the elixir's ingredients include Tantrum energy drink, banana, Funyons, and ginger
- The origins of the "Big Fudge" nickname coming to light in "Rally": we learn that Marshall somehow ate an eight-pound block of fudge in twelve minutes when he was accepted into Columbia
- *The Wedding Bride Too!* in "Vesuvius" — and learning that *The Wedding Bride* has become a smash Broadway musical
- The scene in *The Wedding Bride Too!* that features "Narshall" eating birthday cake, a stab at Segel, who took a swipe at the show in a 2010 *GQ* interview, and then later in his *This Is the End* cameo, when he voiced his worry that Marshall and Lily's relationship dynamic would be reduced to tired sitcom tropes ("What happened to the birthday cake?" ". . . *What* birthday cake?")

- The fact that after a same-sex kiss in "Rally," all in an effort to wake up a drunken Barney, Lily is suddenly over her attraction to Robin — only for Robin to suddenly have a crush on Lily
- The tracking shot that ties up all the loose ends at the close of "Gary Blauman," including Kal Penn's return as the worst therapist ever (how many of his patients does he get involved with?)

taking life and turning it into a series of crazy stories
THE EPISODES

9.01 the locket

For a wrap-up season, the first episode of the year has a surprising number of introductions to make.

First, we have the idea that the entire season is going to take place over the weekend of Robin and Barney's wedding. That is neatly accomplished by the "55 hours before the wedding" title card. We also get Future Ted telling us that the weekend changed the lives of a lot of people, and the three-way split screen gives a solid sense that there are a few threads of action happening in this episode. But it also serves as an indication of what we can expect over the year, although given the number of subplots and back-and-forths through time, limiting it to three is underselling the season a little bit.

As Marshall makes his way back home from Minnesota, we are introduced to Daphne. After getting the two of them (well, three, including little Marvin) kicked off an airplane, Daphne becomes Marshall's road trip buddy in an effort to get home to New York over a holiday weekend in the only way possible — by car. Daphne (as played by *The View*'s Sherri Shepherd, *very* memorable from her turn as Tracy Jordan's wife, Angie, on *30 Rock*) is a great foil for Marshall's sweet-if-sometimes-doltishly-optimistic worldview. However, I was worried from the start that we wouldn't get to see Marshall interact with the gang for the bulk of the season . . . with the exception of Lily's creepy Marshpillow 2.0. I suppose that this is the price to pay for the narrative roulette wheel of setting a whole season over a single weekend, but with the amount of time given to Daphne in this episode (and subsequent ones), I started to wonder if the producers should have promoted Shepherd to the status of regular cast member.

Thinking about things ending, we get a sense that Barney and Robin's relationship might not make it to the wedding when they discover that they might be blood relatives. Barney is repulsed by the notion of even kissing his bride-to-be when he thinks they are family, which seems a little out of character — not that I think he is a fan of incest per se, but given his storied and extensive sexual history (to say nothing of his mother's heroically epic carnal past), there is a sufficient likelihood that he already has dipped his toe into the Stinson gene pool. It's more likely that this early threat to Robin and Barney's relationship is meant as off-handed foreshadowing, given how things wind up for these two down the road. (Wait, should I have prefaced that with a "spoiler alert" warning?)

We are led to believe that Marshall and Lily's relationship is in jeopardy — due to the fact that their trip to Italy is threatened by Marshall taking a New York judgeship without consulting Lily — but, like their breakup in the first season, it's never a true threat to their relationship. Perhaps there's an implied threat to Marshall's personal safety because we *know* there is going to be a huge fight, but these kids are meant to be together for the long haul. Can a little thing like one spouse's dream job infringing on the other's really bring everything to an end for them?

Meanwhile, Ted has spent the entire episode ostensibly preparing to give Robin her much-treasured locket as a wedding gift, one that is construed by Lily as an oblique attempt to derail the wedding (or at least put a cow on the tracks). By the end of the first half hour, we're almost lulled into a false sense of security with the final revelation that Ted isn't giving the titular locket to Robin. To all appearances this suggests that Ted is actually over her and ready to give her and Barney his full platonic blessing. But in yet another flashback, we see that Ted *has* gone out to Los Angeles in search of that cursed locket. Maybe there will be more than a few wild cards over the course of the season.

empire state building fun facts

- Spoiler alert! Florian van Otterloop, the Dutch buckle-smith whose life story Ted regales Lily with at the start of the episode, isn't a real person — although who wouldn't want to visit the historical home of a guy who revolutionized the belt business?

9.09 platonish

In this flashback episode, Barney suggests that platonic love can only occur between two people if "in the next twenty minutes, there is no chance of them hooking up." He prefaces this theory with a call of "Symposium," which isn't as catchy as one of his standard cries (like "challenge accepted" or "true story") and makes you wonder if he even knows what the word means.

No one would believe that Barney is *actually* trying to convene a seminar, but Carter Bays and Craig Thomas (along with the episode's author, George Sloan) get full hoity-toity, smarty-pants, college-boy points for a slam-dunk literary allusion.

As you might think, the concept of "platonic love" is named after the philosophical titan Plato. While he never coined the term, it was explored in depth in his work *Symposium*, in which two sides of love (Vulgar Eros and Divine Eros — I'll let you sort out which is the naughty one and which is chaste) are examined through a serious of speeches by men at a drinking party. To round out the reference, naturally Barney is offering his notion of platonic love — and the only true example of it that he knows — while drinking at MacLaren's.

Barney is likely right, at least as it pertains to the gang, when he states that Marshall and Robin's is the only truly platonic male-female relationship in existence. The fantasy scenario that Barney dreams up to prove this feels like a logical explanation of the relationship between these two. When Lily walks into the bar strapped with TNT and gives the direction that unless Marshall and Robin make out, the whole building will go up in flames, we believe that both would rather let the bomb detonate than actually lock lips. This sequence also proves that the Marshall-Robin dynamic has been sorely underused throughout the whole series. Sure, we saw them thrown together a couple of times (most memorably at the Hoser Hut), but I can't be the only person who thinks that the lack of Marshall-Robin storylines is a genuine loss for fans of the show. (If they could have figured it out for the last season, I would have much preferred to see these two thrown together in a desperate attempt to drive out to Farhampton.)

Speaking of genuine losses, Marshall and Ted discuss the latter's unavoidable, undying love for Robin all while rooting for the biggest losers in all of sports, the Washington Generals. Only these two would root for the team that was essentially created (in various names and formations) to lose against those showboating Harlem Globetrotters. Maybe the Ted and Robin story is less one of platonic love and more about a particular brand of self-punishment that only could be understood by a fan of a team that lost 2,495 games in a row before a freak win on January 5, 1971.

Still in flashback, Barney accepts a number of *actual* challenges from Lily and Robin tied directly to picking up women (natch). While obtaining a girl's phone number while only making sounds like a dolphin may seem like a stretch, the literary thread begun with the idea of platonic love continues when Barney is challenged to pick up a woman while engaging in a lipogram (a form of "constrained writing" game) where he can only use words that don't contain the letter *e*, the most frequently used letter in the English language (which means that he can't say words like "hello," "sex," or even "Barney").

While watching Barney complete this series of challenges is enjoyable for its own sake, more importantly it provides him an opportunity to meet the Mother (trying to get a number while carrying a pack of diapers). But she sees straight through his game and provides insight into why Barney has filled his time up with so many challenges of late: he is trying to fill the void left by not being with Robin with as much effort and noise as possible. We learn that it is the Mother's trenchant comments that put Barney back on the path to winning Robin over, which leads, of course, to their impending wedding.

Between the realization of how much of an impact the Mother has had on the gang's life and Ted's dawning realization that he will never *entirely* be over Robin (hence the "platonish" of the title), this is one of the better episodes of the season. It neatly maintains a balance between the broad comedy and the sweet heart at the core of the whole show, even if the whole episode being a flashback feels like a bit of a cheat given the locked-in weekend-of-the-wedding conceit.

Still, it's enough to make anyone disappointed with the eighth season fall right back into Divine Eros with the show.

empire state building fun facts

- One of the greatest lipogram achievements is *Gadsby* by Ernest Vincent Wright, a 50,000-word novel written entirely without the letter *e*: no word on whether the author was ever able to use it to curry favor with the ladies.

9.12 the rehearsal dinner

If all good things must come to an end (or, as Geoffrey Chaucer originally wrote, "There is an end to everything, to good things as well," which, I think you'll agree, doesn't work as well on a funny coffee mug), then the same must be said about *How I Met Your Mother*'s long-running digs at Canada. While this episode may appear to be about how Barney may not *truly* be ready for marriage (something we're forced to consider when he continues to insist that Robin is preparing a surprise laser tag rehearsal dinner), in the end it is little more than window dressing for an epic wrap-up of the show's jokes at the expense of the Great White North.

When recalling the compromises she's made regarding the wedding, Robin mentions how she wanted to have the ceremony in Canada, a notion that is met with the standard Canuck-shaming from the gang. Two jokes about mittens result in a withering response from Robin, but two jabs that use the band Crash Test Dummies as a punchline go by without a remark.

However, there is a nice symmetry in one of Marshall's jokes: for the only time since the original Canadian joke in the first season, Marshall makes a reference that actually makes the country sound like a place many would like to live ("What, is everyone going to have access to universal health care so no one has to choose between going bankrupt and treating a life-threatening illness?").

Sadly, we also see the last of Robin Sparkles — in a rather underwhelming fashion. While it might have taken a little work to arrange it, it would have been nice to see Robin actually inhabit the role once again (maybe a failed reality show documenting Sparkles in her post–Robin Daggers attempt to rise from the ashes à la, let's say, Lindsay Lohan in *Lindsay*?). Of all the wellsprings of Canadian humor on the show, Sparkles was one of the richest, and it is somewhat disappointing that the last time we see her is when Barney's brother, James, portrays her in half-drag (his other half is dressed up as a Mountie, of course).

Otherwise, we are left with the heartbreaking realization that we will no longer get to hear jokes at the expense of the following Canadian standbys:

- Tim Hortons
- snow
- hockey
- cold
- Alan Thicke (singing a Barney-centric version of the Crash Test Dummies' international hit "Mmm Mmm Mmm Mmm")

- moose
- skating
- health care
- ice

". . . To good things as well" indeed.

~~Empire State Building~~ Canadian Fun Facts
(AS LISTED BY BARNEY IN AN INFORMATIVE TURN AT THE END OF THIS EPISODE)

- Dr. Frederick Banting *did* discover insulin.
- Manitoba's native son Norman Breakey *did* invent the paint roller (although Richard Croxton Adams held the first U.S. patent and claimed to have developed it in his own basement).
- Louise Poirier *did* develop the Wonderbra in the early 1960s, while working for Moe Nadler at the Canadian Lady Corset Company, resulting in the Model 1300 plunge push-up bra.
- Instant mashed potatoes *were* developed by a Canadian — Edward Asselbergs, a Dutch-Canadian food chemist.

9.14 slapsgiving 3: slappointment in slapmarra

This episode, the fourteenth of the season and the last of the "Slapsgiving" extravaganzas, exhibits both the best and worst impulses in the *HIMYM* canon. Whether trying to pay tribute to the long line of slaps that have come before or to their penchant for kung fu films, Carter Bays and Craig Thomas manage to create an episode that combines much of what we like and what we find distracting about the show.

the good
Starting the episode in *The Matrix*–style super slow motion, with Marshall in the middle of letting loose an epic cheek-burner of a

slap (all to the bombastic strains of "O Fortuna" from Carl Orff's *Carmina Burana*, itself an adaptation of a thirteenth-century poem that was a protest against the whims of fate) is as good an episode opener as any of the series. Wordless and full of drama, the scene wrings a great deal of entertainment out of the look of furious enjoyment on Marshall's face and slack-jawed terror on Barney's.

Perhaps the best thing about this episode, as we can tell from the over-the-top opener, is that Marshall's interminable road trip has come to an end and he is finally in Farhampton with the rest of the gang, where he should have been long ago. No offense to the hugely talented Sherri Shepherd, but for a long-running ensemble series coming to an end, it's important to have the core cast together under the same roof as much as possible.

The wordplay that the slap theme inspires also generates a great deal of fun, from Marshall wanting to learn the art of "slapistry" to his admission that he has a "slappetite for destruction," another sly Guns N' Roses reference (a happy reminder of season six's "Architect of Destruction").

In fact, music cues in this episode generate the richest laughs. From the opening music to the use of Samuel Barber's "Adagio for Strings" (a heart-rending piece perhaps best known in recent memory for appearing in Oliver Stone's *Platoon*) as Marshall finally delivers the mega-slap at the end, music plays a key role in this slappointment. Not surprisingly, the show's coda — featuring members of Boyz II Men kicking out an old-school slow-jam version of "You Just Got Slapped" — is quite satisfying.

the bad

While there is a need to bring the Slapsgiving episodes to a rousing close, the biggest issue with this entry is that it doesn't serve anything *but* that end. Not only do we not see the Mother in this installment, but we derive no further understanding of the core characters or their interpersonal dynamics, unlike in the previous slapisodes. Remember the reconciliation of Lily and her dad Mickey in season five's "Slapsgiving 2: Revenge of the Slap"? Or a troubled Robin and Ted re-bonding over their "General Idea" joke in the first "Slapsgiving" from season three? We don't see anything like that in this episode and, perhaps worst of all, we don't get to see Neil Patrick Harris spin around in another of his cataclysmic pratfalls after receiving a slap (although the slow-motion face-smushing is a reasonable runner-up).

the slappy

Summed up in one hashtag? #HowIMetYourRacism.

The idea of casting the core members as martial arts masters may have felt like a way to include everyone in a wild storyline, and maybe it even worked as a cost-cutting measure, but the complete tone deafness of casting non-Asian actors in Asian roles upset many and inspired the #HowIMetYourRacism hashtag that caused the showrunners a few headaches.

Now, internet outrage is easier to come by than tangled wire hangers at the back of your closet, but even a jaded viewer such as me found it a little off-putting. With Robin and Lily taking the roles of Red Bird and White Flower, there was no attempt to make them look Asian, outside of wardrobe choices. It was Ted as The Calligrapher, complete with a Fu Manchu moustache, who came perilously close to reaching a blackface level of racial insensitivity.

On top of that, the bittersweet aspect of this final season is completely lost in this exaggerated farce. Sure, it gets a little wiggle room in that it is a story Marshall tells for the sole purpose of putting the fear of slap back into a supposedly jaded Barney, but a slapping tree? That's really pushing it.

empire state building fun facts

- The inspiration for the title of this episode is John O'Hara's novel *Appointment in Samarra*: the book's epigraph, from W. Somerset Maugham, details a Baghdad servant frightened by the sight of Death who tries to escape his bony clutches by hiding in the village of Samarra only to find that he has fulfilled his own grisly fate: "I was surprised to see him in Baghdad," Death says later. "For I had an appointment with him tonight in Samarra."

9.22 the end of the aisle

Both Robin and Barney are in panic mode thirty-two minutes before the wedding — and who can blame them? Joining with someone for the rest of your life is not an easy step to take but, as both Future and Present Ted state, it is the best thing that we humans do.

In a way, everyone in the gang has taken vows. Marshall and Lily of course took theirs years ago, but, as Barney happily points out (while going through the *Gone with the Wind* drafts of his own vows), they've broken every one. As the flashbacks show, this is merely a matter of day-to-day life getting in the way of romantic ideals. How can you hope to live up to an earnest altar proclamation when you've each seen the other hunch on a toilet or pick at her teeth with the corner of the *TV Guide*?

As much as Barney likes to think that this failure to live up to ideals makes vows a silly notion to entertain, in actuality it proves that the intention behind the vows is what's important. As anyone who has been in a long-term relationship knows, you don't prove the strength of your love when everything is going swimmingly but when the overdue bills stack up while the basement is flooded.

That's why Marshall's idea of revisiting vows with Lily is the only thing that makes sense in a marriage. Changes crop up in any living, breathing relationship, and it seems to me that by revisiting these vows every five years or so, these shifting dynamics could be addressed. When children show up, suddenly keeping a fresh tube of mango love butter in the house doesn't carry the same weight it once did.

While Barney is worried about writing the perfect vow, Robin is more concerned with the mistake she fears she is making by trading vows with him. Throughout much of the season, we see

Ted struggling with a great deal of anxiety about whether or not he is genuinely over Robin, but this is the first time we've considered that maybe Robin isn't quite over him either. While this doesn't play for very long, and it ultimately becomes clear that Robin wondering if she should be marrying Ted is more of a release valve for her than an action she'd likely consider, it does tug at our heartstrings a little to wonder what might have been if it weren't just Ted who was moon-eyed at the thought of them getting back together.

While watching this episode — and this season in general — I couldn't help but feel that too much energy was devoted to going over this well-traveled road. Maybe I should have given more credit to Carter Bays and Craig Thomas and their overall vision for how the show was to conclude, but for most of the year it felt like we were spinning our wheels. In this episode, however, it was pleasing to watch Robin wrestle with the unusual connection she'd made with Barney and mourn for what she'd had (and lost) with Ted. And that means that the whole locket scenario may have more weight than we originally thought, given how things ultimately wind up between them.

As things wind up on this episode, which ends with Robin and Barney getting married, we finally see the end of the long-standing Slap Bet. Although this smack may feel anticlimactic when compared to other wallops doled out over the years, there is something very pleasing about Marshall using this bet-concluding slap to rid Barney of his pre-wedding jitters. Unfortunately, we don't get to hear what the married couple's wedding vows actually are, blocked out as they are by Future Ted ruminating on what a long and bumpy road it had been getting to that spot. While this feels like another mild lost opportunity, Future Ted saying that we can never vow to be perfect but can only promise to love each other with everything that we've got is as sweet a vow as we'll ever hear.

empire state building fun facts

- When Ted mentions that he won't be a part of a third

runaway bride situation because it's like ". . . the dude in that documentary who kept having women show up dead at the bottom of his staircase. I mean sure, did they all trip? But do you want to hang out with that guy?" he is referring to *The Staircase* or *Soupçons*, an exhaustive 360-minute French documentary about author Michael Peterson (*The Immortal Dragon*, *A Bitter Peace*) defending himself against the charge of murdering his wife.

- Marshall vows to stop petitioning Paul McCartney to allow Weird Al Yankovic to perform his parody *Chicken Pot Pie* to the tune of *Live and Let Die*: this is true, and while Yankovic could perform the song and simply pay out the royalties, he has a standing rule to only go ahead with a parody once given the blessing from the original artist (which is why we've never heard any Prince parodies from Mr. Yankovic).

9.23 & 9.24 last forever, parts one and two

Pulling off a final episode that will satisfy fans but not feel like a cut-and-paste "happy ending" is no walk in the park. Good thing that Carter Bays and Craig Thomas made a point of watching finales of other sitcoms in preparation for writing their own. Better still that they stuck by their original plan to end the show from a draft they wrote way back in 2006. Because if you're going to finish what is likely your biggest artistic accomplishment to date, you may as well make *yourself* happy — because God knows you're never going to manage that for everyone else.

Judging by the swift and immediately divisive reaction to the finale, Bays and Thomas couldn't have upset more fans of the show if they had ended the whole thing in a terrorist attack on MacLaren's that left everyone torn in half by C-4 explosives.

Before we get to the ways people were displeased, it would do us well to consider the very fact that people were miffed by the whole enterprise. In an episode that skipped over so many years that it felt like a tenth season crammed into a single hour, it says a lot about the emotional heft of the show and commitment to the characters that people cared so much about how it all wound up. There aren't many long-running comedies that managed to wring as many laughs and tears from the big wrap-up as *HIMYM*. Shows like *Friends* and *The Office* come to mind, but it's hard to imagine such a sentimental ending to *Two and a Half Men* or *The Big Bang Theory*.

While many complained that Bays and Thomas gave short shrift to the characters they had created (or, as suggested by Todd VanDerWerff of *The AV Club*, that they were "shitty long-term planners"), few could get past their own sense of personal betrayal and get to the meat of the nut: life doesn't give a hoot for your plans. People who you would never consider compatible come together while the couple you *knew* would make it split up quickly enough to get an annulment. Friends move to the suburbs while others stay in the city, and that group that you thought would always be there for each other get pulled to opposite ends of the globe. In the end, the show is less about Ted meeting and marrying the love of his life than it is about the crazy times we all have in our youth — times that inevitably must come to an end, even when that's the last thing we want.

For me, the biggest hurdle to get over (upon first viewing) is how quickly Robin and Barney's marriage ends. After spending so much time trying to get them to the altar, it is a left-field development for the two of them to announce their divorce fifteen minutes into the final episode. But consider how much time the episode covers and how much business it has to tend to before the final curtain. When we get to a certain age, we all know of people who don't last three years together in the same apartment, never mind married, and considering the overall dramatic thrust of the episode — that nothing turns out the way you plan — it makes perfect sense that they wouldn't last. How many times has a couple not survived when one's career takes off while the other's stalls? (Even a few years in the future, Barney's lifestyle blog with its daily boner jokes doesn't seem like much of a home run, occupation-wise.) Sure, it would have been good to see more of Robin and Barney trying to make things work, but we'd need a few more seasons to do so, and that's simply not in the cards. I mean, we'd *all* like to see a return of Fat Barney, but at this late date, time is of the essence.

When Barney and Robin's split signals the true end of the gang's attendance for all the "big moments," it's funny to see how this affects each member. Robin's career takes off and she's whisked around the globe, but it is pretense: she can't contribute to the gang's activities as much as she once could because it represents so much pain for her. While Lily takes it the hardest, it is Marshall who is the least sympathetic to Robin's feelings. When Lily remarks that a genuine "Scherbatsky sighting" is as momentous as spying Sasquatch, Marshall remarks that Robin is more like the Yeti, "cold and aloof." Can't he see how much heartbreak "the gang" represents for her, what with an ex-husband and a guy she likely *should* have wound up with, who has since met the love of his life and started a family?

Robin's storyline in the finale was another element that surprised me. While we've all been waiting for Ted to meet the Mother and fall in love, we have failed to see what kind of life Robin has in front of her. Certainly there is success in her career, but there are as many regrets as there are stamps on her passport. There is a pleasing symmetry to how we see her in the episode's final moments — in an apartment with five dogs once again — and the identity of the gentleman caller at her front door makes even more of an impact when we consider not only everything *he's* gone through but the road Robin has traveled to get there as well.

A two-hour finale would have been more appropriate. Maybe then the show could have paid the proper tribute to its cinematic romantic-comedy inspirations. We could have seen more of what we felt was brushed away too quickly. We might have seen something of Marshall and Lily's year in Italy, as an example. Of all the characters poorly served in the finale (more on the Mother in a minute), these two had the least amount of serious screen time. We find out that Marshall has gone back to corporate law for a while, is offered a judgeship again, and then decides to run for Supreme Court (heralding a change of nickname from "Judge Fudge" to "Fudge Supreme"). But other than another baby, we don't get much of a sense of time passing for these two, and that is a real shame. For all the ink (and pixels) spilled about how poorly the Mother was treated in the finale, little attention was given to this fun and funny couple and what happened to them throughout the years.

Which, kids, brings us to the Mother. Or, more accurately, Tracy McConnell. Again, the upset that her untimely end caused is a testament not only to the character as created by Bays and Thomas but as inhabited by Cristin Milioti. And I don't disagree with the sentiment that the way her death was dealt with felt like more of an afterthought than the dramatic crescendo befitting of someone we've come to love. But thinking about this only leads me back to Robin. Yes, we've spent a year getting to know Tracy and falling in love with her, so we can understand how Ted can go head-over-heels at the first sight of her. But still, we've only known her for a year. How does one year with Tracy somehow trump nine years with Robin? Ms. Scherbatsky isn't dispatched with in the same manner as Tracy, but I was genuinely surprised how much loyalty fans of the show seemed to have to the latter over the former. Why does an alternate cut of the finale, which appeared online shortly after the initial broadcast and removes Tracy's passing, make people happier than the idea of Ted and Robin finding happiness together?

I'm still scratching my head about that one. So strong was the response that Bays and Thomas included an alternate ending to the series on the season nine DVD set. That feels to me like caving in to the wrong kind of pressure, but then again, given the amount of footage apparently cut out of the final episode, it's understandable that after nine years together, the show's creators would want to give as much to the fans as they possibly can.

As for me, I'm not displeased with the ending. I'm sorry to learn the fate of Tracy, but Ted and Robin have always belonged together, and I've said good-bye to the show happy in the knowledge that they finally wind up together. Along with that blue French horn.

empire state building fun facts

- During Barney's return to King of the Horn Dogs, he creates *The Playbook II: Electric Bangaloo*, which is a tight nod to the finest title for a movie sequel ever created, namely *Breakin' 2: Electric Boogaloo*.
- As many as eighteen minutes of the finale were cut to fit the running time: included were an introduction to the mother of Barney's daughter (the delightfully named "#31"); Lily repaying a bet to Marshall over Ted and Robin ending up together; the genesis of the Pineapple Incident; Ted and Robin having lunch after running into each other in front of the GNB building, with Robin telling a story about her run-in with a bull in Spain; and, perhaps saddest of all, Robin Sparkles appearing at the reception, complete with Robin wearing her former alter ego's jean jacket over her wedding dress while singing "Let's Go to the Mall" with the wedding band: with any luck, we'll get to see it on the DVD/Blu-ray release.

house guests

- Sherri Shepherd (*The View*, *30 Rock*) as Daphne, Marshall's unexpected road trip partner in the first half of the season
- Roger Bart (*The Stepford Wives* remake, the *Young Frankenstein* Broadway musical) as Curtis, the front desk clerk at the Farhampton Inn

- Edward Herrmann (*Annie, Gilmore Girls, The Lost Boys*) as the disapproving Reverend Lowell in "Knight Vision"
- Rhys Darby (*Flight of the Conchords*) as Hamish, the night clerk of the Farhampton Inn, in "No Questions Asked"
- Jon Heder (*Napoleon Dynamite*) playing Narshall in *The Wedding Bride Too!* in "Vesuvius"
- Tracey Ullman (*The Tracey Ullman Show*) as Genevieve Scherbatsky, Robin's never-before-seen mom

The rest of the House Guests are returnees from previous seasons:

- Wayne Brady as Barney's brother, James
- Ben Vereen as James' father, the Reverend Sam Gibbs, who officiates Barney and Robin's wedding in "The End of the Aisle"
- John Lithgow as Barney's dad, Jerome Whittaker, in "The End of the Aisle"
- Frances Conroy as Barney's mom, Loretta, in "Mom and Dad" and "The End of the Aisle"
- William Zabka as spurned best man William Zabka
- James Van Der Beek as Robin's old boyfriend Simon in "Bedtime Stories"
- Alan Thicke as himself in "The Rehearsal Dinner"
- Stacy Keibler, Nazanin Boniadi, April Bowlby, Katie Walder, and Eva Amurri Martino as a selection of Barney's old conquests in "Slapsgiving 3: Slappointment in Slapmarra"
- Sarah Chalke as Stella in "Sunrise"
- Bill Fagerbakke as Marshall's dad, Marvin Eriksen Sr., in "Sunrise"
- Tim Gunn as himself
- Bryan Cranston as Hammond Druthers in "Platonish"
- Abby Elliott as Jeanette
- Chris Kattan playing Jed in *The Wedding Bride Too!* in "Vesuvius"

- Lucy Hale as Robin's sister, Katie, in "Vesuvius"
- Marshall Manesh as Ranjeet
- Kyle MacLachlan as The Captain in "Daisy"
- Chris Elliott as Lily's dad, Mickey, who travels with Marshall and Lily to Italy as their nanny in "Daisy"
- Taran Killam as Gary Blauman in "Gary Blauman" and "The End of the Aisle"
- Rachel Bilson as Cindy in "How Your Mother Met Me"
- Ashley Williams as Victoria in "Sunrise"
- In "Gary Blauman," we see the return of Jennifer Morrison as Zoey, Kal Penn as Kevin the therapist, Alexis Denisof as Sandy Rivers, David Burtka as Scooter, Jorge Garcia as The Blitz, and Jai Rodriguez as James' partner Tom, all as a part of a long camera pan meant to tie up many loose ends from the series in one single shot
- Ray Wise as Robin's dad in "Rally" and "The End of the Aisle"

maybe it's the booze talking
REACTIONS TO THE SEASON

It's hard not to gauge the ninth season through the polarizing filter of the finale, but it is important to remember that there were twenty-two other episodes before it, some of which were as conceptually risky as the final moments of the finale.

Max Nicholson of IGN titled his sum-up of the season "The Big Fat Misdirect," which might indicate that he wasn't a fan of how the final season played out. While he was (like yours truly) a fan of the final episode (saying that he knows this puts him "in a very small bracket"), he wasn't as convinced that the chancy narrative gamble of the season-as-weekend framework truly worked. "Mainly," he says, "because the wedding had *nothing* to do with the ending. Moreover, the execution of these episodes was all over the map."

In fact, Nicholson suggests what I think most fans felt: that the first half of the season was a mess, while the second half regained the savvy mix of humor and gravitas we had come to expect from the show, especially as it hurtled toward the end of a nine-year run. He even suggests of the finale that "there was easily a whole *season's* worth of material in 'Last Forever' and that while going down a different road would have led to a different finale, "it certainly would have made a lot more sense to make *that* the storyline for season 9 instead of Barney and Robin's wedding."

Todd VanDerWerff of The A.V. Club is more forgiving of the season-long weekend conceit, suggesting that while it could have felt "stilted and inorganic . . . instead, it feels weirdly organic."

VanDerWerff feels that, more than any other series, *HIMYM* (and its creators, Bays and Thomas) understands how, when we look back on our lives, we tend to view the events as we would a novel, judiciously selecting all the elements that support the ending we have come to accept. In making this argument, he likens the show to the work of grouchy German philosopher Arthur Schopenhauer, which has *got* to be a first for *How I Met Your Mother* . . . or any other sitcom, for that matter.

In fact, VanDerWerff makes the case that any other approach to this season would have been a betrayal of the roots of the show, one that has "always flirted with this concept of time, the way stories can dart in and out of each other," and that such a radical approach to time is in *HIMYM's* DNA. Worried less about the distractions that such time-shifting might have inspired, he avers that the show "works best when it embraces the idea that this is a story, that it is heading somewhere, that there is something wonderful at its end . . . but the fact remains that this is a story about a man who was missing something, then found it all of a sudden on a rainy platform on Long Island."